Advertising

Advertising does not ~~ed~~ ~other graduate!

Whether you are an aspiring advertising creative, designer, account manager, PR / publicity consultant or marketing manager, *Advertising* is an engaging source of inspiration for those dark, idea-less days and a motivator when those job interviews or placements seem in short supply. Its companion website at **www.routledge.com/textbooks/advertising** supports the book with further examples and ideas to inspire as well as offering up-to-date advice.

This book is filled with numerous visual examples of advertising thinking, with words of advice and guidance from some of the industry's most respected practitioners, as well as insights from graduates who faced the same challenges you soon will in securing that elusive first job.

Add to that an extensive supply of hints and tips to enhance your creative thinking processes, which take the work you do beyond what you think you are capable of and, crucially, gain an edge at job interviews.

Maybe advertising doesn't need another graduate, but then you won't be just another graduate will you?

Andy Tibbs is Senior Lecturer in Advertising at the University of Gloucestershire. He has worked for over 20 years as an art director and designer across many business sectors, with a list of clients including: Volkswagen UK, Bovis Homes, HBOS, Gleneagles Golf Resort, British Gas, Hilton Hotels and Capital One – among many others. Andy also works as a freelance trainer, inspiring secondary school teachers to include insightful, relevant creative teaching in their art & design programmes.

Advertising

Its business, culture and careers

Andy Tibbs

Foreword by Trevor Beattie

Routledge
Taylor & Francis Group

LONDON AND NEW YORK

First published 2010
by Routledge
2 Park Square, Milton Park, Abingdon, Oxon, OX14 4RN

Simultaneously published in the USA and Canada
by Routledge
270 Madison Avenue, New York, NY 10016

Routledge is an imprint of the Taylor & Francis Group, an informa business

© 2010 Andy Tibbs; with the exception of the foreword, © 2010 Trevor Beattie

Designed and typeset in FS Albert by Keystroke, Tettenhall, Wolverhampton
Printed and bound in Great Britain by Bell & Bain Ltd, Glasgow

British Library Cataloguing in Publication Data
A catalogue record for this book is available from the British Library

Library of Congress Cataloging in Publication Data
Tibbs, Andy, 1964–
    Advertising : its business, culture and careers / Andy Tibbs.
        p. cm.
    Includes bibliographical references and index.
    1. Advertising—Vocational guidance. I. Title.
    HF5828.4.T43 2009
    659.1023—dc22

ISBN 10: 0–415–54468–8 (hbk)
ISBN 10: 0–415–54466–1 (pbk)
ISBN 10: 0–203–86595–2 (ebk)

ISBN 13: 978–0–415–54468–9 (hbk)
ISBN 13: 978–0–415–54466–5 (pbk)
ISBN 13: 978–0–203–86595–8 (ebk)

For Tina, Rowan, Daisy and Theo with love.

For advertising students everywhere. Good luck!

Contents

Acknowledgements

I owe massive thanks and mentions to what seems like the whole of the world. So here goes. If I have missed anyone, please accept my apologies.

Trevor Beattie for his fantastic foreword and support. Antionette de Lisser at Beattie McGuinness Bungay for her help and support (and for nagging Trevor!).

Tina, Rowan, Daisy and Theo Tibbs for their unerring support, encouragement and patience.

Aileen Storry at Routledge for her belief in me and for helping my words become more readable.

Amy Kingsbury at Bartle Bogle Hegarty for persuading their creatives to talk to me.

Jessica at Mother for getting people there on my side.

Frank Holmes at the University of Gloucestershire for the use of his address book.

Sir John Hegarty for making me love advertising more than I thought possible.

Then to all the following lovely people who agreed to share their experiences and contribute (in no particular order):

Sam Barratt at Oxfam

Mark Terry-Lush at Renegade Media

Martin Moll at Honda (UK)

Louise Goldstein at BDR London

Neil Anderson at Cadbury World

Gillian Challinor at Gyro HSR

Rob Ellis at Agency Republic

Pete Goold at Punch Communications

Chris Pitt at Ecclesiastical

David Sloly at Mason Zimbler

Charlotte Driscoll at Mason Zimbler

Lucy and Darren at Wieden+Kennedy

Paul Graham at Anomaly London

Lucy-Anne Ronayne at Work Club

Darren Bailes at VCCP

Marc Giusti at GT

Gwyn Jones at Bartle Bogle Hegarty

Dave Trott at CST

Robert Minton Taylor at Leeds Metropolitan University

Lindsay at Paradigm Staffing

Carol Fisher at Central Office of Information

Rob Engelman at Engelman Management Group Inc.

Johanna Fawcett at Sheactive

Michael Welch at Black Circles

Simon Williams at Carat Ltd

Selina Hull at Periscope, Creative Recruitment LLP

Also the following people for additional snippets of inspiration:

Jon Fox – Copywriter, BBH London

Mareka Carter – Art Director/ Copywriter, BBH London

Damien Bellon – Creative, Mother

Stuart Outhwaite – Creative, Mother

Jaimin and Waldemar

Katharine Mansell at Dairy Crest

Peter Harbour at Unilever

Lindsay Strachan at Scottish Widows

Tim Dixon at More Th>n

Finally, thanks to all those who have allowed their words and imagery to be reproduced. If any words or images have been inadvertently reproduced without the correct permission or been miscredited in any way, the errors will be rectified in future editions of this book.

Foreword

Trevor Beattie

Take it from me. It's worth it. Worth it all. Worth the grief and the anxiety. Worth the late nights and the early mornings. Worth the current screaming heebeegeebees that the ad industry is about to implode. Worth the insecurity. Worth the inherent random instability and unfairness of the creative placement scheme (no one has yet designed a better way). Worth listening to what you might now regard as the bonkers advice of Andy Tibbs. Worth going without sleep for. Worth splitting up with the person you met at Uni and thought you were going to spend the rest of your life with. Worth twice whatever it costs.

Make getting a job in advertising your single, abiding goal. Forget WHERE you would like to work. Concentrate on WHEN. Think job. Not company name. Go get. And when you get it (and you will), feel free to party like a bastard. You will have deserved it. You will be the proud owner of the best job in the world.

Take it from me. The advice, that is. Not the job.

You'd have to kill me to take that.

Trevor Beattie
Beattie McGuinness Bungay

Image courtesy of Will Wintercross/BMB

I Does advertising need another graduate?

Now that is an unnerving statement to start a book for young people embarking on a career in advertising with, so I had better explain what I mean. You will already have made a decision in your own mind to follow a course of study in Advertising and Media communications in one of its many forms. Some of you may have explored the possibilities of advertising as part of your Media or Graphic Design A-Level; others may have chosen a BTEC course in Graphic Design, Media or Business and Marketing. Many of you will be at university on one of a multitude of courses that include advertising in some form. Advertising Photography; Business, Marketing and Communications courses; Public Relations; Graphic Design; Media Communications; Creative Advertising or Advertising Design – to name some of the most popular. Whatever you are currently studying, you will be excited by a career in advertising and at the same time daunted by the prospect too.

I would be lying if I said that the course you are on and the qualifications you receive will be enough on their own to get you that first break in advertising. They won't. So what will? Essentially, you. Your personality, enthusiasm, ideas and understanding of the expectations of the advertising and media industry are your greatest assets. I can say absolutely honestly that a career in advertising is exciting, diverse, fulfilling and ultimately well rewarded. After well over 20 years as an art director, and for the last ten or so a lecturer in Advertising too, the whole business and process of advertising still excites me and it always will.

Of course in picking up this book for the first time you will want to know exactly what it takes to kick-start your career in advertising and media communications – that is not an easy task. Ask 100 people in advertising to give you their interpretation

of what it takes and chances are you will probably get 100 different answers. Many of you may find you are confused enough already and need some more practical guidance in defining your career aims and then setting about achieving them. That is exactly what this book is intended to help you with: I want to try and offer you some insights into how advertising works as an industry and guide you past some of the half-truths and mystique that seem to surround it. You may then be able to see more clearly how your talent and enthusiasm can fit into the plethora of jobs advertising and communications can offer bright, motivated, creative and inspired young people like you.

Your tutors and lecturers will play a massive part in shaping your thinking whilst you are studying and may also have an impact on your future career decisions. As an advertising tutor I know very well that I cannot hope to give my students a definitive education that delivers everything they need to know; neither can your tutors. The process of developing your skills and knowledge to prepare you to work in advertising and media communications is based around the acquisition of experiences, in my opinion. Soak up, reflect on and act on everything you learn on your current course and milk your tutors and lecturers dry. Make sure you have asked all the questions you can and trained your mind to think critically based on the vast range of techniques and experiences that they can possibly impart. When you have

done that, search for even more experiences. Compare, contrast and learn from what I have to say. Absorb every last drop of advice and insight you can from the industry practitioners you come in to contact with as part of the course. Never accept that you now know all you need to begin your career. The learning process at college or university is just the beginning of the journey. You will need to start learning all over again when you secure your first work-experience, placement and, hopefully, permanent job. Students who adopt an open-minded philosophy and a determination to spend the rest of their lives exploring and learning from new experiences will be successful in advertising and media communications.

Oh, and yes, advertising very definitely does need another graduate. All advertising agencies, design studios, publicity firms and marketing strategists constantly need to reinvent themselves with frequent injections of fresh ideas to present their clients with challenging, creative thinking that moves their brands and businesses forward. After all, that is how they earn their fees and maintain their reputations – you are a vital part of that process.

A piece of advice before I go any further, though. Unless a career in advertising and communication means more to you than anything else in the world, rethink your future. To be successful and well rewarded in the industry requires passion, dedication and ambition – a skin as thick as a rhinoceros might be useful too. Now

3

put this book down for a moment and take a hard look at yourself: you know advertising and communication is absolutely where you want to spend your working life but which kind of job are you best suited for? Later chapters will define in more detail the role of the creative team – art director and copywriter – the backbone of advertising. Perhaps your marketing, communication and presentation skills lend themselves to your becoming an account executive at an advertising agency or a brand manager working for clients? Do you have the kind of analytical mind which account planners need to understand the profiles of consumers, customers and brands? As a talented designer you could be just what studio and production teams need, or will your efficiency and organizational talents be perfect for media planning and buying? It could be even that your engaging and persuasive writing and verbal skills draw you towards Public Relations where you can support advertising agencies as part of clients' marketing strategies.

By reading through this book and being inspired by its images and learning from the contributions of advertising and communications practitioners, I hope you will find that your career dreams look more achievable. With energy, desire and a talent for ideas you can get there. Good luck, the world is yours for the taking if you want it badly enough.

But enough about what is in my book – why should you read it? In my opinion the single most important piece of advice I can give any student of advertising and communication is to spend every waking moment with all your senses open and in receive mode. The critical role of any piece of advertising or media communication is to deliver its message in precisely the way its target audience are most likely to be receptive to it. For you to play a part in achieving that successfully, it is vital to be both creatively stimulated and to understand the way in which potential consumers think, speak and behave. Throughout this book I will demonstrate ways in which your minds can become an Aladdin's Cave of ideas, inspiration and knowledge. Equally, I believe it is important to understand as fully as possible the ways in which others have gained their first career break or what different types of employers look for when recruiting graduates. By speaking with professionals across the industry, I can give you the chance to share some of their secrets and to prepare yourself better with their advice and observations.

Don't be fooled, no book can be definitive and I don't own a magic wand. What I would like you to believe is that you can never know too much. Your teachers, tutors and lecturers will all have their knowledge to impart; my book will supplement that and offer you some more directions and inspirations.

2 Resisting the usual

Resist the usual. The inspirational mantra of Raymond Rubicam, one of the twentieth century's most innovative and pioneering ad-men. All of you who aspire to a career in advertising and communication would be well advised to tattoo those words on the back of your hand. Advertising thrives on a need to think independently and

differently with a desire to explore new ways of delivering messages – so should you. Picture the scene, you are in an interview room with at least ten other interviewees, all of whom have the same qualifications and similar education. What is there to separate you? Who will get the job? In my experience, when all ten have gone and there are tough decisions to make, the person who had the most inventive ideas, an engaging and enthusiastic personality, and above all stood out as being a thinker who is just a little different to the rest wins every time.

Throughout your studies and your future careers the continual absorption of new creative stimuli and inspirational points of reference will be a vital part of who you are and help make you special in the eyes of potential employers. To help you along with that lifelong learning process, I've identified some of advertising's ground-breaking and thought-provoking idea inventors. Whilst these are people who have inspired me in my career, I accept that some of their work and thoughts may seem a little dated and out of step with advertising in the twenty-first century. Don't be so blinkered as to feel they are irrelevant to the way you are taught to think and act on your courses, though; much of what these great people have achieved still shapes the way advertising is created. Also, don't stop where I stop either: looking at influential advertising from around the world, exploring the thinking behind it and being inspired by the people who created it is an integral part of making you stronger. I firmly believe that the best advertising people are the best informed – I'm not telling you what to think, just simply telling you to think.

The origins of the advertising species

To make sense of the kinds of sophisticated, targeted advertising messages we are all surrounded by and bombarded by every day of our lives, I think it is useful at this point to take stock of how advertising became such an incisive, persuasive marketing tool. Whether we like it or not, advertising is inextricably linked to the way we live in the twenty-first century. Our towns and cities are ring-fenced with powerful billboards, and their walls and shop fronts decorated with seductive, enticing brand messages – they fill our ears, impair our vision and even appear under our feet. When I meet new students during their induction week I set them a challenge. Along a prearranged route between the advertising studio we first meet in and a city centre rendezvous, I invite them to participate in the *Great Ad Race* – armed with a sheet of paper their mission is to list all the different types of advertising they encounter along the route. The current record is over 100 in an hour!

That little bonding exercise doesn't even begin to include the direct mail you receive in your daily post, the advertising you see in newspapers and magazines or the messages you hear on your radios. Socially, your television is peppered with commercials and sponsored stings across the multitude of channels you can now receive. Your evening at the cinema is spent being entertained by yet more commercials and trailers, and when the main film starts it frequently assaults the

The chaotic clutter of contemporary advertising messages in a Hong Kong street.

senses with product placements – if it's good enough for James Bond in his *Tom Ford* suits and *Omega* watches then it's good enough for you. Did you spot the *Nike*-clad Wildcats in *High School Musical 3: Senior Year* as they rehydrated themselves with *Dasani*? And *Sex and the City*, the movie and the American TV show, had almost as many featured brands as it had dialogue. Many brands are viewing placement as being increasingly important to their advertising strategies, and continuing relaxation of the UK regulation of such placement will see this increase to levels that have been commonplace for some years in the USA. Also, no doubt many of your evenings out are organized via email, social networking sites or texting – try counting the ads next time you are arranging to meet at 8.00pm!

Little did the Ancient Egyptians and Greeks who made posters and sales messages from papyrus know what a monster they were creating. Evidence of advertising communications has been found among almost all the ancient civilizations. The ruins of Pompeii and ancient Arabia have concealed trade and political messages, whilst painted advertisements on walls and rocks in Asia, Africa and South America can, in some parts of India, be traced back to 4000 BC. When towns and cities became more densely populated in the Middle Ages, advertising communications were largely visual symbols (because most people were unable to read) – footwear for a cobbler, sacks of flour for a miller or horseshoes for a blacksmith. Tradesmen also used street callers or town criers to attract customers, an unrefined form of cold calling perhaps?

It is surprising there is any room left for a story line with the sheer volume of products strategically placed for advertising purposes in recent James Bond movies.

Image courtesy of Danjag, LLC, United Artists Corporation, Columbia Pictures Industries Inc.

By the seventeenth century literacy had improved, as had the ability to print multiple copies of sheets of paper. As a result, advertising became more sophisticated, handbills with words were commonplace and weekly newspapers began to feature advertising, often for books or medicines. The growth of businesses, advancements in industrial mechanization and a need for businesses to shout louder than an increasingly growing range of competitors led to a greater demand to advertise and promote mass-produced products. In 1836 the French newspaper *La Presse* became the first publication to include paid-for advertising – this meant it could lower its cover price and sell more copies – and it wasn't long before all newspapers had followed suit. The next logical step was for advertising to become a more organized industry, and the first moves were made towards forming advertising agencies. At first their businesses centred on the brokering of advertising space for newspapers, then in 1869 a Philadelphia company became the first to offer its customers a creative service. NW Ayer & Son effectively became the first full-service agency by writing and producing advertisements, then booking space for them in appropriate newspapers and charging a commission – remarkably this practice still exists today when buying media space. The principle is that the publication quotes its rates for varying sizes of space, the advertising agency passes this cost on to its clients and the publication then offers the agency a percentage commission for booking space with them.

Forward-thinking clients took advantage of developments in printing techniques that allowed the inclusion and mass reproduction of illustrations, and the use of colour became feasible too. The relationship between a brand, its values and the advertising messages it communicated to consumers and customers began to grow.

A Victorian-era example of full-colour press advertising for Pears soap.

Pears soap recognized that they needed to be far more proactive and even aggressive in pushing their products under consumers' noses. After marrying into the soap-making family, Thomas J. Barratt developed techniques that will be familiar to twenty-first-century advertising strategists by launching a series of advertisements based around artistic images of cherubic children. He used these charming and visually engaging visuals to reflect and reinforce the brand's core values of quality, purity and simplicity. In a precursor to modern-day advertising and its use of slogans and catch-phrases, Victorians adopted the phrase 'Have you used your Pears soap today?' often in response to a verbal greeting such as 'good morning'. Meanwhile, the pottery manufacturer Josiah Wedgwood foresaw the challenges facing the manufacturing industry in post-Industrial Revolution England. The ability to mass-produce his firm's products in factories meant he had more pottery stockpiled than he had customers for it. It was evident that he needed to increase demand for his products. Using a variety of inventive marketing techniques he presented his well-defined product range in a number of segmented ways – for example, kitchenware, bathroom, decorative and personal products were brought to their respective marketplaces independently rather than under the unwieldy, all-encompassing umbrella of chinaware. He also targeted his potential consumers in smaller social groups according to class, age, gender and profession. Once Wedgwood had this early strategic data at his disposal he tempted these consumers with money-back guarantees and free promotions, delivering his message via every advertising outlet available to him – from newspaper adverts to handbills and posters to public relations events. In order to move his rapidly developing brand to a more upmarket, classical position he created a pastiche Roman vase which he showed publicly and gained press coverage in doing so. Hard to imagine that Victorian England was home to one of the world's first inventive marketing and PR practitioners!

By the end of the nineteenth century advertising was a fully fledged industry with its own creative values and unique practices. J. Walter Thompson and Co. was a pioneering American agency of the time and still operates today. Other businesses were suffering like Josiah Wedgwood's, manufacturing volumes of products for a too-small customer base. Advertising agencies offering their services as experts in commercial communication were manna from heaven for the manufacturing industry. They were able to focus their energies on making products, whilst paying their chosen advertising agency to promote and sell greater volumes of products to wider audiences, using ever more sophisticated strategies and persuasive messages. In 1906 WK Kellogg placed his first adverts for Cornflakes in six regional American newspapers; by 1915 his advertising budget had increased to $1 million. The advertising agencies continued to go from strength to strength, and when world war broke out in 1914 they were approached by their respective governments to organize national advertising campaigns, or propaganda. In Britain, government advertising implored British men to fight for their country and attempted to persuade Americans to join and support Britain. Hitler later concluded in *Mein Kampf* that Germany had

An advertising / propaganda poster from wartime Britain.

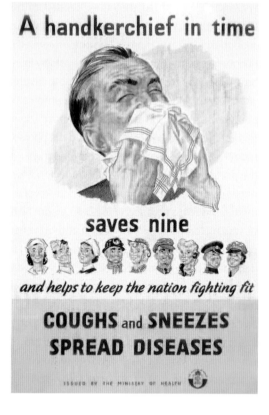

been outsmarted in the propaganda battle and consequently lost the war. With mechanization in manufacturing increasing still further following World War I, the volumes of manufacture and the costs associated with upgrading factories put businesses under further pressure to increase their sales. The advertising agencies stepped up to the plate once again – from the 1920s the agencies changed their creative approach from the factual (mostly!) expounding of product benefits to more subtle, persuasive techniques – convincing the consumer it now *needed* the product advertised with a variety of emotional lead-ins.

The post-World War I period provided mixed fortunes for the advertising industry. It was very quick to take full advantage of the rapid developments in mass media – using cinema and particularly radio. The first radio stations appeared in the early 1920s established by radio-equipment manufacturers and retailers, initially to boost sales of radio sets. In 1922 AT&T's radio station, WEAF in New York, offered 10 minutes of air time to anyone prepared to pay $100. A real-estate firm, Queensboro Corporation from Long Island, has the distinction of purchasing the first commercial radio spots in advertising history – their 15 spots at $50 each publicized a new apartment complex at Jackson Heights. Advertising was enjoying a successful integration with the wider business communities, and the reputations of its practitioners were forged. In 1923 John Orr Young and Raymond Rubicam opened Young

& Rubicam in Philadelphia, moving to New York shortly afterwards. Meanwhile in the UK, Lintas (Lever International Advertising Services) was formed as the house agency of Unilever a year later.

However, boom has a nasty habit of turning to bust. The Wall Street Crash and the subsequent Great Depression across the USA hit advertising hard, and by 1929 the total revenue the industry enjoyed of $3.5 billion had sunk to $1.5 billion. Business endured a torrid time throughout the 1930s culminating in the outbreak of World War II, although this created opportunities for advertising agencies to once more be employed by governments in the propaganda effort. Significant names continued to emerge though – George Gallup joined Young & Rubicam as Director of Research and developed a widely utilized opinion poll system and in 1935 Leo Burnett started his own agency in Chicago.

The post-war era of advertising is considered by many to be its golden age – the advent of television turned the process of communication on its head. It could be argued that the creative practice of advertising has been radicalized on perhaps four occasions by technological advances in the media – the ability to include illustrations and colour in the printing process, the invention of radio, the mass availability of television and the establishment of the internet. In conjunction with each of these events advertising people have demonstrated remarkable invention

By the 1950s advertising took full advantage of the idea that women were responsible for household purchases. This went hand in hand with the emergence of large-scale supermarkets and convenience foods. Horribly stereotyped imagery, but at that time, strategically perfect.

Madison Avenue, New York. The epicentre of the American advertising explosion.

and innovation in maximizing these advancements for their clients' brands and products. I'm going to leave this chronological résumé of advertising alone now, continuing the advertising story by focusing on how individuals and their agencies have revolutionized the way business sells its products and consumers perceive the brands. These advertising legends have, during the past five decades, defined and shaped advertising history into the electrifying industry you so desire to be part of.

Actually, no, let's not talk about advertising legends quite yet, I've just realized, you are probably feeling all argumentative with me. What are you thinking right now? I'm guessing, but I bet some of these questions might have popped into your mind. What is the point of looking at ancient Pears Soap ads? Who cares about the impact of the invention of television on modern advertising? So what if the Madison Avenue advertising agencies changed the way advertising was created? Why harp on about the internet revolution? – I've grown up researching stuff and being bombarded with ads on the internet. They are all perfectly valid questions. No doubt your teachers, tutors or lecturers have shown you plenty of old advertising – weird metallic aliens advertising mashed potato, arty Guinness commercials, shady men standing on street corners smoking long-forgotten brands of cigarettes, or odd-looking 1980s computer ads. If you've seen them, or other ads like them, they probably made you laugh (but the person who showed you them laughed even more, right?). To answer those questions I need you to think about why it is you want to study and work in advertising. Most prospective students I meet tell me that they have always been excited by advertising and for as long as they can remember have enjoyed watching the commercial breaks on television almost as much as the programmes which surround them. This passion for watching television commercials grows into a love for billboards and magazine ads and fuels a burning desire to understand more about how these seductive, glossy and persuasive communication pieces come into being. That brings me right back now to why I think you should explore the ideas, invention and creative thought that have shaped twenty-first-century advertising. To appreciate the radical thinking of the past is to be inspired enough to influence the future. As far as the advertising and promotion industry is concerned, you are very much part of that future and, in order to live up to that expectation, I firmly believe you must start by learning all that you possibly can from others. Advertising and design students are a little unique here, in that they often have a slightly arrogant belief that to be genuinely original in their creative work, it is best not to look at the work of others. Yet all fine-art students will embrace the history of art. Literature students could not comprehend a course that did not include Shakespeare or Dickens. Drama students learn from the work of film and theatre's most revered actors. So why do creative advertising and design students believe such an understanding of their culture creates boundaries around their work? Surely accumulated knowledge gives you the fuel with which to light your own creative fires and to develop your own techniques, styles and ideas? Here are some of the people who have inspired me in different ways by constantly being alive to exciting ideas and who never flinched when questioned or even ridiculed about the validity of their thinking.

Bizarre metallic aliens with an aluminium laugh reinvigorated the instant mashed-potato brand *Smash* in the 1970s.

Image courtesy of BMP DDB

Raymond Rubicam

Raymond Rubicam was born in Brooklyn, New York in 1892. Despite his natural talent for writing, which came from his trade-journalist father and his poetry-writing mother, Rubicam held down numerous jobs in the hope of saving enough to fund a college education in law. At the same time he clung to an ambition to become a writer, and at 19 years old decided to broaden his experiences by literally earning his way along the road from New York to his family's ancestral hometown of Philadelphia. During the course of a year he turned his hand to everything, from a theatre usher to a bellhop and cinema projectionist to door-to-door salesman. On arriving in Philadelphia, he began writing short stories, and on the back of a number of freelance newspaper stories he'd written, won himself a job as a reporter with the *Philadelphia Inquirer*.

After deciding to marry, Rubicam left his job at the newspaper to become a car salesman, a job he was good at but disliked intensely. Whilst working in sales he became more aware of advertising and decided it fulfilled his objective to be a writer and also provided sufficient income to support his new wife. He applied for a job as a copywriter at the then Philadelphia advertising agency F. Wallis Armstrong. His patience wore thin as he awaited a reply, prompting him to write a letter to the head of the agency which would either gain him an instant interview or finish his career before it even started. He got his interview and spent three years learning his trade without ever really enjoying his time at the agency. His decision to move to N.W. Ayer, the largest, most prominent agency in the USA, proved to be inspired and he built his reputation on seminal campaigns such as 'The Instrument of the Immortals' for piano-maker Steinway and 'The Priceless Ingredient' for Squibb.

Raymond Rubicam worked on 'The Instrument of the Immortals' press advertisements for piano-maker Steinway as he learned the advertising craft.

Four years later and now in his early thirties he teamed up with a dynamic account executive named John Orr Young to found Young & Rubicam, which started on a shoe-string budget and grew to be among the largest, most lucrative advertising agencies in the world. Rubicam was among the first to fully realize that outstanding creative thinking was vital to the success of the fledgling agency. Only six months into Young & Rubicam's existence they were winning awards for their campaigns for General Foods and sealing their reputation as a creative advertising agency. In 1926 they moved to New York and set up shop in Madison Avenue, investing large sums into expanding the agency with extra creative copywriters and Vaughn Flannery, America's top art director, which set new standards in American advertising for style and taste. Raymond Rubicam was also the first in advertising to recognize the need for research as part of the creative process and he hired George Gallup to measure

the readership and relative impact of adverts and to establish consumer likes, dislikes and their reading and radio-listening habits. From this research the agency established campaign guidelines which would lead to their campaigns becoming among the most read in America. Rubicam's mantra for this radical new approach was *the way we sell is to get read first.* He also defined his agency's creative work as being strong in selling to the consumer but also remembered longer as being an *admirable piece of work.*

Rubicam always sided with creativity and innovation as being the driving forces behind Young & Rubicam's success and never tired of stressing the need for advertising to be created around fact. 'Try to know more than your competitors do about the market,' he said. 'Then put that knowledge into the hands of writers and artists with imagination and broad human sympathies' (Young & Rubicam). He retained enormous empathy with creative people yet frequently infuriated them with his annoying tendency to reject creative work virtually as the account executive was leaving to visit the client. He justified this particularly maddening habit by claiming that clients remembered exciting creative work long after they had forgotten the deadline had been missed.

John Orr Young retired from his agency in 1927, leaving Raymond Rubicam to take over his presidential mantle, retiring himself at the age of 52 in 1944. He always retained enormous respect from employees at Young & Rubicam with his generous sharing of the credit for outstanding creative work and some equally generous profit sharing. When he left the agency he also left behind his legacy – there were no agency rules and his aphorism 'Resist the Usual' reverberated around the Madison Avenue walls, or as Rubicam's chief copywriter Roy Whittier put it, 'In advertising, the beginning of greatness is to be different and the beginning of failure is to be the same.'[1]

Bill Bernbach

Bill Bernbach was born in 1911 and graduated from New York University with a degree in English Literature. Whilst working in the mailroom of New York firm Schenley he attracted the attention of the chairman, Grover Whalen, who was instrumental in developing Bernbach's talent for writing. When Whalen left to head up New York's World Fair, he took his young charge with him to write his speeches. Bill Bernbach had by now been bitten by the publicity bug and at the end of the World Fair joined the respected advertising agency Weintraub as a copywriter, where he worked alongside the art director Paul Rand, a creative free spirit who had spent time at the seminal Bauhaus art school.

Following a period of service in the American army during World War II, Bernbach returned to advertising at Grey in 1945, rising rapidly to become the agency's

1 D. Ogilvy, *Ogilvy on Advertising*, London: Prion, 1983, p. 198.

creative principal. After four years he had accumulated enough confidence and a modest, yet sufficient investment sum to start his own agency with Ned Doyle, Doyle Dane Bernbach's account supervisor, and Max Dane, who ran his own small agency. Doyle Dane Bernbach quickly established itself as one of the most creative and style-led agencies in New York, growing over the years to establish itself among the top ten advertising agencies in the world. Although the agency publicly stated that no commas separated their names on company stationery because nothing could come between them, Bernbach was the driving force behind its success. His presence within the creative departments was spellbinding, and under his guidance creatives were able to flourish and their talent and reputations soared. At the same time he was an absolute perfectionist, spending hours cutting up and repositioning layouts to exacting standards.

His unfailing belief that his copywriters and art directors were absolutely key to the success of Doyle Dane Bernbach was backed up by an intuitive skill in integrating words and images into the agency's campaigns. Bernbach is credited with the invention of the modern advertising creative team, bringing together copywriters and art directors to work on campaigns as a single creative unit. Other agencies quickly followed his lead, recognizing that their creative departments were being out manoeuvred. Most of these agencies had previously believed that either campaigns should be conceived and created by copywriters, with art directors being passed the idea to make it look good, or that copywriters should be somehow subordinated to art directors. New York creatives aspired to work for Bernbach – he was their mentor, the man who defended the principles of originality and elegance against any client who dared to disagree with him. In arguments about creative approaches he was a formidable opponent, rarely admitting he was wrong. One of the stories passed down to generations of creatives at Doyle Dane Bernbach was that he carried a card with him bearing the words *Maybe He's Right*.

Looking back at the wonderful advertising produced by Doyle Dane Bernbach it is clear that the more conservative tastes of the food and other packaged-products clients were restricting and constraining to Bernbach's unorthodox approach, and his work for them was less successful. Contrast that with the seminal campaigns created by Bernbach, chief copywriter Julian Koenig and art director Helmut Krone for Volkswagen ('Think Small', 'Lemon') and Avis ('We Try Harder'), where his principles of clever and original advertising, but always with the product

Doyle Dane Bernbach changed the way advertising was made with campaigns like *Lemon* for Volkswagen. Devasting simplicity and razor-sharp copy made DDB the envy of the creative world.

Lemon.

as the hero, really broke new ground. On seeing the touches of creative genius that Doyle Dane Bernbach was consistently producing, other, less exciting agencies naturally made frequent attempts to poach his top creatives. But Bernbach was often heard to say that his people would be helpless without his hand to guide and inspire them.

When you're only No.2, you try harder. Or else.

Little fish have to keep moving all of the time. The big ones never stop picking on them.

Avis knows all about the problems of little fish.

We're only No.2 in rent a cars. We'd be swallowed up if we didn't try harder.

Avis can't afford to relax.

There's no rest for us.

We're always emptying ashtrays. Making sure gas tanks are full before we rent our cars. Seeing that the batteries are full of life. Checking our windshield wipers.

And the cars we rent out can't be anything less than spanking new Plymouths.

And since we're not the big fish, you won't feel like a sardine when you come to our counter.

We're not jammed with customers.

© AVIS RENT A CAR SYSTEM, INC.

DDB's strategy for Avis was to use their market position as the second-largest car-rental firm in the USA as a selling point, turning the strategy upside down to great effect.

This softly spoken family man was a genuine inspiration to all those who worked alongside him, a true creative genius in advertising and also in the way he organized his agency. He possessed an uncanny ability to understand creative people and was consistently able to encourage them to create well beyond their own expectations. He died in 1982 after witnessing many changes in advertising, the media and the way consumers absorb messages, but his core belief that creativity is at the heart of great advertising was never diminished. I hope and expect that it never will. Last words go to Bill Bernbach himself, when writing in 1949 about the 'creative revolution': 'let us prove to the world that good taste, good art and good writing can be good selling'.[2]

2 B. Garfield, *Top 100 Advertising Campaigns*, Online. Available HTTP. http://www.adage.com/century/campaigns.html (accessed 26 February 2009).

David Ogilvy

Like Raymond Rubicam, David Ogilvy spent part of his early career as a salesman, but with a significant difference, Ogilvy enjoyed it and was to base the principle of his advertising career around selling. He was born in Surrey, England, to a Scottish father and Irish mother and inherited his father's intellect, gaining a scholarship to the famed Fettes College in Edinburgh at the age of 13. The depression of the 1920s hit his father's business as a financial broker hard, and in 1929 Ogilvy was fortunate to be offered a second scholarship to allow his studies to continue, in History at Christ Church, Oxford. He struggled with his studies, and left Oxford in 1931 to become a trainee chef at the Majestic Hotel in Paris. A year later, he returned to Scotland and found a job selling Aga cooking stoves door to door. He had a natural talent for selling and was asked by his employers to write a training manual for other salesmen, *The Theory and Practice of Selling the Aga Cooker.* A document that was still used over 30 years later as a shining example of sales technique.

His elder brother Francis, meanwhile, was employed by London advertising agency Mather & Crowther, and he showed his brother's sales manual to his bosses; and as a result, David was offered an account executive's position at the agency. The young Ogilvy was a blossoming talent – when a hotel owner walked into Mather & Crowther with a small budget wanting to advertise his hotel's opening, he was handed to the still wet-behind-the-ears Ogilvy to look after. He responded by recommending that the hotelier spend his whole budget on a set of postcards, to be sent to as many people as possible from a telephone directory. The hotel opened fully booked and Ogilvy had his first taste of a successful Direct Response campaign, an advertising technique he was to use to enormous effect throughout his career. By 1938, he persuaded the agency to let him go and work in the USA for a year. He decided to set up home there and moved on to George Gallup's Audience Research Institute in New Jersey. He fell under the spell of Gallup's research techniques and later was to apply all that he learned about meticulous consumer research and consumer reality to his own advertising thinking.

During World War II, he worked in Washington for the British Intelligence Service using Gallup's research models in matters of diplomacy and in analysing the behaviour and nationalism of the American people. By the end of the war General Eisenhower's Psychological Warfare Board had put many aspects of Ogilvy's research and reports on human behaviour into practice across the battlefronts of Europe. After the war, Ogilvy settled into a farmer's life in Pennsylvania living among the Amish people. He realized after a few years that an agricultural lifestyle, though cleansing, serene and content, was not for him, so he moved back to New York.

With the backing of his former London employers, Mather & Crowther, he started his own advertising agency, Ogilvy & Mather, in 1949, which he based on the principles of advertising as an effective selling tool underpinned by solid consumer research. He quickly built a reputation for incisive and insightful copywriting created from his painstaking research into what he perceived American consumers really expected from the products he advertised. At the same time he often infuriated his creative teams (especially the writers, whom he still felt were the linchpin of creative advertising) by rejecting creative work he believed would not elicit above-average responses from consumers. His philosophy of research before creative work gave his agency the edge in understanding the types of words, images and messages that would most effectively stimulate consumers to read Ogilvy & Mather advertising.

David Ogilvy was an absolute master of long persuasive copy. He was also pretty handy with headlines, images and captioning pictures.

Before any creative work could begin, he insisted on understanding all that he could about the product and its likely consumers – this near-scientific approach is naturally commonplace among all advertising agencies today. After winning the Rolls-Royce account, he spent three weeks reading about the car before writing the legendary headline, 'At 60 miles an hour the loudest noise in this new Rolls-Royce comes from the electric clock', and supporting his claim with some 600 words of fact-based copy. His belief that the best way to win new business was to produce admired and effective advertising for other clients was borne out by later winning the Mercedes-Benz account. His first task for the new client was to send a research team to Stuttgart to interview the car manufacturer's engineers; again the creative result was a campaign of long, factual adverts that increased Mercedes-Benz sales

fourfold. Conversely, he is also quoted as saying that 'informal conversations with half-a-dozen housewives can sometimes help a copywriter more than formal surveys in which he does not participate'.[3]

Along with Bill Bernbach at Doyle Dane Bernbach, Ogilvy strongly believed in the concept of brand personality, advocating the idea that products have personalities in the same way that people do. At Ogilvy & Mather these personalities were drawn out from combinations of the product name, its packaging, its cost, the advertising style and, most importantly, from the nature of the product. These factors, Ogilvy insisted, should be carefully presented with an aura of quality – inferior-quality advertising would forever tarnish the product as being inferior too. Ogilvy's ideas on how advertising should be done had branding, along with research, at their core. During the 1950s it was becoming obvious to him that brands should be applied not just to products, but also to consumers, who were becoming increasingly willing to affiliate themselves with products they used, desired and aspired to. These new breeds of consumers were willing to pay a premium for products which suited their lifestyles and which made statements to others about their lifestyles. This basic branding principle still holds true in the sophisticated, complex world of twenty-first-century brands.

Ogilvy & Mather often gave their advertising campaigns a brand personality by using characters as the main visual focus.

Ogilvy & Mather succeeded in building strong, definable and accessible branding for Schweppes tonic water, American Express credit cards, Dove soap and Shell gasoline and fully realized that every piece of advertising should be thought of as making a contribution to the brand itself. Ogilvy's world-famous adverts for the Hathaway Shirt Company are a perfect example of using advertising to build a brand. Despite his usual desire to find out all he could about a product, there was little to say about shirts in the 1950s – essentially Hathaway shirts were much the same as anyone else's; they had sleeves, collars and buttons and were made of fabric. Ogilvy's creative response was much better – let's not focus on branding the shirt, let's brand the man wearing the shirt, he thought.

The man in the Hathaway shirt

He also recognized that most men's shirts were, at the time, bought by women for men, therefore advertising for Hathaway had to have an appeal to female consumers whilst retaining a strong appeal for the men who were to wear them. His friend George Wrangell seemed to fit the criteria well as the face of the brand,

3 D. Ogilvy, *Ogilvy on Advertising*, London: Prion, 1983, p. 12.

but several attempts to have him look engaging yet distinctive failed in the photographic studio. Someone, no one seems quite sure who, had the idea of having the model wear an eye patch to add, as Ogilvy states, 'story appeal', a talking point or hook. Even Ogilvy was mystified as to why this simple prop addition became synonymous with a shirt brand, and completely redefined it. 'Exactly why it turned out to be so successful I shall never know. It put Hathaway on the map after 116 years of relative obscurity. What struck me as a moderately good idea for a wet Tuesday morning made me famous. I could have wished for fame to come from some more serious achievement.'[4] The adverts featured Ogilvy's trademark long copy and large, captioned images, and the Hathaway brand was firmly established and intrinsically branded with its eye-patch sporting gentleman, who was clearly not on his way up, he had already arrived.

In 1973 Ogilvy retired from his agency to France, though he kept in touch with its activities. His death in 1999 leaves behind a legacy that has influenced the way advertising agencies conduct their business. His revolutionary brand-building techniques, unfailing thirst for research and inventive copy are still in evidence across the industry today. He was notoriously fastidious and a ferocious list compiler and insisted on using his clients' products himself. He maintained that he couldn't expect to be able to persuade anyone else to buy them if he wouldn't use them himself, so he drove a Rolls-Royce and very likely washed with Dove soap and wore Hathaway shirts too. He extended this insistence to Ogilvy & Mather staff too, particularly account handlers, and he was proud of the fact that they very often knew more about clients' products than clients did themselves. It is not uncommon for advertising agencies to be loyal to their client by buying its products – I worked for an agency myself whose major business came from Volkswagen and all of the company cars were purchased from that manufacturer – but Ogilvy went further than that. For him it was about research and empathy with the brand.

John Hegarty

Advertising creatives who have made their name and influenced subsequent generations of advertising people in more recent times took their decision to work towards a career in advertising much earlier than Rubicam, Bernbach and Ogilvy. Very often they trained in some form of visual communication rather than find themselves in advertising after a number of false career starts; John Hegarty is no exception. He grew up in modest surroundings in North London and was fortunate enough to gain a place at Challoner Grammar School in Finchley. He left there to continue his education at Hornsey Art School and the London College of Printing, though he left before completing the course, as he felt his work had so much of an

---

4 D. Ogilvy, *Confessions of an Advertising Man,* New York: Atheneum, 1963, pp. 116–17.

advertising bias he would fail anyway. He began his advertising career in London as a junior art director at Benton & Bowles in 1965, leaving to become an art director, working with Charles Saatchi as copywriter, at Cramer Saatchi in 1967 – which became the world famous Saatchi & Saatchi agency in 1970. A year later Hegarty had risen to the position of Deputy Creative Director, a position he held until 1973 when he left to co-found TBWA, London, as Creative Director. Under his creative stewardship, TBWA, London was the first to be voted *Campaign* (the UK's leading advertising magazine) Agency of the Year in 1980. He left in 1982 to found Bartle Bogle Hegarty with his partners Nigel Bogle (who is still the agency's Chief Executive) and John Bartle. The agency has grown to a worldwide operation with offices in London, New York, Singapore, Tokyo and São Paulo, and Hegarty continues to be heavily involved as the agency's Chairman and Worldwide Creative Director. He appears frequently in the media talking eloquently and passionately about his first love – advertising.

Highly regarded in the industry as a 'creative's creative' his hands-on involvement in some of the UK's finest creative advertising has been an inspiration to many aspiring young art directors. Bartle Bogle Hegarty have been frequent winners of *Campaign* magazine's Agency of the Year accolade and Hegarty's personal achievements include two D&AD Golds and six Silvers, Cannes Golds and Silvers, and British Television Gold and Silvers. He was awarded the D&AD President's Award for outstanding achievement in the advertising industry. In May 2005, the International Clio Awards awarded him a Lifetime Achievement Award for his outstanding contribution to the industry. In 2007, he received a knighthood in the Queen's birthday honours. Hegarty has also been appointed to the New York's One Club Hall of Fame and in 2008 was inducted into the New York Art Directors Club Hall of Fame.

But such high-level recognition from his advertising peers has to be earned, and Hegarty's own creative philosophy has always been for his and his agency's work to stand out from the crowd, to break out and explore new ideas. Bartle Bogle Hegarty will perhaps be best remembered for the long-running campaigns they have conceived for Levi Strauss, many of which Hegarty worked on personally. Since the now legendary 'Launderette' commercial appeared in 1984, the agency has become the master of compelling, entertaining commercials that invite consumers to belong to the brands it promotes. Yet successive campaigns for Levi Strauss have consistently helped reinvent the brand and remain fresh and cutting-edge through literally dozens of commercials. Hegarty's understanding of popular culture, coupled with slick well-conceived production and brilliantly inventive ideas, have been instrumental in the agency's ability to retain the Levi's account for the best part of three decades. The unforgettable image of Nick Kamen dropping his jeans and the glorious retro styling of 'Launderette' together with an unswerving affinity to the brand and product caused a sensation. The lead actor became a minor pop and media star in his own right, and successive commercials had soundtracks that became re-released No. 1 hit singles. My personal favourite is the second in the series, which presented the

In the past quarter of a century, Bartle Bogle Hegarty have continued to surprise consumers by extending the boundaries of the Levi Strauss brand. This example comes from 1985.

Levi 501 product as having 'shrink-to-fit' benefits. The commercial was beautifully photographed in what the viewer perceives to be a typical 1960s New York apartment block, and has the delightfully simple image of a handsome, style-conscious American hunk slipping into a hot bath in his jeans to shrink them around his perfectly formed waist and legs. All the while, Hegarty's belief in the importance of music in his commercials was borne out with the faintly rebellious 'Wonderful World' by Sam Cooke providing the soundtrack. Who would not be seduced into an affinity with the brand and the lifestyle it presented? As a 20-year-old design student, I certainly was.

As Levi 501s dropped out of fashion, Bartle Bogle Hegarty completely redefined the brand and created Flat Eric, a surreal furry yellow puppet, to sell Levi's Sta-Prest range of casual trousers. Flat Eric first appeared alongside a slightly geeky guy being pulled over by an American police car, coyly switching the prototype-techno soundtrack to something more sedate as the officer approached the car and finally satisfying him by producing a driver's licence with his own yellow face on. The UK went crazy for Flat Eric, and he too became a star for a while. In many ways, these two commercials embody Hegarty's view that one of the principles of advertising success is to give a brand fame; he of course supported that with some brilliantly original ideas which cemented his and Bartle Bogle Hegarty's reputations as among the most exciting creatives in the business.

Unlike Rubicam, Bernbach and Ogilvy, Hegarty and his contemporaries had a new consumer phenomenon to overcome – the sheer volume of advertising that swamps consumers almost to the point of total disinterest. He understands that

consumers don't really need another mobile phone, or a car or even more toothpaste products, and no longer believe that one product contains any more of a magic ingredient than any other does. The challenge is to keep a brand in the minds of consumers, and Hegarty's view is that this can now only be achieved by image; with most competitive products being equal in their benefits, the only thing left is lifestyle. So much of Bartle Bogle Hegarty's work focuses on the thought that consumers only buy brands they believe in and are happy to be seen with – a world of subjective taste and fashion where only brilliantly clear creativity and innovative thinking will triumph. This has also changed the way in which consumers behave: in a multimedia society they no longer expect to wait for information to be delivered, they actively seek it out. Advertising must therefore adopt a new mindset to develop creative thinking and to plan media strategies. The result is that advertising must increasingly form a part of a consumer's entertainment and not simply be high-handedly offering information and expecting to be read, seen or heard.

The agency that gave us 'Vorsprung durch Technik' to personify the Audi car brand and the Lynx Effect, both of which defined the thinking and brand-building aesthetics of 1980s advertising, has had to shift its strategies away from sole reliance on the traditional mainstay of television. Hegarty maintains that television is still among the most powerful media available in advertising, which it is – television shows like Channel 4's *Big Brother* and ITV's *X-Factor* still command enormous media attention. He has been among the advertising forerunners in creating

This BBH press advertisement majors heavily on Audi's brand statement. It makes the car look quite good too!

campaigns which operate across many media platforms, largely because he is convinced his agency should create entertaining advertising that should be seen by people, not missed. Hegarty has always been one of advertising's boldest and most daring creatives; this proactive mindset is one of Bartle Bogle Hegarty's most cherished resources. The £16 million campaign they unleashed for Vodafone, 'Make the Most of Now', began with an ambitious television launch across 200 channels simultaneously in which viewers saw thousands of clock parts rain down on streets in London and Glasgow, a spectacular commercial simply bursting with creative ideas and sublime production. Whilst 200 channels were airing the TV commercial, online users of eBay, Google, MSN, Rightmove, Pricerunner and YouTube witnessed the web pages they were viewing folding up into tiny squares which disappeared into a graphic of a mobile phone. Stunningly creative, not just visually, but also as examples of communication strategy.

Once again, Bartle Bogle Hegarty were able to make the brand they were advertising more famous by showing consumers something interesting. Hegarty defines his agency's strategic approach as being as vital as their sparkling creativity, using television to create the fame he so frequently alludes to, creating billboards that constantly converse with consumers and harnessing the internet to interest and excite on a more personal level. Hegarty's legacy will be the fusing of startling, original creative ideas which entertain with brilliant strategic thinking that takes control of the media consumers are excited by.

Jay Chiat

'Good enough is not enough' – the mantra of, arguably, advertising's most prominent maverick. Morton Jay Chiat was born in the Bronx district of New York in 1931 but he grew up in New Jersey. After graduating from Rutgers University he joined the US Air Force as a public information officer and he found himself in California. Following his discharge and a short time working on recruitment advertising, in 1958 he joined the Leland Oliver Company, a small advertising agency in Orange County, California. He rose to the position of Creative Director before leaving in 1962 to open his own agency, Jay Chiat & Associates. In 1968 after less than an hour's conversation with Guy Day at a Los Angeles Dodgers ball game, the two men agreed to merge their agencies to form Chiat/Day. So began a famously rocky partnership that saw Guy Day leave and return twice, before finally leaving in 1986 – he would often say of Jay Chiat that 'the guy is a born gambler'. Chiat had an equally fractious relationship with Chiat/Day staff, who often became factionalized into two camps. On one side, there were those who were inspired by his uncompromising opinions on what constituted great advertising and who bought into Chiat's creative philosophies – they were fiercely loyal to him. Others were deeply frustrated by his refusal to appreciate and listen to different viewpoints, which on many occasions led to the agency losing clients. He pushed himself, the people around him and the agency's clients to the edge and challenged them all to find a way to fly – Chiat trod the finest of lines between genius and madman.

When reflecting on the achievements of Chiat/Day, he would often muse that losing clients was his real talent, and many global brands came to try for themselves Chiat's unorthodox methods and challenging thinking. American Express, Apple, Honda, Nike and Reebok all sampled aspects of his genius and subsequently retreated, disillusioned with the inconsistency of the results and in some cases simply scared away. No client, no matter how conservative, could fail to be impressed by Chiat/Day when they were perceived to have got campaigns right – then, the results were spectacular. During the Los Angeles Olympic Games in 1984, the city was virtually pasted over by huge Nike posters of athletes and saturated by a near-rotation commercial featuring an infectious rendition of 'I Love LA' by American singer Randy Newman. America believed, completely as a result of Chiat/Day's campaigns, that Nike was the Olympics' official sports footwear sponsor, despite the fact that Converse had invested $4 million for that title. This kind of advertising excitement was Jay Chiat at his very best. He was absolutely convinced that compelling brand advertising had to be liberally soaked in art, design, music and every other aspect of popular culture to deliver aesthetically correct advertising messages. Then, by embodying the brand with irresistible cultural statements, it would simply sell products and secondary merchandise in larger volumes.

The coming together of Chiat's iconic brand-building ideas and the design and culture-led mission statements of San Francisco's Apple Inc. should have been a

Chiat/Day's groundbreaking Super Bowl commercial for Apple Computers was controversial yet instrumental in defining the Apple brand.

creative marriage made in advertising heaven. The relationship, in retrospect, gave birth to arguably the most celebrated television commercial of the past three decades, but it so nearly didn't run. To introduce the Macintosh computer, Chiat/Day created *1984*, to be aired during Super Bowl XVIII in January 1984. The commercial, unbelievably given its legacy, ran only once and was a striking, consuming visual spectacular given life by Ridley Scott, the director of *Alien*, *Blade Runner* and, more recently, *Gladiator*. To fully comprehend the cataclysmic visuals and, proposition behind this commercial, it is necessary to understand something of the year 1984 itself. In 1948, George Orwell created a visionary and prophetic masterpiece in the form of his novel, *1984*. The story described the experiences of Winston Smith, a freethinker, at a time when all the world's nations were kept perpetually at war. The activities, thoughts and desires of ordinary people were monitored by Big Brother, an autocratic dictator, who saw all from a network of television screens on the streets and in people's homes. The Party, overseen by Big Brother, continually rewrites history to fit its manifesto, and by a system of political and sociological conformity crushes all individuality and personal freedom out of all those who dare to think for themselves.

The commercial opens with mindless, vacuous humans marching through a transparent corridor towards a large assembly hall where Big Brother rails against insubordination on huge video screens. As the crowd stares passively at the screens, an athletic young woman waving a sledgehammer bursts into the hall with Thought Police in hot pursuit. With Big Brother's rhetorical ranting reaching a crescendo, she throws the hammer with all her might at the screen, which explodes in a blinding flash of light that envelopes the confused crowd. The commercial closes with the words, 'On January 24th, Apple Computer will introduce Macintosh. And you'll see why 1984 won't be like "1984"'. Chiat/Day's creative thinking and Ridley Scott's visual homage to German Expressionist cinema had delivered a 60-second spot described by Apple co-founder Steve Jobs as 'insanely great advertising'. But this was not just advertising, this was an event; yet Apple's cost-concerned board of directors were deeply nervous. Focus groups and other market testing had delivered very poor responses to Chiat/Day's opus, and Apple's marketing team instructed their agency to cancel the advert. According to Chiat, one of the two 60-second spots was sold (the ad was scheduled to run twice) but the second spot remained unsold; the board reluctantly agreed the commercial should be shown. American media pundits were confused – was it a commercial or was it a movie? *Advertising Age* rates it as the Commercial of the Decade of the 1980s and it won a top prize at the Cannes International Advertising Film Festival. But *Entertainment Weekly* denounced it as 'just so pretentious' and 'the most overrated commercial ever' and not surprisingly it was not featured in their Fifty Greatest Commercials of All Time (3 March 1995).

As an event, it achieved what plenty of advertising has striven for and fallen short of – it got talked about a great deal. *1984* took its place in the consumer's cultural consciousness and will be remembered as forming part of a consumer lifestyle, not

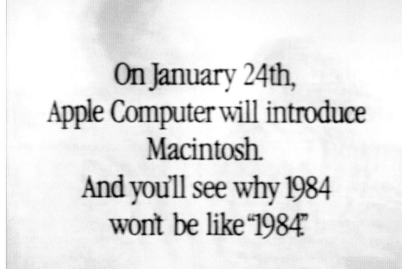

On January 24th,
Apple Computer will introduce
Macintosh.
And you'll see why 1984
won't be like "1984."

Endscreen from Chiat/Day's *1984* commercial.

as the technological innovation it clearly was. This was precisely what Chiat/Day intended, and a Super Bowl slot was chosen because Americans expect to see and to enjoy the advertising on display, and most importantly to see and to be seduced by something totally new.

In time-honoured Jay Chiat tradition, Apple returned to his agency in 1985 to launch its Macintosh Office product systems. Chiat/Day presented *Lemmings* in which we see a new line of human drones in business suits, blindfold and climbing a hill. At the top, each jumps over the precipice blindly following their leader; the final drone pulls off its blindfold to deliver a product message. The proposition is clear; other computer brands (especially IBM) exist only for brainwashed clones. Yet the commercial failed as spectacularly as *1984* had succeeded, in offering no resolution and no cultural or lifestyle influences. Chiat/Day lost the Apple account amid accusations that this is what happens when advertising loses sight of the product and focuses exclusively on an entertainment event. Consumers will only talk about advertising when they find it stimulating and interesting and the product has a perceived value in their lives.

Jay Chiat's legacy is twofold. Firstly, he successfully fired advertising deep into the heart of popular consumer culture. Secondly, he changed the way American advertising agencies operate when he hired specialist Account Planners to explore and implement research into the creative process, a common practice in British agencies but very rare in the USA (remember David Ogilvy?). Chiat/Day's roots in the late 1960s were the essential ingredients of an agency that dared to behave

differently to conventional advertising business – they pioneered open-plan working spaces, lauded the unconventional and had a genuine zest for the work they produced. Chiat/Day was an industry-acclaimed agency, with 1,200 employees at its peak in the early 1990s, but it was plagued by expansion strategies that proved to be expensive failures and the business battled with significant debts. Jay Chiat was a true innovator but with the kind of fearless bravery that meant he often got things badly wrong. In 1995 he reluctantly agreed to relinquish control and sold out to the Omnicom Group, which merged Chiat/Day into TBWA International. He left his beloved agency to invest in internet-based businesses, forming Screaming Media in 1998 to provide content for other websites. Ironically, as Chairman of Screaming Media, he hired an advertising agency in 2000 and was quoted in an *Adweek* interview as saying, 'Now that I'm a client, I understand what a jerk I was.' He died from cancer-related illness aged 70 in California in 2002.

Andy Laws and David Abrahams

In a neat twist of advertising fate, Jay Chiat charged Andy Laws and David Abrahams with the responsibility of merging Chiat/Day with TBWA in London. This sour experience was the catalyst for St. Lukes, the most dynamic, progressive advertising agency London had seen in years. The journey towards St. Lukes began with a telephone call to Andy Laws, then Managing Director of Chiat/Day. It was Jay Chiat, informing him that the agency was to be sold to the Omnicom Group and to set up an urgent meeting with TBWA to agree the detail of the merger. Prior to this Laws had given up the luxury lifestyle of an advertising executive at the so-called 'cathedral of creativity', Collett Dickenson Pearce, whose legendary 'Happiness Is A Cigar Called Hamlet' campaigns ran for almost 25 years. He left because he felt the chance to work for the extraordinary Jay Chiat was too good to pass up. After winning the prestigious Midland Bank account in 1990, Laws persuaded former Collett Dickenson Pearce colleague David Abrahams to join him at Chiat/Day. However, Jay Chiat's American model of inclusive idea development, where the whole team is involved, didn't sit comfortably with everyone at the London office. Creatives were used to being kept away from business discussions and clients and there was a rapid turnover of staff; this allowed Andy Laws and David Abrahams to become instrumental in hiring exactly the right people – those they felt would rise to the challenge of an innovative, forward-thinking advertising agency. In 1992 the pair were offered the chance, by Jay Chiat, to research and develop the concept of what an advertising agency might look like in the future. After worldwide visits to all Chiat/Day agencies, Abrahams authored a report entitled *Something Else Is Going On,* which spoke of the ways in which business relates to society and highlighted The Body Shop and Ben & Jerry's as companies which were profiting properly from their roles in consumer society. It also implied, to Chiat's dismay, that the agency should be rebranded and restructured as a charitable organization. Although, perhaps unsurprisingly,

Chiat/Day did not act upon the report, many of its ideas formed the basis for the founding of St. Lukes (though not the charity plan). The internal trauma at the London office of Chiat/Day worsened, and suspicions that Jay himself was losing his way in the USA, too, heightened the uncertainty. Laws, Abrahams and the rest of Chiat/Day London had worked hard to build their reputations as highly creative, original thinkers with a taste for the unusual. Now, with the proposed sale and merger with TBWA, they had visions of being sucked back into the corporate worlds they had striven to escape from. The London team was put under pressure to buy into and accept the takeover, by a variety of high-powered Omnicom executives. Nothing doing. Laws and Abrahams stuck to their guns and finally agreed a deal which allowed them to buy Chiat/Day London for £1, with a £1.2 million 'earn out' payable over up to seven years. A council of war was called to plan a strategy for the newly founded independent agency, which officially bought out of Omnicom on 31 August 1995. Abrahams presented the whole agency with a strategic plan inventively entitled *The World Does Not Need Another Advertising Agency*, with its thrust being the need to be fundamentally different to any other agency, to retain its status and avoid being swallowed up, as Chiat/Day had been. Laws and Abrahams were opposites who complemented each other – Laws the visionary and blue-sky thinker and Abrahams the strategist with a unique talent for fusing innovative ideas together into workable structures.

St. Lukes was named after discovering that medieval trades and guilds named themselves after saints. St. Luke was discovered to be the patron saint of creativity

This St. Lukes commercial for British Telecom was centred around 'real' people speaking about communicating in an amphitheatre setting.

and doctors – he fitted perfectly with an agency who planned to use their exciting ideas to cure sales or image problems. This was an agency determined to operate in a new and very different way, as well as carry those principles forward into its work. The agency was set up as a littleknown business model called a QUEST (Qualifying Employee Shared Ownership Trust), essentially owned by each and every member of staff. St. Lukes held its launch party on 18 October 1995 – yes, you've guessed it, St. Luke's Day.

Clearly, St. Lukes did not entirely race ahead from a standing start. The nucleus of the team was already in place and some clients had agreed to come along too, in particular the lucrative Midland Bank business (which is now absorbed into HSBC). New clients too were curious to explore the energy, vitality and air of nonconformism St. Lukes was generating around London and beyond. Some carefully written press releases and well-chosen interviews with *Campaign*, the most influential advertising magazine, enhanced the mystique of St. Lukes. Agencies and clients alike were desperate to learn more about this co-operative which challenged the advertising status quo like no other agency before them. The 35 staff who started St. Lukes were stakeholders, each owning an equal share in the business and each having an individual voice. Every decision the business made was debated and contributed to by the stakeholders. Laws inspired and instigated their ideas and Abrahams brilliantly moulded the resultant innovations into fully functioning systems and practices.

A project team, who worked ambiently in project spaces uniquely devised and designed for the brands they worked for, looked after each client. Ikea, Fox's Biscuits, British Telecom, Clark's Shoes, Boots and Eurostar clamoured to be part of the St. Lukes creative movement. Creatives Tom Childs and Ed Morris, with their project team, created outstanding campaigns for Teletext, which had an almost mystical quality to it. Other agencies sniffed at how such creative chaos could work, wondering how anyone could function within an environment of 'hot desking', no hierarchies and project spaces that often resembled children's playrooms. Creative director Dave Buonaguidi was totally at home in this 'new world' where everyone was creative. 'Our methodology doesn't make sense to most people in this business and that really frustrates them. They know what we are doing is great, they know our product is great; I mean everything we do is talked about. Everything. They know it's good, but they don't know why. They think we have a secret formula. Like Coca-Cola. Everyone loves Coca-Cola but no one knows what's inside. All they end up saying is that we are like the Moonies. Fine. I like that.'[5]

The work of St. Lukes was stunning, an ironic, witty and spectacularly inventive portfolio of advertising that had people laughing and engaging with the surrealistic humour of the Clark's Shoes campaigns or the philosophical rhetoric of Eric Cantona in television commercials for Eurostar. The irreverent and slightly sinister Ikea work

5 A. Laws, *Open Minds*, London: Orion Business, 1998, p. 184.

The work St. Lukes produced for Ikea was laced with their trademark wit and irony.

established the bold Swedish retailer as the store of choice for style-conscious households. But Britain was to undergo a sweeping change in 1997. Tony Blair led Labour to government for the first time in a generation, on a wave of optimism and media know-how. I vividly remember being on a train to London for a meeting at Abbot Mead Vickers the morning after the election and people were smiling and talking about the positive impact this was to have on their lives. The *modus operandi* of the entire country had changed overnight and the effect on the British public was similar (albeit on a smaller scale) to the effect Barack Obama's election as President of the USA had on the American public. The Government had plans, big ideas and innovations that it needed to share with British people, it had to promote and advertise those ideas – who better to do that than St. Lukes, a new-age advertising agency working with a New Labour Government? Perfect. Gordon Brown and Peter Mandelson were spellbound by St. Lukes, and the campaign created for the Labour Government's *New Deal*, a young persons' training and development programme, was among the finest of the late 1990s. The campaigns were concise and informative yet offered young people a brand they could readily identify with. In one, a wily Scots finance officer reels off unfeasible numbers of zeros as he puts figures on the amount the Government was investing in the *New Deal* programme. However,

one particular piece of creative invention came unstuck. The agency proposed a commercial showing young people at work interacting with their bosses: playing jokes, laughing and wiggling their fingers above the head of a boss as he spoke to the camera about the fabulous young people he had offered opportunities to in his company. Even the slick, polished, people-savvy new Government couldn't be persuaded to buy into the subversive undercurrent of that commercial, believing that it went too far in demonstrating young people enjoying their work. St. Lukes shrugged their shoulders, refused to compromise on what they perceived was the strongest idea yet and shelved the commercial.

To understand and be inspired by St. Lukes, in truth, has less to do with the work they produced and more to do with the environment and culture in which they created it. Andy Laws and David Abrahams will live long in advertising's memory as two people who genuinely challenged the old order and shook its foundations. The irony is, St. Lukes is now completely accepted by clients, media and other agencies alike as being a dynamic, slightly quirky, ideas factory and takes its place alongside its contemporaries as they all vie for similar new business. Just as Tony Blair lost his flavour and the British public turned on his charisma, charm and considerable communication skills, so advertising grew used to St. Lukes, tolerating its idiosyncratic behaviour but no longer considering it revolutionary. For similar reasons, Andy Laws and David Abrahams are no longer at St. Lukes, preferring to seek new challenges in other fields, before their ideas became too 'establishment'.

Trevor Beattie

If I was asked to name one single person in advertising who I felt represented the perfect aspirational role model for students, it would have to be Trevor Beattie. The archetypal bad boy made good, whose disdain for the established order and love affair with controversy have made him one of advertising's most recognizable personalities. The darling of the advertising trade press also frequently found himself justifying his actions within the pages of the mainstream tabloid media. To put that into some sort of context, the effect Beattie has had on *Campaign* magazine closely mirrors the relationship Peter Doherty has with the *NME*. Both also attract similar levels of pious criticism from the UK tabloids for their outspoken and unconventional activities. In fact, Beattie, like Doherty, is a seemingly endless supplier of salacious column inches and outspoken rhetoric. Maybe in some cases it is true that, as copywriter Tom Monahan once said, 'advertising is the rock 'n' roll of the business world'.

 subliminal advertising experiment

Beattie's seminal work with FCUK was always edgy and raised plenty of consumer eyebrows.
Image courtesy of Beattie McGuinness Bungay.

Trevor Beattie is a car mechanic's son and was born in Birmingham in 1959. His road to advertising success began at Moseley Art School and a graphic design and photography course at Wolverhampton Polytechnic. After graduating, he won a 'Creative Scholarship' place at his first advertising agency, Allen Brady & Marsh, and was soon working on the *If You Know What's Good For You – OK* campaign for Weetabix. He took a while to find his feet in London – here was a working-class Brummie lad mixing it with what he perceived as 'a posh middle-class world'. By his own admission his upbringing helped him get into advertising. 'I was always the drawer of the family but I didn't know there was such a job as writing the adverts. I used to call them cartoons and sing the cartoons. I was clearly never going to get a proper job.' Beattie does not look or behave like the stereotypical ad-man; his long curly hair, leather jacket and jeans are a million miles from the Gucci and Porsche image normally associated with advertising 'royalty'. Yet his career has included a 15-year stint, much of it as creative director, at worldwide 'super agency' TBWA. He walked away from TBWA in 1997 after, he says, failing to be consulted over a merger with another agency. He was hired by GGT as creative director soon afterwards, only for GGT to merge with TBWA a year later. Ironically, once again, he found himself creative director at TBWA. Since May 2005 he has devoted himself to working as a partner at his own advertising agency, Beattie McGuinness Bungay (BMB), which was started with a simple objective – to use creativity to solve business problems. BMB is an advertising agency and makes no attempt to disguise the fact, but through its creative work it strives to widen the definitions clients hold of what advertising is. Beattie says about BMB, 'we don't hope to reinvent the wheel, we would like to turn it a bit faster'.

His personal work mantra is 'get noticed'. Possibly one of the understatements of all time, when you realize that this is the creative force behind the shape-shifting branding campaigns for French Connection UK, otherwise known as FCUK. The origins of this brand revolution were quite simple. Beattie had received a brief from French Connection Chief Executive Officer Stephen Marks which simply read, 'make French Connection the most talked-about fashion brand on the high street'. But the idea to restyle the brand as FCUK wasn't wholly Beattie's. His version of the story is that when the newly opened store in Hong Kong began faxing the London head office, addressing its correspondence to FCUK from FCHK, the answer was literally staring Beattie in the face. The campaign theme FCUK FASHION was presented, and French Connection bought into the idea with scarcely a second thought. Since 1997, this evocative, highly enticing theme has been the lifeblood of eight separate campaigns and the brand has grown on an epic scale with stores in over 20 different countries. And then there are the T-shirts: over 1 million emblazoned with FCUK have been sold at around £20 a time. This was genius branding at work: provocative and sufficiently rebellious to allow young people to feel that here was a brand they could take complete ownership of. Their parents would look on disapprovingly as their sons and daughters went out proudly displaying the FCUK logo. Of course, time softens the blow and parents now happily buy their teenagers FCUK Christmas gift packs from any supermarket without raising an eyebrow. I would not mind betting, though, that if you saw someone walking towards you in the street with a T-shirt that read FUCK FASHION, it would take some seconds to register that it actually was not an FCUK shirt. Back in 1997, though, Beattie's work was denigrated by many advertising industry traditionalists, and dismissed as crass and vulgar. The tabloid press had a field day addressing their readerships on the morality of FCUK; this may even have happened in the columns adjacent to the pictures they published of semi-naked models or the images of drunken celebrities. Double standards anyone?

Beattie's work went beyond the single dimension of creative copylines and images; his creativity extended into the juxtaposition of creative thinking and mixed media. When the boxer Lennox Lewis fought Evander Holyfield for the world title, his shorts featured the slogan FCUK FEAR. What was this? Was it an advert, a product placement, sponsorship or a PR stunt? Best of all – as the fight was televised across the world – was it a 30-minute global TV commercial? Again, advertising traditionalists dismissed the work as gimmicky and insubstantial, yet Beattie would argue that this and other ideas like it helped make FCUK a global player. The branding on the new world champion's shorts was supported by a poster campaign featuring Lennox Lewis on a black background next to the words:

finally
crowned
undisputed
king

TBWA's outdoor campaigns for Wonderbra quite literally stopped traffic.

Image courtesy of Beattie McGuinness Bungay.

This outdoor poster is typical of Beattie's irreverent creative style.

Image courtesy of Beattie McGuinness Bungay.

Beattie's star was in the ascendancy, consolidating his creative reputation. This was in contrast to being dismissed as a 'flash in the pan' in 1994 following the infamous *Hello Boys* campaign for Wonderbra, featuring copious portions of the model Eva Herzigova, created by TBWA (even though Beattie didn't write that particular line himself he appeared to get all the credit). This work had also been lambasted by the industry and the press as vulgar, yet he was always willing to talk to the press, which of course lit his name with even brighter lights and, more importantly, created plenty of free publicity for the brands he and TBWA advertised. Controversy has

seldom been far from any advertising campaigns with Trevor Beattie at the creative helm, and another storm was brewing. TBWA was appointed to handle Labour's advertising campaigns in the run-up to the general election of 1997, the start of the rise of Tony Blair. One poster in particular stood out and an enormous furore blew up over the copyline: 'The day Tory sums add up', with images of the heads of Conservative Party leader Michael Howard and Shadow Cabinet member Oliver Letwin superimposed onto the bodies of flying pigs. Both men are Jewish, and a row broke out about Beattie's alleged anti-Semitism. He remained undeterred, believing that the publicity resulting from campaigns is as vital as the advertising itself. In the 2001 election campaign, he enjoyed much publicity with his celebrated image of William Hague sporting Margaret Thatcher's hair.

Needless to say, Beattie's creative forays into British politics were no less controversial than his work for FCUK and Wonderbra.

Image courtesy of Beattie McGuinness Bungay.

French Connection CEO Stephen Marks was once unconvincingly quoted as saying of the FCUK campaigns that 'there was no thought of it being rude'. Beattie has tested the patience of consumers and advertising people frequently, and one political commentator wrote prior to the 2001 election that 'no advertisement has done as much as Beattie's squalid play on words [FCUK] to degrade our public space. If the Prime Minister [Tony Blair] had an ounce of moral sentiment, he would never go near a creep like Beattie.' Harsh words and typical of the polarized opinions Trevor Beattie attracts, and his work often fell foul of the authorities. The Advertising Standards Authority (ASA) banned the putting up of any new posters for FCUK without their prior approval following a series of billboards promoting French Connection's latest website: fcukinkybugger.com. The ASA also went on record saying that it was shocked when French Connection 'had the gall' to send in a script using the exact same website promotion for a television commercial.

Actually it is perfectly feasible to talk forever about Trevor Beattie. Something in the man's nature demands attention, courts controversy and inspires or irritates in roughly equal proportions. There is no doubting that given the right client and positive stimulation Beattie will create spectacularly effective advertising campaigns and, more often than not, one hell of a stir to go with them. Without doubt, Beattie is a talented creative and persuasive word-spinner, but his legacy in contemporary advertising will unquestionably be his intuitive talent to push ideas beyond the boundaries of accepted good taste. Strangely, the general public is relatively ambivalent and tolerant of his work – it's the tabloid press and the ASA whose skin

he really gets under. Or does he? Let's not forget his early career was kick-started by his 'media-magnetism'. The press saw in Beattie someone who could certainly fill a few column inches with his antics; conversely, Beattie saw in the press an additional string to his advertising bow. Why stick to posters or TV when a few deftly conceived provocative headlines and images can generate seemingly limitless free publicity?

Trevor Beattie is a man of our times; probably it's no accident that his star began to ascend at roughly the same time as New Labour's. His friendship with Peter Mandelson, Tony Blair's media guru, is a clear indicator of an advertising mastermind taking full advantage of the mass-communication tools available to him. And then some.

That's a handful of names and a few choice quotes and innovations to get your mind racing. A place to start and absolutely not a place to finish – please do explore the work of my personal hall of fame in more depth but look much further too, not just within advertising. Find out what makes very special creative minds work and be inspired by their methods. Perhaps you will decide cutting-edge thinkers are risk-takers, or maybe egotists, possibly attention-seekers, or sometimes lunatics. Could they just be talented ideas people taking full advantage of their environments? Your call.

Other keywords, searches, soundbites and eye-openers

Here's just a few more pioneers, creative mavericks and thought-provokers; plenty have had nothing whatever to do with advertising, but all have made people sit up and take notice of their ideas. They are fighters, left-field thinkers, and all share a single-minded vision that they are prepared to believe in the face of criticism and adversity. All, too, have changed the worlds in which they work and made life for the next generation just a little easier.

- Heston Blumenthal
- Nelson Mandela
- Pete Townshend
- Peter Doherty
- David Lynch
- Luke Sullivan
- Maurice and Charles Saatchi
- Tracey Emin
- John Lydon
- David Bowie
- HHCL and Partners
- Vaughan Oliver
- Aldous Huxley
- Neville Brody
- Tony Wilson
- John Peel
- Jack Kerouac
- Richard Hamilton
- Kazimir Malevich
- Wasily Kandinsky
- Morrissey
- The Bauhaus
- Bob Marley
- Moholy-Nagy
- Damien Hirst
- Che Guevara
- George Orwell
- Muhammad Ali
- Andy Warhol . . .

Some websites to visit

Some general sites to explore more:

Wikipedia (obviously)
www.adage.com
www.ipa.co.uk

Some specific sites explore the legacies of my advertising mentors

Raymond Rubicam / Young & Rubicam
www.yr.com

Bill Bernbach / Doyle Dane Bernbach
www.ddb.com

David Ogilvy / Ogilvy & Mather
www.ogilvy.com

John Hegarty / Bartle Bogle Hegarty
www.bbh.co.uk

Jay Chiat / Chiat/Day
www.tbwachiat.com

Andy Laws and David Abrahams
www.stlukes.co.uk

Trevor Beattie
www.bmbaagency.com/www.tbwa.com

Some books to read

The Young & Rubicam Travelling Creative Workshop
Hanley Norins

Bill Bernbach's Book: A History of the Advertising that Changed the History of Advertising
Bob Levenson

Confessions of an Advertising Man
David Ogilvy

Ogilvy on Advertising
David Ogilvy

Creative Company: How St. Luke's Became 'the AD Agency to End All AD Agencies'
Andy Law

Open Minds: Twenty-first Century Business Lessons and Innovations from St. Luke's
Andy Law

FCUK Advertising
Trevor Beattie and Bill Bungay

Adland: A Global History of Advertising
Mark Tungate

Get involved

The world would be crushingly dull if everyone else adopted my heroes and inspirations. Visit our Facebook and Twitter pages and post a hero you think other advertising students would be excited by learning more about:

* search Facebook for 'Advertising Its Business Culture and Careers'
* www.twitter.com/adculture

3 Making the disinterested interested

If you are reading this book, you are probably plotting ways in which you can work in the advertising and promotion industry. You have no doubt discussed this with your friends and family; of course your parents are hugely supportive of everything you want to do, but others are perhaps less convinced. Am I right? How often have you heard variations on these statements? Delete as applicable.

> Why do you want to do that? Nobody ever reads/watches/takes any notice of advertising.

> When the commercial break comes on I make a cup of tea/go to the loo/phone a friend.

> Advertising? What a total waste of money.

> Advertising has never persuaded me to buy anything.

The list goes on and on. In fact, many people would openly state that those who work in advertising are just in it for the money and would do well to get a proper job. Substitute advertising for lawyers, bankers, estate agents and any other profession that people seem to love to hate. Sorry, am I making you feel uncomfortable? Did you think everyone loves you if you say you work in advertising? Welcome to the world of popular disposable culture. Advertising is arguably the only profession in the world that charges considerable fees to make a product that will be discarded in a few seconds. Direct mail tossed unopened into a waste bin; a commercial missed while its intended viewers pop out and put the kettle on; billboard posters pasted over within a week or computers with spam and content filters and the option to disable pop-up windows. All that carefully planned, crafted and conceived creative thinking cast aside or completely ignored. Or is it?

JUST DO IT

Wieden+Kennedy's poster campaigns for Nike accurately reflected the British consumer's love of sporting icons.

Image courtesy of Wieden+Kennedy London.

If you were to go out into the town or city centre where you live and ask people for their views on advertising, most of the statements and arguments I have just hinted at would be mentioned, and a few more choice comments besides. But before you rush off and throw yourself under the nearest bus (complete with its multitude of advertising messages), consider the realities of advertising. In simplistic terms, advertising must generate results or companies the world over would not continue to spend large sums of money on promoting their brands and products. Therefore, we can safely assume that the seemingly disinterested public must be taking notice after all. How can we assume that? Easy, they give themselves away far too often. Over the years the happy refrains of *I Feel Like Chicken Tonight* or *Do the Shake N Vac* have been hummed by people everywhere. Celebrity sports stars have been enthusiastically identified from Nike or Adidas campaigns and without question many did indeed want to buy the world a Coke in the legendary campaigns of the 1970s. The pure entertainment advertising explored by Fallon, in their work for Cadbury's Dairy Milk, has made for exceedingly popular viewing. The drum-battering human gorilla and the quirky schoolchildren with their wonky eyebrows are show-stoppers. The kind of TV commercials that have people rushing into a room to watch them, not falling over themselves to get to the teapot or telephone.

Fallon's work for Cadbury's Dairy Milk entertained consumers and crucially got them talking about the brand.

Image courtesy of Fallon.

This commercial for Cadbury's Dairy Milk was watched as frequently on YouTube as it was on television.

Image courtesy of Fallon.

The consumer public actually do buy into advertising messages when they are presented to them with deft creativity and engaging tones of voice. But just go back for a moment to our city-centre straw poll: we have established that consumers will happily deny their interest in advertising, but suppose you ask them how advertising benefits them in their daily lives? Again, in no uncertain terms the general consensus will be a vigorous denial of any advantage at all. Here is where I can provide you with some arguments with which to defend yourselves when you tell people you are hoping to pursue a career doing the 'devil's work'. First of all, consider the reasons why businesses advertise themselves. Ultimately, it is to sell more goods and to increase their income – that is a blinding glimpse of the obvious. But how does that impact on consumers?

Taking supermarket chains as an example, the volume of advertising commissioned by the UK's big four – Tesco, Asda, Sainsbury's and Morrisons – adds up to a significant annual advertising spend. As I write against a background of worldwide recession, Tesco delivers strong messages of useful, everyday products at no-nonsense low prices, supported by familiar celebrity voice-overs. Asda takes an even tougher line, by comparing the cost of its product lines with those of other supermarkets, and spinning the data to deliver a message based on how many more products it can offer more cheaply than its competitors. Sainsbury's takes a slightly different approach, presenting its range as one of superior quality suitable for use by celebrity chef Jamie Oliver, yet at prices slightly more discerning consumers will still consider realistic. The chain's *Feed your Family for a Fiver* campaigns have been enormously successful, consolidating the brand as the quality, value-for-money supermarket. The involvement of Jamie Oliver provides an interesting aside though. His presence in Sainsbury's advertising campaigns has without question been instrumental in reinvigorating what was seen several years ago as a failing brand: struggling to compete with Tesco, floundering without a focused proposition and confusing to its target consumers. Customers returned, confident that the brand represented value for money and happy to buy into the *if it's good enough for Jamie Oliver it's good enough for me* proposition the campaigns so successfully presented. Across the UK, Oliver's chirpy, enthusiastic style struck a chord with consumers, though at times his breezy London accent and persona failed to impress certain target groups in the north-east of England, resulting in some further research and campaign adjustments based on these geographical reactions. A short study of supermarket advertising suggests some very motivating benefits to consumers. By vehemently advertising products, supermarkets are able to sell much greater volumes but at greatly reduced prices. So, it may be argued that advertising can directly benefit consumers, by offering wider ranges of goods at extremely competitive prices. The bottom line here is, because retailers realize the impact advertising can have, consumers are offered goods at cheaper prices. There are of course other factors, such as sourcing cheaper goods to sell, buying in enormous volumes from abroad and driving down manufacturing costs by using Far East factories and labour, but advertising certainly has a major role to play.

Everyone needs some entertainment in their lives and here's where the advertising industry can help again. Much of the entertainment media we now consume has advertising built into it, both directly and indirectly, using product placement and sponsorship. The average cost of a thick, glossy magazine is in the order of £3.50 or so; within its inviting pages are many full-page, full-colour adverts, and in some publications a scattering of smaller, cheaper adverts too. Many of the articles, in particular fashion spreads and cooking or DIY features, feature products which are priced and the shops selling them are name-checked too – magazines are often able to sell advertising space on the back of these features. Of course, what all this means is that publications can generate significant revenue from advertising and this maintains a realistic and affordable cover price. If all the advertising was taken away, magazines would need to double or triple the selling price to stay in business. The same logic can be applied to internet content too. By the inclusion of sponsored links, banner advertising and pop-up windows, all the major search engines like Google or Yahoo as well as price-comparison websites can provide their extensive range of services absolutely free of charge to users and still make large profits. Social Networking sites such as Facebook, Bebo, MySpace, Twitter or YouTube are also available at no cost to the user because of the advertising space they can sell.

Jamie Oliver's presence in Sainsbury's supermarket advertising turned the brand's fortunes around.

Image courtesy of Abbot Mead Vickers BBDO.

Television is no exception either. In the UK three out of five terrestrial channels are available completely free because of the revenues they generate from commercial breaks and sponsorship stings. Many digital channels are free to view, in conjunction with a set-top box, because they are advertising-funded too. BBC channels are an exception because a licence fee is payable, which funds much of their activity. Other subscription satellite and cable television channels still use advertising revenue as a major income stream to allow them to sell various levels of subscription at relatively modest prices. So consumers once more directly benefit from heavily subsidized retail prices, because the products they purchase are able to gain significant portions of their income from advertising and other sponsorships.

Asda has used celebrities to great effect in its commercials. This Christmas commercial featured British actress Julie Walters in the guise of an Asda employee.

Image courtesy of Fallon.

It might also be argued that jobs depend on advertising to a certain extent too. Most private-sector businesses advertise in some form or other to increase their volumes of trade. From the relatively simple use of direct mail letters or websites, right through to global television campaigns. As businesses increase their trading opportunities through various advertising activities, workforces can be maintained and increased to reflect the additional demand created by this advertising and promotion. Whilst that may sound a little naïve and simplistic, it is a fact that advertising has a demonstrable economic impact – it is as much a part of business as manufacturing or customer service, and has been for more than a century – remember Josiah Wedgwood?

The future careers to which graduates aspire in advertising and promotion rely on the continued existence of the business activities I've discussed above. The media industry needs to sell its space and create exciting messages to fill it with to remain viable and to be in a position to offer jobs or placements. Hopefully, you may now start to feel you can deal a little with the insecurities I began to foster in you earlier in the chapter. It is unfair to suggest the average consumer despises you for studying and hoping to work in advertising – that is actually a great exaggeration. In my opinion, consumers do not give a great deal of thought to advertising on a day-to-day basis. Sometimes it is a source of huge irritation to them; at other times it provides valuable streams of entertainment and even vital information. The job of advertising is to strike up dialogues with people at different times, in a variety of environments, and engage with them – in fact, to approach them in such a way that they become genuinely interested in what advertising has to say. A slightly stupid, yet true analogy would be to think back to times when you needed to talk to your parents about something you were uneasy about. It may be to tell them about some misdemeanour or just to ask if you could go out late – either way, you are not confident about the outcome. How do you go about it? What goes through your mind? Certainly, picking the right moment is important, as is the environment (useless ringing your Dad at work as he is at his least receptive then), and then, of course, using the right tone of voice and language. In order to be successful in your objective, preparing what you say and broaching the subject when your parents are relaxed and in good humour are essential. My view is that advertising has to be just as careful and considered when approaching consumers: understanding what they may wish to hear, and in which environment, are at the very heart of advertising strategy.

Consumers are fickle and not as easily manipulated as advertisers often like to believe. Yet, the media in its plethora of guises is capable of influencing and shaping the way consumers think. That's done it, I have opened a big can of worms now by mentioning *the media*. Advertising's best friend and most feared enemy in equal measures I suspect. Harnessing the power of the media, using it to place strategic advertising messages and persuading it to talk about those messages make it a useful ally. However, on a daily basis the tabloid press and celebrity gossip magazines can turn very nasty, picking up a morsel of a salacious story and making a very large meal of it. The media needs to be handled with care and treated with some respect. It is common for publicists and PR consultants to spend as much of their time trying to prevent certain stories appearing in the media as they spend trying to place stories. Advertising campaigns can be totally strangled by disparaging media coverage – yet can also be enhanced. The Wonderbra campaigns created by TBWA grew in stature every time the tabloid press drooled over Eva Herzigova and searched for titillating stories hidden behind the poster headlines. On the other hand, the Volkswagen Polo campaign aired on television early in 2008 was removed from the schedules to avoid adverse press coverage following complaints received by the Advertising Standards Authority. The commercial featured a dog cowering at its owner's feet until it sat in the front seat of a Polo. At which point it became superconfident and burst into a rousing rendition of 'I'm A Man'. Callers to the ASA expressed misgivings about the maltreatment of the dog, prompting Volkswagen's PR people to issue press statements to the contrary. Yet still, the campaign was halted to ensure the potential

PR disaster was averted. Bad press relating to advertisements featuring children or animals will usually negate any success the campaign otherwise may have had. Yet certain commercials aimed at young people can often benefit from a battering from self-righteous tabloid newspapers to raise their coolness profile and, thanks to YouTube, we can still watch them, banned or not. Very much the same sort of logic that saw the Sex Pistols' 'God Save the Queen' rocket to the top of the singles chart in Silver Jubilee week 1977 following a BBC ban. Be aware though, there is a very fine line here. Controversy can be the making of some brands, yet spell the end for others, and there is no magic formula for getting it right.

In the twenty-first century, television, the press and the internet appear to have taken partial control of our lives – this is a double-edged sword. On the one hand consumers are better informed and 'media savvy', on the other hand, at times, it seems people have almost stopped thinking for themselves. Culturally, we live in an 'instant hit' society where information is required to be accessed quickly and without having to do any work to get it. I believe this is beginning to have an effect on students' research and learning capacities. Google, Wikipedia and other encyclopaedia-style websites are fantastic tools for gathering knowledge and information, but are perhaps less good for stimulus. If you know what you are looking for, internet search engines will get you there very quickly, but if you are looking for ideas and inspiration, who knows what you might miss. I think what I am trying to say is that student eyes and brains are being trained to be more one-dimensional and only want to see what they expect to see – trawling through books or magazines with an open mind is becoming less common. That is a dangerous state of mind for any creative person. The moral of this story is this: fishing around with Google or staring vacantly at YouTube is a pretty good way to find oneself being stimulated and inspired by much the same thing as the next person. Definitely not a good thing in advertising. The image or word that triggers a chain of ideas just simply by coming across it is a state that is more difficult to replicate with an internet search. This does not totally surprise me, though, as modern culture operates on a similar 'spoon-fed' basis and is perpetuated by the media. Consider this soundbite I heard on the radio recently – a decade or more ago young primary-school-age girls, when asked what they would like to be when they grew up, often answered a pop singer or an actress. Now, the answer more typically is just *famous*. But famous for what? Increasingly it seems to be famous for doing very little. Television shows like *The X-Factor* or *Britain's Got Talent* and the plethora of other 'vote at home' talent shows tap into the 'instant hit' culture by offering a route to fame that cuts out much of the need to put in any hard work. Reality television is another level still, cutting out the need for building a reputation and, in many cases, talent of any sort. Tragic as the Jade Goody story is, her celebrity status stemmed from being portrayed by the media as stupid and finishing fourth on Channel 4's *Big Brother* television programme in 2004. The celebrity gossip magazines lapped her up and a career in 'being famous for being famous' was launched.

Volkswagen advertising has a heritage of understated wit stretching back to the work of Bill Bernbach's creative teams.
Image courtesy of DDB London.

Whether we like it or not, as advertising people we have to understand what consumers are thinking and talking about. If it turns out to be Jade Goody, Alexandra Burke or any another 'temporary' superstar, advertising has to buy into that zeitgeist. The most successful advertising captures aspects of popular culture and invites consumers to join in too. Advertising creatives, planners and publicists who can instinctively tune into what consumers are thinking and wanting will have a very long and successful career ahead of them. Advertising research can be highly effective in understanding consumer lifestyle, behaviour and habits – often this information is gathered by questionnaires answered in the street, over the telephone, on the internet or by mail. Useful certainly, but a little faceless in determining what genuinely excites consumers. More proactive researchers will sometimes suggest that more can be learned about the expectations of different social groups by eavesdropping on or striking up conversations in pubs or coffee shops than from multiple-choice questionnaires.

Inside the hothouse

By now you should be beginning to open your eyes a little wider and switching your brains more fully to receive mode. Understanding, exploring and storing snippets of popular culture for use at a later date will make you a better and more interesting advertising person in the future. But who are these mythical creatures you dream of becoming one day? Where do they hide and what do they do? A little tip before we look more closely at that question. Even in the major advertising centres like London, New York or Tokyo, the advertising community is very tight and surprisingly small. If you are on the placement or employment trail, find out which pubs the advertising types drink in and just sit in and soak up the vibes, gossip and possible opportunities. Anyway, that is off the point a little; what I really wanted to get across here are the kinds of jobs available in an advertising agency. Size doesn't matter – a large agency will have several people doing similar jobs for different clients, and a small agency might have one person doing more than one of the jobs. Whichever way around, the principles are much the same.

Creative teams

Usually advertising creatives hunt in pairs. Historically a team would be an art director and a copywriter, but in modern advertising the lines are very blurred – visuals and headlines are the result of two brainstorming minds. Their mission remains the same though: to seek out exciting, original ideas and concepts that can be developed into effective, persuasive advertising from a brief supplied by the account management team. The creative teams are expected to work alongside production people to see the idea through and work under the creative director, who assumes overall

"Can I phone an Economist reader please Chris?"

The long-running outdoor campaigns for *The Economist* have been a copywriter's dream.

responsibility for the agency's creative output. No pressure there then, as ultimately agencies are hired and fired for their creative work.

Account management teams

Account executives, managers and directors provide the communication lines between the agency and its clients. Typically, account teams will have a small roster of clients to look after, which means sound relationships can be developed. Once strategies and budgets have been agreed with the client, the account teams will project manage and liaise with all other departments to supervise the campaign to a conclusion. In addition, securing new business and presenting concepts to clients are also the account team's responsibility.

Account planning teams

The point in an agency where research and creativity collide to create communication strategies. Planning teams have an almost telepathic understanding of consumers and their relationship with the brand being advertised. A successful strategy needs a total understanding of consumer habits, behaviours and desires. Detailed research is vital, and planning teams will organize market research of all types and focus groups in order to understand consumers and brands as deeply as possible. A creative brief to fulfil all of the client's advertising needs can then be developed for the creative team to work on.

Media planning teams

In its own way, media planning can be a highly creative position, too, searching for and developing new ways of exploiting the media to fulfil the strategic objectives of

a campaign. Media planners are specialist people who truly understand how various media can be blended efficiently and cost-effectively to achieve maximum impact. They regularly deal and negotiate with TV, press and outdoor poster companies to secure the best space deals.

Production teams

Highly trained, skilled people whose job it is to turn ideas into reality. Production teams may specialize in graphic design, film direction and editing, or digital and internet design and programming. They will work closely with and under the direction of creative teams to ensure that their interpretation of the creative concept is correct. Production managers will also work with outside companies and freelancers to bring in all the right specialized design, film and special effects or internet skills into the agency – taking care to find the best people at the best price. Production teams are also pressure fiends, working to tight deadlines, knowing that if any work is late their department will get the blame.

Working on the client side

The important consideration as you work through your chosen course of study is to understand and undertake your own research into the career opportunities the advertising industry in its broadest context can offer. Any full-service advertising agency contains within its very fabric a wealth of talented creative people with diverse skills. They all must have one thing in common to be successful – dynamism. Advertising demands proactive, confident communicators who are open-minded, receptive and initiators of new types of thinking. That is not just limited to creative concepts for campaigns, as I hope you can now appreciate. Effective, dynamic and persuasive advertising is the result of creative use of the media, intelligent research that is imaginative in its scope, exciting new interpretations of brands and their values, and an all-powerful desire to say something new in new ways.

Successful advertising extends beyond the advertising agency – though, for many students and graduates the roles I have just outlined are extremely attractive – but advertising in its broadest form extends deep into the service industries and beyond too. Any proactive business keen to present its messages and values to as wide an audience as possible will consider other forms of advertising and promotion to supplement and harmonize with the work its chosen advertising agency is producing. I think it is vital in this book about working in advertising to talk about graduate opportunities outside the advertising agency. All agencies have clients, and generally speaking those clients have their own marketing people whose job it is to devise marketing plans and to implement them. In essence, marketing can be described as the planning and execution of the development, pricing, promotion and distribution of goods and services to carefully targeted customers. Some businesses wish to

communicate directly with consumers, others aim to communicate with other businesses. Clearly a retail organization such as a high street chain of shops or car manufacturer will focus its marketing strategies directly upon the end-user – the shopper or car driver. Manufacturing businesses, however, would usually wish to sell their products to other forms of related industries – this is often referred to as business-to-business marketing. For example, a manufacturer of paint for vehicles may invest much of its marketing budget in promoting its product to vehicle manufacturers or perhaps retail outlets that sell car paint. Clothing manufacturers would wish to market their products to high street clothing retailers, yet simultaneously they may also wish to present their brand values to the consumer directly. Sportswear brands like Nike or Adidas do have a limited number of flagship retail outlets of their own. But primarily, the main thrust of their marketing is to grow their brands in the minds of consumers, who in turn make secondary decisions on which retailer to purchase these branded products from.

For many advertising and marketing students working 'on the client side' is a favourable career choice. Long-term, the chance to work in account management or account planning at an advertising agency would still remain an option. In fact, it is not uncommon for marketing managers to move into agencies and vice versa. Many of the skills required for marketing management are similar to those of agency accounts teams. But, going back to the client side for the moment, marketing managers need to immerse themselves totally in a company's brand and product values, and the ability to find creative, new ways of presenting those values is a desirable attribute. A total understanding of what the products are, the ability to explain them clearly and to convince consumers to buy them are prerequisites of a marketing manager, but identifying reasons why consumers would benefit from them is the subtle art of successful marketing and the most difficult. Once understood, turning those benefits into a creative marketing plan and implementing it are the cornerstones of a successful career. Naturally, the execution and communication of that plan put the excitement into a marketing team's day. Here is where you could find yourself working with new-media specialists to develop online communications, advertising agencies to create persuasive campaigns, graphic-design consultants to create brand images and company literature, and PR consultants to keep the company's name in the minds of customers and consumers. For any company, no matter how large or small, keeping a complete focus on the customer or consumer is absolutely essential. As a marketing manager you will be required to have sufficiently strong verbal communication skills to actually talk to customers, competitors and suppliers. This will help in the implementation of marketing strategies – genuinely having empathy with customers' needs, understanding their complaints or misgivings and being fully up to speed with developments in relevant industries are solid foundations from which to build a plan.

Getting the media to work for you

Bill Gates once famously said, 'If I was down to my last dollar, I'd spend it on public relations.' It is pretty unlikely Microsoft's founding father would ever be stony broke, but he has got a point. The role of PR in a company's marketing strategy is key in managing the image and reputation of businesses and basically there are two distinct approaches a PR consultant may use. The first is generating positive news stories that build the profile and increase awareness of brands, businesses and individuals. The second is responding to crises; in other words, using the media to negate the impact of 'bad press'. In truth, managing the media is just one aspect of a PR consultant's role, which would typically involve the writing and distribution of news stories to online, print, radio and television media. According to *The Economist*, as much as 50 per cent of the content of national newspapers is PR instigated; in the business pages of the broadsheet newspapers this figure is likely to be much higher. Any business launching a new product or service would submit an article about it to the business sections of local newspapers, trade magazines and sometimes the national press too. The hugely increased influence of the media over the past decade or so means that PR consultants have become instrumental in the careers of celebrities. Look at the role Max Clifford played in the magazine and television career of Jade Goody or the way the Labour governments since Tony Blair have managed the media. Consequently, a PR consultant will be required to write and initiate feature articles and even stage-manage photo opportunities.

PR consultants will also be required to manage communications with a client's internal and immediate audiences. Larger companies often use an intranet to keep employees in touch with all aspects of the business and to enhance their sense of belonging and participation; this needs careful writing and management. Organizations with memberships will often distribute newsletters and magazines – again these have to be carefully written and photographed to maintain members' involvement. Public Relations is the provision of a 'clear voice' and, as such, consultants, as with all facets of advertising, need to be strong communicators with a talent for sharp, persuasive, concise writing. Organizational skills are also a given, to sustain effective relationships with the media, to manage promotional opportunities and to organize public events and conferences.

Worship the brand god

I am conscious that I have used the word *brand* rather frequently during this chapter. What is a brand? That is a dangerous question to ask. I could write a whole book about branding, so I will just offer a taste of how branding influences advertising communications. Brands can be shrouded in mystery and hidden by smoke and mirrors as companies strive to engage with and buy into consumer lifestyles, and there is a lot of over-inflated nonsense talked about branding. What is a brand? That is also a foolhardy question to ask. Consumer reaction to brands is so personal it can be hard to express succinctly. Stop reading and think for a moment about some well-known brands whose persona is well established and developed. Try to distil everything you feel and understand about these brands down into one single word:

> Volvo
> Cadbury's Dairy Milk
> Levi Strauss
> Apple iPod
> Guinness
> Coca-Cola

Hard isn't it? Even though you know inside exactly what each of these brands represents, formulating that into an all-encompassing word or even a phrase is extremely difficult. But don't worry, there is no right or wrong answer, the question was more to get you to appreciate how nebulous a brand is. In advertising and marketing, a brand and its equity are perhaps the most valuable entity, priceless even. Compare a brand to a valuable painting – Leonardo da Vinci's *Mona Lisa* for example – there is only one of it, it takes a great deal of time, skill and patience to create it and money simply cannot buy it, it is so valuable. Yet one moment of carelessness can damage it irreparably. Hold on there for a second, what was that expression I used just now that you probably chose to ignore? Brand equity. When advertising people are presented with an existing brand to work with it comes complete with a full set of conceptions, preconceptions and downright miscon-ceptions – some are accurate, some are totally misplaced. Still, this slippery indefinable *brand thing* is the single biggest asset available to work with. A brand name is featured on the box or tin, but that in itself is not the brand, neither is the product contained inside the packaging either. The brand is a melting pot boiling over with history, imagery, words, perceptions, potential and hearsay all of which float around in the target consumer's consciousness. Working with this delicate, extraordinary asset is a breathtaking experience. One false word, ill-chosen image or misunderstanding can shatter it into a thousand fragments. The best you can hope for is to just help it along a little more. In the earlier words of Trevor Beattie, 'we don't want to reinvent the wheel, just help it to turn a little faster' (www.bmbagency.com).

Amongst all this confusion, consumers have no desire to sit around thinking about brands and defining what they believe about them. Consumers know precisely how they feel about a brand, they just don't know why, nor do they care. Advertising and marketing have to define what a brand means and find ways of conveying that to consumers. Dan Wieden, of advertising agency Wieden+Kennedy, says that brands are verbs – doing words, if you remember English-language classes. Here come some similar answers to the little brand quiz earlier – Nike exhorts, IBM solves, Sony dreams. Brands represent consumers' hopes, expectations and lifestyles. Why do students

Vodafone has created a visual and cultural brand that consumers can readily identify with.

Images courtesy of Vodafone.

pretty much always wear Apple iPods, not other brands of MP3 player? Could it be because they identify with Apple's sense of brand style, design innovation and all-round coolness? To what extent do their contemporaries influence them?

I think what I really need to get across here is that in advertising it is probably much more important to understand brands, not *branding*. Don't use valuable creative thinking time trying to define what you think you should be saying about a brand. Spend the time turning the brand over, under and sideways, look at it from every angle and find a new way of expressing what you and your agency understands about that brand. Explore what works, what doesn't, what could and what could never. Their owners fiercely protect brands and advertising respects that. They are more than just logos or icons; they are the owner-company's personality.

But if brands are more than just logos why do companies spend so much money on logo development? Corporate identity is important to every business and the visual appearance of company stationery, packaging, signs, brochures, websites etc. is an integral part of the brand message. Think about how Vodafone would appear if its packaging, logo and shop interiors were bright green, not red – its persona would be very different. What if its use of colour was not consistent: sometimes green, and sometimes red? The brand communication would be confusing and lose definition. Much of this corporate identity work would be undertaken by a graphic-design consultancy; typically they would also create a set of guidelines that travel with the logo. This creates a uniform visual structure including the logo itself and how it may be positioned and used. Company colours would also be defined, as would fonts and how and when straplines may be used. Larger organizations would often include within their guidelines examples of stationery and brochure layout or photography styles. These corporate identity rules and regulations are sacrosanct – marketing managers defend them with their lives and any creative work, design and logo use must adhere closely to the guidelines to create consistency and to support the brand image.

In summary, if advertising is considered to be a big umbrella encompassing all forms of marketing and promotion, then bright, dynamic people like you can be spoilt for choice when it comes to choosing a career pathway. Which one is right for you? Marketing management, brand management, a PR consultant, an advertising creative, account manager, planner, media buyer, designer? Even if you are a photographer, new-media programmer, illustrator or filmmaker, advertising wants your skills too.

Making the media work harder

There can be no doubt that advertising is at its most effective when stunning creative ideas link seamlessly to inventive ways of placing messages in front of people. The choice of media at campaign launch will make or break it. When T-Mobile launched its *Life Is For Sharing* campaign featuring 'flashmobbing' at Liverpool Street Station,

advertising agency Saatchi & Saatchi booked a full-length commercial-break spot during Channel 4's *Celebrity Big Brother* to run a version of the advert which ran for over 3 minutes. Subsequent airings featured various 30-second edits. It was also no coincidence that T-Mobile was the sponsor of the television programme too.

Saatchi & Saatchi's inventive 'flashmob' commercials for T-Mobile encouraged consumer interaction with the brand.
Images courtesy of Saatchi & Saatchi.

In considering the strategy for an advertising campaign, a sound understanding of the target audience usually suggests the most appropriate advertising media to communicate with it most effectively. The increasingly inventive use of ambient media, guerrilla techniques and digital advertising has expanded the range of options creative planners and media buyers can select from. Traditional media such as press, TV and posters are still widely used but in harmony with newer forms. The T-Mobile campaign was launched using television but a posting on YouTube demonstrates how the commercial was choreographed and shot to add value to the campaign.

Outdoor advertising

Traditionally outdoor advertising still focuses on posters in a variety of sizes and locations. The M40 route into central London, via Hangar Lane, has some of the largest poster sites I've seen – the spectacular creative work executed and then exhibited at that size is just jaw dropping. Billboard posters are pasted into place using a number of overlapping sheets of paper. The size of the site is still referred to by the number of prints used to create the full image – 16-sheet and 48-sheet posters are typical of the rectangular posters seen in every city centre; 96-sheet posters are enormous. Long, thin rectangular sites that dominate their immediate environment – these are found more typically in major cities and the approaches to airports, stadia and other gathering points for large groups of people. Some sites rotate now using vertical or horizontal strips between three or four posters or can display two advertisements when viewed from different angles. Outdoor poster media can also include *Adshells* – 4-sheet posters contained in back-lit boxes displayed at the ends of bus shelters or at railway stations, underground stations and airport foyers. These create their own distinct creative opportunities – readers normally have a little more time to absorb these messages as they are often waiting in proximity to them for a period of time. Creatives and media planners have also devised some unusual three-dimensional outdoor sites – a campaign for *The Economist* featured a light bulb protruding from the billboard that lit up as people walked past it. Outdoor posters represent an on-going dialogue with potential consumers, offering brief reminders and snapshots of the campaign message, which are seen frequently. The most successful poster campaigns are usually those that use simple concepts, uncomplicated imagery and few words. Their positioning is vitally important. It is no accident that posters advertising children's foods, clothes and toys appear along the routes to schools. Alcohol brands and other 'male-orientated' products may well line the approaches to football stadia. Book and newspaper posters are frequently sited at railway stations and airports. Once again, the media strategy behind a poster campaign contributes heavily to its potential success.

This is a news story that puts into context the power of outdoor media and the impact it can have across other media platforms. In June 2009, David Beckham mania took over one of Britain's busiest streets as the footballer attended the unveiling of a huge poster of himself wearing only underpants. Emporio Armani's new underwear campaign stars the footballer, and a poster in which he is pictured clutching a rope as he models the snug-fitting pants was unveiled outside Selfridges in London's Oxford Street.

Cheers and screams from hundreds of onlookers greeted Beckham, more fully dressed in a suit, as the poster was revealed at the store.

Beckham, 34, was asked if he enjoyed the experience and said he did not mind the photos being taken, but added: 'When they're unveiled it's a little embarrassing'.

He said he did not go on special diets for the pictures but 'obviously I work out before these shoots'. He was introduced onto a stage by sports presenter Gabby Logan, who congratulated him on the England football team's 'brilliant' 6–0 victory over Andorra the previous night. Beckham said: 'It was a big, big win for us. It was a great game for us to play in. A lot of hard work's been done. The team's in great spirits. There's a lot of togetherness and it shows on the field.'

An object lesson in how to create powerful advertising posters and then harness the persuasive, attention-grabbing opportunities presented by an ambient advertising 'stunt' and PR. This news release was taken from the website of Sky News, but was covered by all major British television channels and newspapers. Maybe the presence of 'brand Beckham' helped a little too!

This Trevor Beattie-led campaign for Pretty Polly used the outdoor poster site to maximize the creative message.

Image courtesy of Beattie McGuinness Bungay.

Where advertising meets celebrity and a public event.

Image courtesy of The Press Association.

Television advertising

For over 50 years television has been the 'glamour boy' of advertising and retains its status among big-hitting advertising agencies and clients as the most potent communication medium. As we approach the end of the first decade of the twenty-

first century television's position is perhaps under threat for the first time as the internet continues to grow. For many businesses prime-time television advertising is out of reach, the cost of airtime and production is prohibitive. For larger companies it remains the best way of increasing their brand awareness. As John Hegarty often puts it, television makes brands famous. Increasingly, commercials are devised to entertain viewers as the surrounding programming would. Advertising's continuing love affair with moving images, dialogue and music creates an industry in its own right. The concepts initially put forward by the creative team can lead to a specialist illustrator being employed to draw storyboards to present to the client. Once the concepts have been put into production, filmmakers, commercial directors, music writers and producers will usually be required to create the final 30- or 40-second film. There could well be the need for special effects or animations to be made, models or celebrities may need hiring, voice-overs might have to be recorded and locations found. By the time the campaign is over the client could easily have spent several hundreds of thousands of pounds.

Advertising has produced some legendary moments of television in its own right. You will all have your own personal favourites, but here are a few I think are well worth an hour on YouTube to search for. No quick trip through advertising's finest moments can miss out Guinness. The awesome *Surfer,* filmed on a huge budget in Polynesia, was an integral part of the campaign created by Abbot Mead Vickers on the theme of 'good things come to those who wait'. This particular commercial features surfers waiting for the ultimate wave, stylishly shot in black and white with some breathtaking post-production – watch those white horses soar. Renowned art director Graham Fitch conceived a spectacular commercial for British Airways during his time at Saatchi & Saatchi which involved choreographing hundreds of people dressed in red, white and blue on a tropical island to form a stylized face. More recently three commercials created by Wieden+Kennedy London for Honda have completely transformed the perception of the brand from cheap Japanese old-person's car maker to a stylish, desirable, aspirational brand. Viewers were transfixed by the two-minute *Cog* campaign films which showed car parts elegantly and painstakingly moving and reacting with each other to deliver a fully built Honda Accord by the end of the commercial. Almost uniquely, the two minutes were silent, apart from the gentle clinks and swishes as the parts rolled and swung across the screen. The follow-up campaign was an animated sequence in bright colours telling the joyful tale of Honda's chief engineer's quest to design the perfect diesel engine against his own better judgement. *Love/Hate* stood out strongly with its totally different visual appeal. Finally, search out the brand-awareness campaign featuring skydivers who left it very late to open their parachutes to reveal the Honda logo. A simple concept which captured audience attention by being aired as a 'live advert'. Much of Bartle Bogle Hegarty's work for Levi's since 1984 is worth a look. See if you can spot a young Brad Pitt in one. My personal favourite is *Spaceman* for sheer sassy style and off-kilter glamour. Television will probably always be the weapon of choice for advertising agencies looking to impress audiences and getting them talking about brands. Some commercials, particularly Coca-Cola's Christmas campaigns and the soap-opera love affair of the Gold Blend couple, have achieved huge audience numbers in their own right by carefully building a campaign of interest in newspapers and magazines prior to their first airings. Television is also probably responsible for the first advertising you became aware of.

Cinema advertising

Advertising in the cinema has seen remarkable changes in fortune over the past five decades. Up until the mid-1960s, the cinema was the entertainment of choice for most people. Before the 1950s and the arrival of television in every household it was the only way to see movies and watch the news. It was as important as television is now in creating fame and awareness for brands. Commercials made in the 1950s and 1960s had an almost cinematic quality of their own. The film-noir of the *You're Never Alone with a Strand* cigarette adverts are some of the most atmospheric ever made. Thankfully, the film industry has undergone something of a resurgence after many years of fighting against the video and DVD industries. The cinema is popular again, especially with 15–25 year olds, and commercials are again being made specifically for the cinema, though Orange seems to dominate the prelude to the main feature. The cinema provides a powerful environment in which to advertise. The movie being shown virtually identifies the target audience and makes it very easy to schedule and buy advertising spots to match brand messages to potential consumers. Better still, the audience is completely captive and in a receptive frame of mind as they wait to be entertained. In fact, the trailers and commercials that provide the prelude to the main feature are as much a part of the cinema experience as popcorn. A well-organized media plan based closely around the movies being shown can be a highly effective way of communicating brand messages to a willing audience. Cinema advertising is very much alive and kicking and should not be written off.

Wieden+Kennedy's work for Honda changed the way car brands are advertised.
Images courtesy of Wieden+Kennedy London.

The mobile phone network Orange has taken almost complete control of cinema advertising in recent years. This example features American rapper Snoop Dogg.
Image courtesy of Wieden+Kennedy London.

Press advertising

Selling advertising space has long been the lifeblood of printed magazines and newspapers; cover price alone is never enough to sustain a title. Advertising has a long association with newspapers, and the rise in popularity of lifestyle and professional magazines has increased the advertising opportunities. The market is fragmented, though, and publications face stiff competition from the wide choice of competitive titles available and increasingly from the internet. Many consumers now read their daily news from websites, a factor that has particularly affected local newspapers. However, with literally thousands of titles available, the ability to advertise directly to tightly targeted audience groups remains a significant part of an advertising strategy. This is where media planners really come into their own and an in-depth knowledge of print titles is essential. Contact with magazine editorial teams is also useful because having advance notification of features that are being planned means space can be booked to take advantage of the readership's interests. For example, a magazine about home furnishing and decoration may indicate that it will print a feature about the latest trends in wallpaper design. An advertising agency working with a DIY retailer will be able to create a message based around its client's range of wall-coverings for that particular issue. That's not rocket science, really, is it? More like common sense, but it's amazing sometimes how common sense can become overcomplicated. Advertising in magazines opens up a wealth of ideas that are difficult to achieve in other media. The first is the distribution of free samples; sachets of hand cream, fragrances impregnated into the page, sachets of hot chocolate and tea bags. In fact, anything that can be sealed in a bag or sachet and fixed to a page is fair game – let your imagination loose on that one! These samples can work in conjunction with an advert or be a cover-mounted freebie. Secondly, it is possible to glue into the magazine fold-out pages so that interested consumers can physically open out the advertisement to reveal even more information. This works especially well in more upmarket lifestyle magazines.

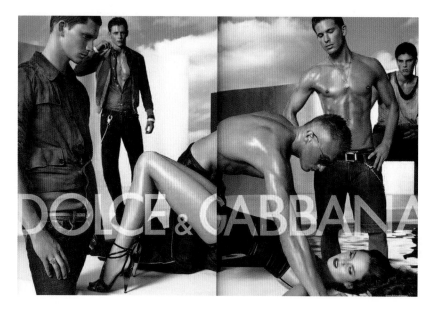

This spread from a women's lifestyle magazine is typical of the way brands continue to communicate with consumers in print.

The important thing to remember is, no matter what brand you are trying to advertise and plan for there is a magazine out there with absolutely the right readership profile. From niche professional titles for every manner of occupation to celebrity gossip and television listings to high fashion. I've missed out everything in between – you can search for those next time you are undertaking a creative or strategic advertising project.

Radio advertising

Since radio networks were deregulated some years ago, a huge number of independent and local radio stations have begun broadcasting. The effect on radio advertising has been something of a double-edged sword. On the one hand it means there are now so many stations broadcasting that listeners and audience ratings have become fragmented into lots of small audiences. On the other hand it means that the cost of radio advertising, especially when compared to television, is comparatively cheap – with so many radio stations offering advertising space, the price has been driven down.

It is fair to say that the heyday of radio advertising was several decades ago, yet it still presents unique and often quite personal ways of communicating with an audience. Prime time for radio is the journey to and from work for most people. A few years ago I was working for an agency on campaigns for Volkswagen Commercial Vehicles; a large slice of the target was small-business people who owned and drove vans. The nature of the work meant that they spent a good deal of their working day out driving and yes, you've guessed it, listening to the radio. Obviously, Volkswagen advertising for vans used several radio campaigns to take advantage of that. In general, radio listeners seem to behave in two ways. They are either creatures of habit, listening to specific radio programmes regularly and predictably – for example, when they are getting ready for work, driving to and from work or even whilst at work. Other listeners are more selective, consciously choosing which station or programmes to listen to. If that choice is made for reasons of entertainment or leisure then the listener is likely to be more receptive and involved in the programme (and of course any advertising).

Good radio commercials are a creative challenge, particularly for writers. They need to deliver a powerful and persuasive message without the use of any visuals. Dialogue needs to be sharp and engaging, sound effects need to appeal without irritating and the use of people needs to leave a lasting mental impression of their personality. The combination of sounds, music and dialogue that radio advertising requires often works well if they raise questions in listeners' minds making them more alert and receptive. These questions do not necessarily refer to the brand or product; they are more subliminal than that. Who is talking? Why are they saying that? What is that sound? By teasing listeners into an involvement with the commercial, they are more likely to remember the brand. Music is usually handled with extreme caution though – if the commercial is to air on a music radio station then it will not necessarily stand out with sufficient clarity. Much as stations will hate me for saying this, daytime music radio is wallpaper for most listeners; they are probably at work or at home using the radio for company, so advertising needs to be very clever to grab their attention for a short while.

Direct mail

The early part of this chapter talked a little about how people react when asked about advertising – their perceptions and prejudices. If there is one form of advertising which 'winds up' consumers more than any other it is direct mail (aka junk mail). Advertising which comes through people's letterboxes is viewed with suspicion and disdain by what seems like everybody; on a level of hatred it is second only to cold-callers who telephone just as you are eating or unwinding after a long day.

A montage of direct mail packs.

Image courtesy of Fitch & Co., Inc. New York.

Why do people seem to despise direct mail so much? After all, at work it is perfectly normal to receive advertising by mail and few seem to mind, but at home things are very different. I think consumers tend to feel a little uncomfortable that discount furniture stores, credit card companies, insurance firms and others seem to know so much about them. Here are a few examples I have heard mentioned recently. A single man in his late 20s who is a schoolteacher moved into a new flat. A few days later he received a large envelope with a letter and a brochure inside from a well-known furniture superstore. The letter addressed him by name and welcomed him to his new home and asked him if he was enjoying his time off from school; it went on to tell him about the great offers they were currently running on sofas and beds. A couple in their mid-forties returned from a holiday of a lifetime in Australia to a direct mail pack from a major credit card company. The pack included a letter, a glossy folded leaflet, an application form, a pen and a comparison card with their and other companies' interest rates on. The letter began by asking the couple if they had enjoyed their holiday and if they had overspent a little. It continued by outlining how a new low-rate credit card could help them along. Finally, a professional man in his thirties fulfilled a lifelong dream and bought himself a brand-new sports car. Shortly after he received a letter, a brochure and a free tax-disc holder from a renowned insurance company inviting him to ask for a quotation on insurance for his fabulous new sports car. Consumers are definitely suspicious that so much seems to be known about them, and if they are not interested in sofas, insurance or credit cards at that moment in time then they consider sending an envelope full of paper to be a waste of time and effort.

So in light of all this consumer resistance, why do advertising agencies continue to recommend direct mail and does it work? The truth is it does, even though the percentage of wastage can be high. In advertising terms the results are also quantifiable: it is almost impossible to be specific about how many people have viewed and responded to a TV commercial or an outdoor campaign, but by using direct mail the volume of responses can be recorded precisely. More importantly to clients, it is also easy to calculate how many responses converted into sales. Broadly speaking, direct mail can be divided into two distinct groups. 'Warm' mailings use databases of names and addresses of consumers who are either existing customers or who have previously expressed an interest in the company's products. Clearly, a direct mail campaign targeted towards a 'warm' mailing list is likely to elicit a better response; these databases can be built and maintained by any business at any level. 'Cold' mailings are much more of a shot in the dark. This type of campaign will be directed towards possible consumers who fit a specific demographic, using a database that is bought for the purpose. For example, a mail order wine club may decide to target people above the age of 55 and use data based on the electoral register of people in that age group. The list of names and addresses provides no information about how many of those people are regular wine drinkers or users of mail order, nor about their more generalized behaviour and buying habits. However, by mailing such 'cold' databases it is possible to test different creative ideas, different styles of mailing pack, and alternative phrasing and messaging, and compare the results. For future campaigns, the agency would have gathered significant research data in terms of which techniques yielded the best results.

As you can see, direct mail is highly specialized and relies heavily on the quality and accuracy of data and research. This data can be subdivided into smaller target groups with even greater degrees of personalization which allow brands to open a dialogue with customers that appears to be offering exactly what the recipient needs at that moment. Major retailers, especially supermarkets, are extremely effective at

this. Customers who hold a loyalty card regularly receive mailings based on their recent buying habits offering vouchers that discount still further the type of products they buy. This level of sophistication makes direct mail a highly effective form of advertising.

Charities and health organizations have become extremely good at maximizing the potential of direct mail and play the long game: building strong, open dialogues with people over long periods of time. Financial organizations also consider direct mail to be a vital part of their advertising mix, often using it in conjunction with TV and outdoor campaigns. Consumers who have become familiar with the poster message and seen the commercial will often respond more willingly to a direct mail pack. Successful mailings must engage and interest the recipient, but at the same time make the response easy too. If a charity embarked upon a campaign to persuade potential donors to contribute a small amount of money by direct debit on a monthly basis it needs to achieve two things. Firstly, it must be persuasive. The pack is likely to contain a personalized letter (with a PS: that summary of benefits at the end of the letter is vital if the letter has not been read fully) and a leaflet to explain the objectives of the charity, visually and with words. These elements are emotive and will aim to convince the recipient that the charity's motives are trustworthy and its aims are beneficial and worthwhile. Once a possible donor believes in the communication message, a quick response is required. By now the recipient will have discovered the application and direct debit forms and may even have the pen contained in the pack too. All they have to do is fill in the form with the free pen and pop it into the pre-paid envelope provided and the mailing has been a success. By delivering the message in stages and making the response easy, the charity has increased its contributions to its cause. Speed is of the essence, really: as soon as that pack is put to one side for reading later or at the weekend, then the chance of a response is lessened.

On a simpler, cheaper level, direct mail items may be devised without personalization. Letters addressed to the householder, or simple colour leaflets and booklets, can be distributed either by hand or via the postal service to promote all types of businesses. A gardener may simply pop his business card through the door, a pizza-delivery firm may slip a menu through the letterbox, retailers may deliver a small product catalogue or electricity companies might even send boxed low-energy light bulbs. These approaches bypass the need for an extensive database but can still be geographically targeted using postcodes and locality to reach the correct audience. Alternatively, agencies might arrange distribution of advertising messages via magazine or newspaper inserts. These are printed leaflets inserted between the pages of publications and sold on a similar basis to advertising space. Again, this can work for small businesses by using regional newspapers (especially the free ones), and by large brands inserting leaflets into glossy magazines. The targeting here is similar to press advertising in identifying titles read by the consumers that brands wish to communicate with.

Direct mail is not the appropriate advertising medium for every type of brand, but the incredible flexibility, and the one-to-one conversation with consumers and creative potential, make it vibrant and effective. For a strategist, the thrill of honing databases, identifying targets and testing different messages is at its most heightened with direct mail. Depending on cost restrictions, for a creative the opportunities are restricted only by ideas and imagination. Over the years I have seen direct mail envelopes that demand the consumer's attention with cardboard pop-ups, sachets of glitter, free samples, earplugs, pens, sparkplugs, stressballs and inflatables. The packs have been made from plastic, paper and card, and included inserts printed on rice paper, lasagne, toilet roll and metal. Each of these items has been included as part of a visually engaging and persuasively written creative concept, personalized to a clearly identified target audience. Look more closely and consider the strategy behind the campaign the next time you are tempted to carelessly throw away a direct mail piece.

Ambient and guerrilla advertising

Very much advertising's new kid on the block, the continuing creative necessity for new brand messages presented in new ways has contributed to a rise in ambient advertising activity during recent years. It is very simply defined as advertising that occupies an environmental space that consumers encounter as part of their daily lives. In many ways, there is a bridge built between advertising and PR, as ambient campaigns can often walk a line between a publicity stunt and advertising. However, the creative possibilities are endless and imaginative strategists can really stretch themselves with an ambient campaign. It can also be used to great effect to support more traditional advertising. On a recent rail journey to Manchester, the slow drag into the main railway station was punctuated by a series of billboard posters promoting different ways consumers could use a Maestro payment card. As I left the train and walked across the concourse to the exit, some of the tiles on the floor were covered with vinyl advertising messages continuing the billboard creative theme I had seen 10 minutes earlier. That is a relatively easy and cost-effective example of ambient advertising. Public transport also links outdoor advertising with an ambient approach by using bus sides and taxis to display messages. In fact, it is very rare to see a traditional black cab anywhere in the UK that hasn't been repainted in an eye-catching colour with advertising covering every surface. On a more unique, attention-grabbing level, Volkswagen's agency, DDB London, planted an ice sculpture of a Polo model in a busy London street to promote the benefits of its air-conditioning system. Even small businesses can get in on the act. Strategically planted vehicles with large messages adjacent to major roads are a common sight. I even saw a garden centre cover a van completely in turf to draw attention to its nearby location. Anything is fair game in ambient advertising. Nightclubbers' hands have been rubber stamped by street-teams as they queue, with the messages still being legible the next

morning. Car-park tickets have messages on the back, trees have been labelled and telephone boxes have made high-visibility advertising spaces. Flags and banners can easily be placed in fixed locations and on cars or planes, giant inflatables are floated above outdoor events and people are hired to wear costumes and hand out leaflets and free samples. A large pan-European stationery company once carried one of my ads on the tops of all its very large delivery lorries to advertise its products to workers in high-rise office buildings.

This alcohol-awareness campaign aimed at young people maximized the possibilities of advertising in and on taxis as they drove the consumer to and from a night out.

Images courtesy of CST.

Ambient advertising is most successful when consumers in unexpected locations see the messages because they naturally become more interested and receptive to the brand message. Advertising agencies are always keen to attract attention to the brands they promote in distinctive ways, and clever ambient techniques fulfil that objective perfectly. A well-conceived ambient concept will get consumers talking; better still if it can get news media talking about it too. Anyone remember the gigantic projection of Gayle Porter's bum up the full height of the House of Commons a few years ago? Creating a dramatic impact and building a 'buzz' among consumers by exploring unconventional media and providing relatively cheap promotional opportunities for brands can be a useful advertising weapon. But be

In reality, guerrilla advertising has been around for years.

careful. Ambient advertising has its limitations. Not all clients would feel it sits comfortably with the brand image they strive to communicate and the 'one-off' nature of ambient events can be limited in their exposure to consumers, which is why they are often used as part of a wider, more traditional media campaign. Stirring up controversy, as ambient ideas sometimes do, can also irritate and alienate consumers. Which leads me neatly on to ambient advertising's feisty, bad-boy alter ego – guerrilla advertising.

There are times when advertising needs to quite literally set a trap for an audience and catch it totally unaware in order to deliver a message it may not even realize it is receiving. By the time it realizes it has just seen an advertisement, it has already been hooked. Enter guerrilla advertising, a term introduced by Jay Conrad Levinson in his 1984 book *Guerrilla Marketing*. Exploiting the environment around the campaign and delivering the unexpected to grab attention and instigate discussion and debate among consumers is at the heart of it. Initially the audience may be totally confused by what is in front of it. Actually, if you think about it, guerrilla techniques have been around for years. Music events have always been promoted by pasting posters illegally onto blank wall space at night. Graffiti and street art have decorated urban environments for as long as I can remember, and when Banksy, the British street artist, became famous for his work, advertising agencies fell over themselves to commission him to create brand messages. Strategically placed stickers and leaflets handed out in the street are commonplace too. Theatres have often dispatched actors in full costume into the streets to raise awareness of performances. My own students have been remarkably creative with ambient and guerrilla advertising too. One team developed an awareness campaign about recycling that used piles of rubbish next to some explanatory signs; another replaced town-centre wooden benches with brightly coloured sofas for a fruit-drinks brand. So whilst it may sometimes be argued that guerrilla advertising is not a new phenomenon, the big brands have taken it to new levels. Microsoft once plastered butterfly logo stickers all across Manhattan, Adidas organized an aerial football match in Japan with players suspended by wires high above city streets in Tokyo and Osaka, and McDonald's hired a model to appear to be asleep in her bed in a busy Hong Kong subway station. All of these activities generated huge levels of debate and controversy among consumers.

By developing a full understanding of how advertising can use the media in new, exciting and creative ways you can challenge yourselves to be more inventive in the work that you produce strategically and creatively; this then makes you more interesting and grabs the attention of potential employers more readily. But wait, I know this overview of advertising media has a fatal flaw – there is no mention of digital advertising. This is so important to contemporary and future advertising that it warrants a chapter of its own. So read on.

Some websites to visit

Here are some sites to help you keep up to date with advertising news and opinion:

www.campaignlive.co.uk
www.businessweek.com
www.brandrepublic.com

These sites feature some of the agencies and campaigns featured in this chapter:

www.loweworldwide.com
www.ddblondon.com
www.wklondon.com
www.fallon.co.uk
www.saatchi.co.uk
www.claydonheeley.com
www.tdaltd.com
www.amvbbdo.com
www.publicis-dialog.co.uk

Some books to read

100 Best TV Commercials: And Why They Worked
Bernice Kanner

Twenty Ads that Shook the World
James B. Twitchell

The Advertising Handbook
Sean Brierley

Graphics: A Century of Poster and Advertising Design
Alain Weill

Best Poster Designs (Design Cube Series)
Zeixs (Editor)

The Radio Advertising Hall of Fame
Radio Advertising Bureau (Editor)

Absolute Appeal: Direct Mail
Pie Books (Editor)

Guerrilla Advertising: Unconventional Brand Communication
Gavin Lucas and Mike Dorrian

Guerrilla Advertising: Cost-effective Tactics for Small-business Success
Jay Conrad Levinson

Advertising is Dead: Long Live Advertising!
Tom Himpe and Will Collin

Wally Olins on Brand
Wally Olins

The Advertised Mind: Groundbreaking Insights into How our Brains Respond to Advertising
Eric Du Plessis

Get involved

This book's Facebook and Twitter page features regular blogs on exciting new campaigns and imaginative use of the media. Please feel free to add comments about the work that inspires you too so everyone can share:

- search Facebook for 'Advertising Its Business Culture and Careers'
- www.twitter.com/adculture

4 The future is bright, the future is digital

To paraphrase the great Orange campaign, the future of advertising is bright, the future is digital, but new ideas are constantly emerging. Many global advertising agencies are establishing secondary agencies to explore and maximize digital and integrated advertising – for example, Ogilvy One from Ogilvy & Mather. Other, new agencies are revolutionizing the industry by being smaller, more fluid and compact to offer clients a more flexible integrated service – Mother, Iris, Publicis and Glue. Notice how they have shorter, funkier names; gone are the letterhead-filling strings of surnames or initials so beloved of advertising agencies.

Many clients are turning the focus of their marketing communications towards an effective (and cheaper) online or viral output. It is increasingly common for businesses to invest their 'traditional' advertising budgets in campaigns to promote websites or other online activity. The same creativity and persuasive thinking is still required, but the objectives and outcomes have shifted. Designers are required to understand both digital and print media, creatives need to explore different communication techniques, and strategists need to comprehend and extend the possibilities of digital media.

As recently as 1999, the American film *The Blair Witch Project* broke new ground with some innovative ambient, viral and online marketing techniques ahead of its general release. Film clips were posted on a website and emailed, with parts of the film being aired on the Independent Film Channel's *Split Screen* TV series in the USA, leading to heated speculation on internet forums as to whether the film clips were real or fictional. Many people were misled into believing that they were viewing genuine footage of missing persons and that the film was a documentary. The teaser poster and other traditional advertising for the film were created to support the 'documentary' concept, reinforcing the suspicion that three young Americans really had disappeared in the woods. Building on this momentum, a fake documentary was shown on the Sci Fi Channel in the USA, *Curse of the Blair Witch*, that claimed to investigate the legend surrounding the movie, immediately before the film's release. The programme contained interviews with friends and relatives of the missing students, paranormal experts and local historians (all fictional of course). This was done so convincingly that the three lead actors were listed for a time as 'missing, presumed dead'. While attending the Cannes Film Festival, the producers put up 'missing persons' posters featuring the three stars of the film, which were removed the next day following the actual kidnapping of a television executive (who was later recovered and returned home safely). By the time *The Blair Witch Project* hit the screens its audiences had been talking about it and debating the publicity campaign for some considerable time.

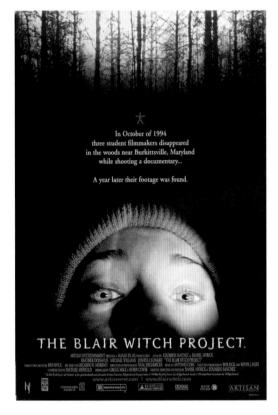

Advance publicity for *The Blair Witch Project* was one of the first online and mass-media campaigns.

Since the groundbreaking *Blair Witch* launch, the scope of digital advertising and the perceptions of advertisers, agencies and consumers have advanced beyond recognition. Like all bandwagons, though, it is all too easy to just jump aboard – the pressure to get into digital advertising because everyone else is presents an analogy with the rise of desktop publishing in the late 1980s. For some time creative companies, particularly graphic designers, were involved in a battle of wills with clients. The sales pitches of IT consultants were partly based around the apparently boundless flexibility of the software packages bundled with personal computers. Some clients were dazzled into believing their sales and marketing teams could take over the design and production of their promotional materials. Consequently, it was not unusual to be confronted by some utterly horrific misspelled design nightmares which did little to advance the presence of the brands in question. In fact, so low were the standards, brands even damaged themselves by allowing their messages to become visually confusing and lacking in definition. Designers fought hard against this – the core of their argument was that whilst computers might provide the tools for designers to express themselves, the tools had no inherent design skills. Thus, expecting people with no design training (or ability for that matter) to take over any businesses communications was naïve at best.

There are distinct parallels here with digital advertising techniques. Whilst businesses can genuinely embark on advertising campaigns and promotional ventures with huge cost advantages, there are big mistakes being made daily. Visual

consistency and 'tone of voice' are vital to all marketing and business communications, from advertising through to promotional literature and business stationery through to websites. Marketing people have learned the lessons of desktop publishing and the days of administrative staff taking on the role of designer have mostly gone except in one key area. Web design. Yes, of course, the companies and marketing teams who recognize the importance of brand communications would treat their website and any other online activities in the same way they would treat other visual communications – they would commission professionals to produce the work for them. Some businesses are less enlightened. Websites are often designed either 'in-house' by marketing people with a bit of computer expertise or by 'surrogate' web designers. These are people who are highly skilled and adept IT people with a wide knowledge of software and hardware, yet who are not and have never been designers or creatives. The results are similar to the dark days of desktop publishing. Whilst technically the work they produce is competent and functional, the design is poor – often woefully over-designed, with little regard for the identity and style of the commissioning business. Once again, technical skill is no substitute for good design. But there is worse to come, the exciting, sexy world of digital advertising is once again compromised by the lack of a consistent message. In short, in the wrong hands, businesses usually do not have anything meaningful to say or a story to tell and then wonder why digital advertising hasn't been their salvation.

Google is held up as an example to all. After all, did it not become one of the world's most familiar brands without spending a cent on traditional advertising? Did it not grow by word of mouth alone? In contemporary digital advertising word of mouth has been sort of superseded by social media, but the principle remains the same. As a consequence, businesses everywhere are quite rightly exploring digital and social media to communicate with customers – for some the results are spectacular, others seem to be completely ignored. Let me tell you a story to illustrate the point a little more. What, I hear you ask? Story? What is he on about now? Think about it, though. Even before Industrial Revolution marketing techniques, medieval signage and symbols, Asian cave painting and Roman posters, people communicated with and passed messages to each other. They excited, delighted, intrigued, persuaded and engaged each other by simply talking and unfolding a story. They still do, but unfortunately not always on social media sites. Here's a completely fictional product (I hope). Meet *Bog's Standard Baked Beans*, a terribly ordinary, shy tin-based food product that has spent its whole life living in the shadow of *Heinz*, a louder, more extrovert character altogether.

Over many years, *Bog's Standard Baked Beans* has reluctantly appeared hidden at the back of lifestyle magazines, hung around on billboards and coyly driven to work with people on their radios. Not many people took very much notice. Even occasional appearances on television didn't seem to change things very much. Everyone liked *Bog's Standard Baked Beans*, but every time it seems that consumers might at last be taking a bit of notice and beginning to take a few more tins home, along comes

Heinz and ruins it all by shouting louder and just being a bit more, well, interesting really. Nothing seemed to work. *Bog's Standard Baked Beans* tried to be clever and funny but not many people laughed. It tried to yell at people, but they just got annoyed. It tried to email people but they got confused and thought *Spam* was emailing them. One day *Bog's Standard Baked Beans* was watching the news on television and saw people discussing something called Social Media. What were these exciting things called Facebook, Twitter and YouTube? It seems that all that was necessary was to make a blog or a short film and soon everyone would be talking about it. So that is exactly what *Bog's Standard Baked Beans* did, and people did seem to be talking about it every few minutes, but usually people were just telling each other what they had eaten for dinner the night before! *Bog's Standard Baked Beans* seemed destined to spend the rest of its life hiding at the back of supermarket shelves. Then one day, someone mentioned how they thought people just liked to see, hear and read stories best. *Bog's Standard Baked Beans* stopped writing blogs about how nice its sauce is and how fat the haricot beans are and began to post stories on Facebook and Twitter about how well it knows *toast*, and people

particularly enjoyed the story of how it first met *egg and bacon*. But best of all, people laughed and wrote lots of messages of their own about *Bog's Standard Baked Beans* adventures with students. How they ate beans cold late at night, how some had eaten beans every day for six months and how some of them even did naughty things with them. Finally, everyone knew about *Bog's Standard Baked Beans*. The moral of this story? Isn't it obvious? Tell consumers something new, interesting and engaging and they will respond in many ways and across many different media types.

The importance of social media sites

By definition the advent of social media was based around the creation of networks where people could communicate, post pictures, share information and send each other messages. Internet chat rooms came first but were little more than a glorified email system. People registered, invented user names for themselves to preserve their anonymity and were able to communicate instantly with a wide range of other users. The messaging was usually conversational and often conducted with strangers; the relationships people struck up were more often than not with others who they only 'knew' from the chat room they used. Certainly, an online community was established and people used chat rooms to openly express their emotions, feelings and fears alongside more trivial conversations. Users generally felt secure in the anonymity of the chat environment, but also chat rooms offered a link to young people for sexual predators and the criminally minded. The bad press chat rooms received was centred on horror stories of young girls striking up online relationships with men (who turned out to be far older than the teenagers they communicated with were). In a minority of instances, girls agreed to meet their online 'boyfriend' with potentially dangerous results ranging from eloping to rape. Even ITV's *Coronation Street* featured a story illustrating the dangers of turning chat-room liaisons into reality. In truth, advertising agencies saw few promotional possibilities in chat rooms other than the straightforward booking of banner and pop-up adverts to surround the website. The MSN system of live messaging devised by Microsoft took the concept of chat rooms a little further and partially appeased concerned parents by building in a friends system which meant it was only possible to 'chat' with people the user had previously accepted as an online 'friend'. It is possible on MSN to engage in online conversations with multiple friends, but once again the advertising potential is limited and the same dangers associated with chat rooms are still present on MSN. As an alternative to live messaging, the idea of a Web Log or *Blog* was also appealing to computer users. This involved setting up a web page to tell your own stories – a kind of online, but very public, diary. These blog sites could include pictures and music to increase their appeal and of course were interactive to allow other users to leave messages. The arrival of MySpace, quickly followed by Facebook and Bebo, turned the concepts of chat rooms and blogs on

their head – effectively combining the two and adding more features. The basic principle is still a friends system – the ability to create and message larger groups and publish photos, films and music to share with other users. I am going to stop there because I am conscious of preaching to the converted here – I don't know a single student who doesn't have a Facebook page and in fact it is an integral part of student communication. But how did the advertising industry recognize the potential of social networking and social media?

Advertising and social networking

Advertising agencies were quick to recognize the strategic benefits of social networking websites, taking advantage of internet forums, podcasts, blogs, Wikipedia and in particular social networking sites. They provide people with a platform to talk about themselves and publish information that interests them and that they wish to share with others. In principle, the world can share the music, films, books and other social activities those individuals wish to publish on their pages. Interesting people can communicate with other interesting people. Importantly to advertising agencies, though, social networking offered them access to an increased knowledge of the behaviour, interests and language of potential consumers in a wide range of social groups. Initially, agencies were able to use this information to place advertising directly in front of highly targeted consumers using banners and sponsored links within the pages of social networking websites. Advertising quickly developed an intuitive understanding of how people communicated on their personal pages and recognized that it was possible to communicate directly with consumers using their language and in a context in which they were receptive. Late in 2007, Facebook founder Mark Zuckerberg introduced an advertising system that made it easy for agencies to tap into the potential of social networking. Styled as *Facebook Ads*, Zuckerberg explained to New York marketing and advertising executives how they could connect with global audiences:

> *Facebook Ads* represents a completely new way of advertising online. For the last 100 years media has been pushed out to people, by now marketers and advertisers are going to be a part of the conversation. And they're going to do this by using the social graph in the same way our users do. The core of every user's experience on *Facebook* is their page and that's where businesses are going to start as well. The first thing businesses can do is design a page to craft the exact experience they want people to see. (www.facebook.com/press/releases)

In advertising terms there are three distinct opportunities to explore: the creation of Facebook pages to connect with audiences, an advertising system that allows the distribution of advertising messages virally and, of significant strategic value, an

Burger King uses Facebook to advertise its brand and maintain an on-going consumer dialogue.

interface that gathers insightful data about consumer activity on Facebook. By its very nature, social interactions within the site create trust and a sense of referral as users share and pass on information between 'friends'. Advertising activity can in effect be supported by 'user reviews' of brands, products and services. By buying into the Facebook community, advertisers can create messages which can be refined and tailored to mirror the behaviour of consumers and talk to them with unprece-dented precision. Brands are now users 'friends' and advertising can be delivered directly to carefully identified users as News Feeds, appear as sponsored links or just simply be positioned within a user's Facebook page. Links from these placed advertising messages very often take users to the brand's Facebook page and not to its usual website to allow a continuity of social culture, style and language. Also, users can post messages, photos and start discussion groups with the brand's page to add increased kudos to other users – and so the 'conversation' grows. Given the correct prompts, people will talk to each other about anything that appears to be of shared interest. It can sometimes go horribly wrong though. Fast-food giant Burger King cancelled a campaign on the strength of protests from Facebook. The idea was that people added and quickly removed 'friends' from their pages in exchange for a free Whopper. The campaign ran with headlines like 'Friendship is strong, but the Whopper is stronger', resulting in thousands of users ditching their 'friends' for a free burger. Every time someone removed a 'friend', a special application programme published an update on both people's Facebook pages. The campaign, called *Whopper Sacrifice*, devised by Burger King's agency Crispin Porter+Bogusky, was cancelled when Facebook disabled the application programme and requested changes that would have negated the concept behind the campaign. Burger King

did, however, successfully get away with running a campaign called *Whopper Virgins* that took the form of taste tests against McDonald's Big Mac with consumers who had previously not tried Burger King food. It also ran commercials under the heading 'Angry Whopper' about burgers raised by a sadistic farmer.

Negative posts on social networking sites have resulted in some high-profile news stories. A fork-lift truck driver was sacked by his employer for posting clips of him performing stunts and 'burn-outs' with his vehicle. An office administrator was sacked for telling her Facebook 'friends' about how boring her job was. Virgin Atlantic fired 13 cabin-crew employees for calling into question the company's safety policies and insulting passengers by describing them as 'chavs' – once again the online conversations had appeared on Facebook. Tread carefully, both personally and professionally: the world is watching, reading and listening.

Advertising as a virus

Viral advertising is good old-fashioned 'word of mouth' gone digital. But viral messages don't just spread by themselves, someone somewhere has to start the whole thing off. A Harvard Business School graduate, Tim Draper, is credited with the term Viral Advertising in 1997, in part to describe Hotmail's habit of adding advertising messages to the foot of its users' outbound emails. The principle is essentially simple – by telling someone who you know will be interested in something, it can be guaranteed that they will tell others. Obvious, yes, but the trick is to ensure that the first people to receive the message are those who will be sufficiently engaged to spread the word further. There are no specific ways in which to instigate a viral campaign – the imagination and creativity of strategists mean the context is continually evolving. In the early days, before Facebook or YouTube, email was the weapon of choice, with written text, html pages or video clips sent to chosen target groups' inboxes in the expectation that they would pass them on. Emails often included links to websites containing animations, films or games. The advancement of mobile phone technology soon expanded the repertoire to allow text messages, picture messages and videos to be distributed to users' handsets – again, hit the right initial users and watch as they bounce the messages on to their phonebooks. By sending a video clip that is just so much fun, so interesting or so intriguing the advertising work is done as the message spreads to an audience of millions. Successful campaigns are those that burrow right into the heart of popular culture and that are placed in precisely the right environment to be picked up by the online and technological communities.

It really is too boring just to continue to drone on about the strategies and techniques that might be used to launch a viral campaign. The necessity to communicate with an audience in the right way, at the right time and in the right place should now be tattooed across the forehead of every reader. Here are some examples of how viral advertising has been effective. At the top of the list is Nike –

its campaign featuring Brazilian soccer star Ronaldinho hitting the crossbar four times without the football ever touching the ground achieved over 50 million hits on YouTube across the world. A discussion both online and in the traditional media about whether the video clip was real or computer generated sent interested viewers flocking to YouTube. A film for Agent Provocateur featuring Kylie Minogue riding a bucking bronco in the brand's lingerie was deemed too *risqué* for its intended cinema audience. Agent Provocateur's brand desire to invite controversy saw this commercial rage across the internet, and five years later it has chalked up 360 million hits. Not bad for a cinema ad!

Now for a couple of classics. In 2006, Ogilvy & Mather (Toronto) created *Evolution*, a commercial forming part of Dove's *Campaign for Real Beauty.*

A screen shot from Dove's successful *Evolution* viral campaign.

Image courtesy of Leo Burnett New York.

The sequence is based around time-lapse photography showing a woman being transformed by a team of stylists into a stunning model. After the makeover a photographer appears to take a series of photographs of the woman. One of the shots is chosen and is then shown opening up on a computer screen into Adobe Photoshop. The image is then manipulated further to lengthen her neck, enlarge her eyes and mouth, touch-up her skin and hair and adjust the curve of her shoulder. The completed image is then shown on a fictional billboard campaign for an invented make-up brand *Fasel,* with the headline, 'no wonder our perception of beauty is distorted'. The film finished by inviting viewers to take part in *Dove Real Beauty Workshops.* To begin with the film was incorporated into the Canadian Campaign for Real Beauty website, later being uploaded to YouTube. The film received 40,000 hits on its first day, rising to 12 million after a year. The campaign was given huge exposure by featuring in discussions on major daytime North American television with plenty of news coverage too. Such was the impact of the campaign it won first prize at the Cannes Film Festival and several other international advertising awards. It also spawned a number of YouTube spoof films, including *Slob Evolution,* featuring a teenage boy being given fast food, alcohol and cigarettes instead of a makeover as he is slowly transformed into a middle-aged overweight 'slob'. On the back of an initial viral launch of only 30 carefully targeted emails, its hits ran into hundreds of thousands in less than a month. Of course, all the while the Dove version was picking up viewing instigated by the parody. A perfect demonstration of how a clever film can be launched virally and then gains massive publicity through other media. The even bigger plus of such a viral campaign is that it lasts almost forever, not just for a month on television screens. It will not have escaped your attention, though, that many high-profile television commercials past and present are available to view on YouTube.

A more recent favourite viral of mine is *Smirnoff Tea Partay*, which I first saw when Sir John Hegarty showed it as part of a lecture he was giving at my university. The film was created by Bartle Bogle Hegarty for a new Smirnoff product, Raw Tea, and directed by music video director Julien Christian Lutz. (www.thirdwayblog.com/smirnoff/smirnoff-tea-partay-preppies-on-youtube) The concept and execution is

shot to feel like a rap video, but with American College preppies rapping instead. It is a brave piece of advertising for what most young people would consider to be an unattractive product – alcoholic ice tea. The visual statements made by the very safe, conservative American students confront the product preconceptions head on and somehow make the equally safe preconceptions of ice tea on the lawn exciting and engaging. The semi-mythical context of American college students in New England or Vermont, set against an environment of tennis, croquet, cucumber sandwiches and preppie-fashion, is then laced with the kind of quirkiness viral advertising demands. Clean-cut students deliver their self-mocking rap (by a band called Prep-Unit) about their American rich-kid lifestyle with humour and panache. The strategy is as clever and as underplayed as the film. It began life hidden on a low-key website that allowed viewers to upload it to YouTube themselves. Over 2 million hits later and the message is well and truly broadcast. But wait a minute, yes you say, as a viral campaign it has clearly been a roaring success but does it sell Smirnoff Raw Tea? Who would want to drink that? General consumer reaction goes something like this. The commercial is very funny and very entertaining but it would not necessarily make anyone buy the product directly. However, if when standing in a bar or liquor store waiting for a cold beer consumers caught sight of Raw Tea, the chances are they would try it just for the hell of it. Judge for yourselves whether that makes it an effective product commercial or not.

Bartle Bogle Hegarty's viral for Smirnoff entitled *Tea Partay* has been a huge success across social network and blog sites.

Image courtesy of Bartle Bogle Hegarty.

You probably all know that Google owns YouTube (which in the space of four years or so has become the core of many viral campaigns). Whilst it's obvious that YouTube is integral to advertising today, not so obvious is the role it plays in more traditional digital advertising. It is possible to include advertising in video clips, although not all videos are eligible for advertising. Around 20 seconds into a clip a transparent advertisement could appear for around 15 seconds in the bottom part of the window; clicking on the image runs the commercial, otherwise it just disappears. YouTube claims that only around 10 per cent of users close the image overlay as soon as it appears, suggesting that most users are not concerned by being fed advertising messages at the same time as viewing video clips. This is in stark contrast to earlier experiments with running advertising at the beginning of clips when it was found many users simply abandoned their viewing. YouTube also strives to prevent advertising appearing within potentially brand-damaging content such as pornographic or violent clips: a problem Facebook once had when its technology allowed established brands to appear on a page created by the extreme right-wing British National Party. No brand needs that kind of association or negativity attached to its reputation.

Managing and maintaining an online brand persona is just as vital as it would be in traditional print or television-based media. Consistency of style, tone and message is important in building consumer responses and perceptions of a brand – we have already discussed how complex and precious an entity that can be.

So what about the good old-fashioned website?

I have often wondered just how many websites exist across the world. How sad is that? It's a mind-boggling thought, though, because a website is as much a part of corporate communication as a letterhead or a business card; every business has one but do they still have a role to play in digital advertising? It is strange to be even saying that, suggesting that websites may not be such a big part of advertising strategy today. The answer is yes; of course they have a role to play. A website is a highly effective method of distributing information to consumers and customers. In order to be effective, as an advertising medium, company brochure and forum, potential consumers and customers need to know it is there. Technologies to increase the flow of visitors or traffic to websites have become increasingly sophisticated. A website provides a permanent resource and ever-present base for other types of online dialogue that brands establish. The platform to maintaining a website as a continuous part of advertising and communication campaigns is to drive up the visitor numbers. The underlying means to this end is the presence of a web address on every last piece of customer or consumer dialogue. Business stationery starts the list off but it also includes traditional advertising, emails, printed literature, PR stories and product packaging. That's obvious, but search engines are of crucial importance too. A huge percentage of internet users make searches at least once a day, and it is generally believed that around half of online purchases are preceded by a search. It is reasonable to assume that consumers are actively searching for a brand's product, service or entertainment offers. The most amazing, content-rich website is a wasted resource if it is difficult to find, and ranking on all the major search engines is absolutely necessary. If the website doesn't appear in the early pages of a Google search, it may as well not exist. The technique used to maximize a presence within search results is known as search engine optimization, the principle of which involves delivering content to the largest search engines to gain more prominent listings on results pages. I can feel you starting to glaze over now so I will not get too technical about this, but here are the golden rules of search engine optimization:

> Build in the best and most appropriate keywords.
> Understand what competitive websites are doing.
> Ensure that pages can be found individually by search engines.
> Ensure the website is deeply scanned by search engines.

These factors ensure that a website crops up every time a consumer puts in a comparable search word. A linking program can also help with the visibility of a website to allow web surfers to visit easily from other websites of related or friendly businesses in other sectors. This can easily be facilitated by an 'I'll link you if you link me' arrangement. Links should also be included with every other online activity such as Wikipedia, social networking sites or banner advertising.

Email can work effectively in conjunction with a website too. The practice of email marketing is not so different from more traditional direct mail campaigns – the consumer response is about the same too. They dislike spam as much as they do junk mail. An effective email campaign should be approached like a mail pack, using inviting, tantalizing creative thinking and an up-to-date, relevant database. The difference is that the response from recipients is instant. A well-conceived, well-designed email with a link to an interesting-looking website is an instant advertising hit in the bag. Strategists can analyse response rates and measure success just as a print-based direct mail campaign does.

Actually, this is all beginning to sound familiar. Surely these are the very same techniques that other types of media advertising use? Yes they are. Millions of people now access their news coverage online using combinations of websites they are comfortable with and a search engine designed to find news. Any good contemporary PR agency is wise to this fact, and promotional stories are distributed to both online and offline media with the added bonus online of being able to include a link straight back to a brand website. A wider presence online, via news coverage or product reviews on other websites, increases the volume of links in search results. Coming back around full circle again, online PR also includes postings on social networking sites and forums. Competitions, promotions and special offers can also be distributed virally.

Advertising in an online environment can also include 'buying in' to someone else's website. In late 2006 Nintendo launched its new games console, *Wii*, in conjunction with Microsoft. MSN and Windows Live Messenger have target user groups ranging between 15 and 34, which also happens to be perfect for the games market. This group of consumers who regularly use online networking are also likely to be very receptive 'gamers', desperate for the next big gaming experience. The advertising technique was quite innovative too – when users scrolled over the right-hand corner of the respective homepages the screen image peeled away to reveal an advertisement for Nintendo *Wii* with, yes you guessed it, a link to the new console's own website.

The newest arrival on the social networking scene is Twitter, a short messaging and 'micro-blog' service that essentially asks for a response to the question 'what are you doing?' Once again advertising is alert to the possibilities of integrating YouTube, websites and other online activity with this emerging environment. As I write, Twitter has an older demographic than Facebook, with users tending to be over 30, with media people and Blackberry users pioneering it. In 2009, Euro RSCG created a media-rich advertisement that occupied YouTube's homepage for Volvo's new XC60 crossover vehicle. The banner advertisement featured the vehicle's auto-brake 'city safety' capability and offered viewers the chance to watch videos, view photographs or play an online game. It also included a live feed of Twitter updates from the New York Auto Show taking place at the same time. Not only do Volvo's target markets fit well with Twitter users; there are also brand similarities. According

to Volvo, their brand is about humanity, and so is Twitter. At the same time as maximizing the latest, most appropriate technology, the advertising banner is the largest currently featured on YouTube and gives the users the option of closing the window.

Euro RSCG bought the YouTube homepage to advertise the launch of the Volvo XC60 with a live Twitter feed.

Image courtesy of Euro RSCG.

Integration, integration, integration

The key to successful digital advertising is the integration of a variety of online media into a cohesive, powerful campaign tool. The media-smart digital advertising agencies are staffed by an exciting blend of creative talent, inventive strategists and innovative programmers and developers. These combinations of skills can truly maximize and expand the media platforms from which advertisers can communicate. The London-based agency Glue was founded in 2001 and is dedicated to providing its clients with new solutions that take full advantage of familiar and emerging media. The concept of integrated digital advertising is best described by looking more closely at a couple of campaigns both created by Glue. The soft-drinks brand Oasis, part of the Coca-Cola family, ran a television and outdoor campaign entitled 'Run Cactus Kid Run', Glue's brief was to expand that successful campaign digitally. The story unfolds within an online virtual world of micro websites and social media sites. The main character, Cactus Kid, is outlawed because of his dislike of plain water, preferring to drink Oasis instead. The campaign tells of his struggle to keep one step ahead of the authorities as he flees, with his girlfriend, through American locations towards Mexico. The web-based microsites appear to have been developed by the characters themselves and all link back to a main website called the 'Official Find Cactus Kid Website'. This site has links to all the major social networking sites which feature blogs written by Cactus Kid's girlfriend. In addition, a YouTube page features uploaded video clips of Cactus Kid 'sitings' and a Flickr page shows images of him in a variety of locations too. Other microsites are designed to look like the websites of restaurants where Cactus Kid has been spotted, together with wanted posters and 'witness' reports. There was even a site dedicated to MACK (Mother Against Cactus Kid), featuring interviews with women campaigning against Cactus Kid. The campaign ended by asking consumers to vote online for a selection of story endings, with the most popular providing the theme for the final television commercial.

Screen shots from Glue's 'Run Cactus Kid Run' online and viral campaign.

Image courtesy of Glue London.

According to Glue's own website, 70 per cent of Oasis consumers engaged with the campaign in some way, and brand awareness rose from 27 per cent to 45 per cent. The video and image content hosted on Flickr and YouTube exceeded 100,000 visitors, and there were 54,000 different users during the life of the campaign. This was a series of digital advertising events that truly explored the potential of online

Screen shots from Glue's web and mobile campaign for the Royal Navy to encourage increased interest in naval careers among young people.

Image courtesy of Glue London.

communication yet retained a synergy with the accompanying television and outdoor media for a complete, integrated brand experience. It also reinforces the views I expressed when recounting the fictitious tale of *Bog's Standard Baked Beans* – that consumers are prepared to engage with multimedia advertising if there is an interesting and engaging story to be had.

Advertising can also take full advantage of the multimedia capabilities offered by mobile phones, especially when the target audience is young, media literate and stimulated by visual communications. In 2007 Glue won a string of industry awards for their campaign aimed at boosting recruitment for the Royal Navy. The campaign was constructed around an application programme devised specifically for use with mobile phones. It was a video application that had the capability for users to send personalized video messages to each other by email and to handsets using Royal Navy hardware – from Sea King helicopters to submarines, dive boats and even Royal Marine Commandos. The host websites also featured some powerful film clips of the navy in action, with personnel discussing their particular roles aboard ship. As I write, the campaign is still accessible online at www.GetTheMessage.net. Have a play.

Away from the internet (nearly)

Digital advertising should not be considered wholly owned by the internet, though. For many years shopping malls have featured interactive kiosks and consoles which offer information points for shoppers on retail outlets, eating and drinking, and where they are located. The display screen can provide an effective advertising platform for the shops and restaurants within the shopping mall, offering information and messages that communicate with shoppers who are, well, shopping. Similarly, plasma screens are a familiar sight in many retail environments. Some are situated in banks and other places that require customers to queue or wait; these generally display digital television channels showing 24-hour news or sport. Most bars now have television screens that screen sporting events. Of course, these examples are simply showing rescheduled television and its accompanying commercial breaks. More flexible and targeted are plasma screens erected in malls to display advertising, with retail brands able to buy space to display their message to consumers to entice them into their outlets. Other advertisers may also choose to buy space to communicate with consumers whilst they are out and about. Basically, these digital screens are rather like electronic poster sites, and outdoor media

providers often sell the advertising space. It is becoming increasingly common to find these screens in other busy locations too. Universities and colleges, railway stations, airports and even large hotel foyers are some examples I've seen recently. All offer advertisers the same opportunity – the chance to reach specific groups of consumers targeted by their location and activity.

On-screen advertising is an increasing feature of shopping centres and other public places where people gather.

Image courtesy of CMD Global.

Direct Response Television – the dark side

Direct Response Television or DRTV is universally despised by advertising creatives and, to some extent, the agencies that employ them. Why? Because this is where advertising meets the shopping channel and creativity is sold down the river at the expense of sales, sales and more sales. DRTV arrived on the advertising scene in the 1990s with the advent of interactive television. It differs from brand advertising, which is designed to generate awareness of a brand's proposition over a long period of time. Whilst there may be a response mechanism or call to action built into brand advertising, the ultimate objective is to build relationships with consumers. Advertising in a DRTV environment is much closer to our much-maligned friend direct mail, in that its primary objective is to generate immediate and measurable responses from consumers. In other words, it wants to sell something and it wants to sell it now. As you might expect, DRTV is huge in the United States and is much more part of consumer culture than it is in the UK, although of course this is changing. Typically, DRTV advertising has found tremendous success in the charity sector, with religious organizations and cut-price leisure goods benefiting too. Pay-as-you-view television channels also use DRTV, often those showing adult content, as the call to action means an instant credit card sign-up can be achieved. The volume of advertising aimed at younger audiences is also increasing because digital television can bring together TV, web and mobile phone communication with a few clicks of the remote control. The media-savvy teenager demands an instant technology hit and can get it without even getting off the sofa.

DRTV advertisers play the numbers game: they are less interested in who sees the advertisements, focusing instead on trying to reach the largest possible number of people within their identified target group. Often DRTV campaigns will focus on cheaper, off-peak airtime but repeat the advertisements frequently to hit smaller numbers of consumers at a time, but by showing the advertisements almost by rotation, the viewing figures quickly multiply.

The creative and strategic secret to DRTV success is to present consumers with a clear, simple and of course persuasive message and to implore them to respond immediately with a free telephone number or website link. A charity, raising money for blind people, called Sight Savers ran a hugely successful DRTV campaign with the proposition: '£15 will restore the sight of a blind person.' Consumers responded well to the call to action that simply asked for a £15 donation with a credit card.

No doubt you are beginning to see why advertising creatives have such an aversion to DRTV advertising. The objective is not to delight, entertain or inspire consumers, it is simply to sell and in large volumes. The look and style is important but grabbing attention immediately is far more so. In the USA, cars, credit cards, insurance, mobile phones and satellite television have all been sold very successfully on DRTV. The DRTV image of dodgy imitation watches and other cheap and cheerful consumer goods is beginning to change (for the better I would hope).

Contrary to the usual approach of amassing bite-sized numbers of consumers with regular off-peak commercials, one of the USA's most successful DRTV campaigns actually appeared during a Super Bowl commercial break. Cash4Gold, featuring a seemingly destitute Ed McMahon and MC Hammer, ran a spot asking for people to send old jewellery, gold teeth, nuggets, parachutes or whatever they liked in exchange for hard cash. MC Hammer was shown exchanging the gold Turkish pants he wore at the height of his pop fame. A national television pawnshop? Maybe, but it illustrates the power of a hard-hitting direct sell and also supports the slightly sleazy downmarket image of DRTV. But then didn't David Ogilvy famously say, 'if it doesn't sell, it isn't creative'?

DRTV is perhaps the creative's least favourite advertising medium.

Image origin unknown.

Having said that, the author George Orwell also described advertising as the 'rattling of a stick inside a swill bucket', an observation many advertising people would wholeheartedly agree with if applied to DRTV. No matter how sniffy anyone

83

gets about DRTV, we cannot escape the fact that shed-loads of products get shifted this way. Despite what advertising types may think, certain types of retail clients of course love it. A suspect-looking contraption guaranteed to give you a six-pack or slim thighs in a week may have creatives running for the sickbag, but clients rub their hands with glee as the cash register rings.

Actually, none of this is any excuse for the brash, noisy sales spots where the more outrageously sleazy the models and breathlessly urgent the voice-over the better. Boasting in a bar about the amazing DRTV work your agency does would be rather like admitting to a previous career in porn films at a job interview. The additional danger for advertising agencies is the sheer accountability of it all. A traditional brand commercial cannot be measured instantly or effectively for success, but DRTV can. Clients simply have to count sales to judge whether the campaign worked or not, so agencies have to tread carefully and achieve sales or they are out on their ear. If only for that reason, risk taking and creative boundary pushing just don't sit well with DRTV. Yet despite all the bad vibes associated with DRTV, it has slowly crept from late-night schedules to daytime slots, and bigger brands have jumped aboard to take advantage of instant sales. A mental image of Homer Simpson sat on the couch armed with a remote control watching shopping channels because nothing else interests him is not so very far from the reality. A percentage of consumers are pretty much addicted and just waiting to hand over their money for the right product. Usually that is a product only available on TV and not in retail stores, or a hybrid version developed exclusively for TV selling. No wonder consumers are hooked on seductive quick-fix goods delivered without challenging their intellects: effective DRTV tells them all they need to know to buy – quickly, simply and without brand baggage attached. To understand clarity and simplicity is to understand DRTV; once you have hooked your consumer, hit them low and hard with a telephone number to call or a red button click to close the sale. The call to action is king – boil the entire offer down into a few seconds of 'buy now before it's too late' style persuasion then stretch the commercial back out into either a 'short form' commercial of less than 2 minutes or a 'long-form' infomercial of anything over 2 minutes. If you can squeeze in a testimonial or two from other satisfied customers then so much the better.

Just before I leave DRTV alone, think about this. Don't just get all arty and pious about it – demonstrating your ability to work strategically and creatively across varied media platforms increases your offer to prospective employers. Like it or not, DRTV is a part of that media variety.

In the time it has taken you to read this chapter the boundaries of digital advertising will already have been extended by a quick-witted, imaginative creative, strategist and programmer somewhere. The pace of development is rapid and restricted only by the limits of the human mind. Creative briefs for student competitions are frequently open-ended in their media suggestions now, which demands that entrants explore all the potential of integrated media campaigns. Whilst you are learning, expanding your minds and developing your portfolio of work and skills, think about how to tap into advertising media in a different or unusual way. Employers no longer expect to discuss ideas based around the more traditional advertising routes. Yes, they will want to see posters or storyboards and no, they will not want to see just ambient campaign ideas. What they will want is graduates who genuinely understand the creative and communication potential of all the media available to advertising. If you can tell them something they didn't already know, then so much the better.

Some websites to visit

In a digital advertising context there are probably millions, but here are some sites to keep you in the loop; Google the rest!

Just for exploring and checking what everyone is doing:

Facebook, Twitter, Linkedin, YouTube, Flickr, MySpace, Bebo.

Specific sites for news stories and blogs:

www.tangerinetoad.blogspot.com
www.blogtactic.com
www.interactivemarketingtrends.blogspot.com
www.adage.com
www.adweek.com
www.business.timesonline.co.uk
www.thirdwayblog.com

These sites feature digital advertising agencies and campaigns:

www.thecarthatstopsitself.com
www.rebelvirals.com
www.agencyrepublic.com
www.bbh.co.uk
www.brand-advocate.com
www.dotmailer.com
www.imagination.com
www.ogilvy.com
www.gluelondon.com
Search digital advertising and integrated advertising for more.

Some books to read

Advertising and New Media
Christina Spurgeon

Visual Creativity: Inspirational Ideas for Advertising, Animation and Digital
Mario Pricken and Christine Klell

Ads to Icons: How Advertising Succeeds in a Multimedia Age
Paul Springer

Branding@the Digital Age
Herbert M. Meyers and Richard Gerstman

*Creating Flash Advertising: From Concept to Tracking-Microsites, Video Ads and More
(Hands-On Guide Series)*
Jason Fincanon

Connected Marketing: The Viral, Buzz and Word of Mouth Revolution
Justin Kirby and Paul Marsden

Grapevine: The New Art of Word-of-mouth
Dave Balter and John Butman

World's Best Online Advertising Campaigns
Marc Phillips

Get involved

Share your links, campaigns and media discoveries:

- search Facebook for 'Advertising Its Business Culture and Careers'
- www.twitter.com/adculture

5 Is creativity in your DNA?

Teaching the advertising business and creative processes to young people just starting their journey towards a career in advertising and promotion gives me a massive buzz. The raw enthusiasm, latent talent and questioning intelligence of the high-quality students my course is fortunate enough to attract are an exciting prospect for me in September of every year. I have tried for many years to define in my own head what makes a great advertising student. That question is far easier to answer once he or she is two years into my university's advertising programme. The ability to communicate well, analyse an advertising brief and interpret it with boundless creativity and boundary-pushing imagination becomes much more apparent once a student has built a clear definition in his or her own mind of the possibilities of the media and the message.

> When I'm struggling to have ideas . . .
>
> *I go to the gym and boil myself in the sauna until I crack it.*
> David Sloly – Creative Director, Mason Zimbler

My question is more fundamental than that – I am searching to understand whether there are any specific personality indicators or intellectual mindsets that young people instinctively have that make them successful advertising people. I once asked Sir John Hegarty what he and his agency, Bartle Bogle Hegarty, look for in a graduate desperate for a career in advertising. He answered quite simply, enthusiasm. That for me is too simplistic a vision. I know what he meant – enthusiasm and desire go a considerable way towards helping people achieve their goals whatever they may be, but is that enough for advertising? Not any more.

Trevor Beattie created some extraordinary visual imagery in his work for Sony PlayStation.

Image courtesy of Beattie McGuinness Bungay.

The days when great creative thinkers arrived at the door of an agency and were hired for their natural ability have (mostly) gone. The training required to mould that raw talent into an innovative advertising practitioner is seldom undertaken from scratch by agency employers any longer – that role now falls to universities and colleges. Remember the story of David Ogilvy earlier in this book? The university drop-out who took to sales and wrote a training manual for Aga stoves, which was so good it got him a job as a copywriter. That would be an extremely unlikely scenario now. The industry has changed beyond recognition and it now expects a focused individual with an appropriate advertising education who can then be trained in the ways of his or her employing agency. Mostly. There is that word again. The industry of course has stockpiles of ready-made anecdotes to dispute that theory. Advertising agencies would maintain that they are on a quest to seek out exciting creative thinkers, and would welcome innovators from any previous background. However, for the benefit of all you student readers – your university experiences, your personality and the work you are capable of are your main weapons.

> When I'm struggling to have ideas . . .
>
> **Talk to colleagues, brainstorm.**
>
> Gillian Challinor – Digital Project Manager, Gyro HSR

Going back to my earlier question – making a decision on whether to accept someone onto a three-year course in creative advertising is almost based on instinct at the final stage. The process of application demands that all prospective students produce a personal statement that talks about who they are and why they are motivated to pursue a career in advertising. A persuasive and convincing statement is usually sufficient to gain an interview. Students of creative arts invariably have to bring a portfolio of work along to their interview – a practice that is a vital part of the job-interview process too. For me, neither of these factors is sufficient in making a selection decision, it is more intuitive and instinctive than that. Some of the most successful students I have had the pleasure to teach have such an aura about them that the decision is almost immediate. After that they would have to work very hard indeed to screw the interview up and not be offered a place. Yet equally, some students grow into advertising people over three years. Still, there is something about them that is convincing enough to be worthy of a place. Maybe Hegarty was right after all; enthusiasm and commitment are very big players in the make-up of advertising people. Certainly, this has a major effect on the first impressions people form when meeting potential employees for the first time. But there is more too – advertising requires bright, questioning minds that tease out solutions to complex brand-communication problems. Then there are communication skills as well – that engaging, clear manner of speaking and interesting personality. Now I am talking myself into an ever-deepening hole. Advertising cannot work from checklists and tick boxes when it comes to selecting the right people – the process is deeply subjective and tightly wrapped in creative talent, boundless desire and a stimulated mind. Throw in an ability to talk to people and a love of the 'team' environment and maybe we are getting close. In order to understand where you need to be to compete for a position in this exciting world, I think it is important to understand more of how an advertising environment works and to be familiar with the creative process.

The advertising brief

Unquestionably the development of a clear, precise brief is the catalyst for creative thinking and it places great emphasis on devising an effective media plan, an inviting proposition, and then persuasive and innovative executions of the strategy. In short, the big marketing idea and the even bigger creative concept are the twin holy grails. Advertising is always a 'team game'; there is always room for mavericks who start

their thinking process from a different mental place to everyone else, but there is no room for lone wolves. Precious, defensive prima donnas with a distorted view of their own self-righteous creative ideas do not succeed in advertising. Clear, innovative 'blue-sky' thinkers who delight in sharing and developing ideas with others to help those ideas grow and expand are very welcome though.

> When I'm struggling to have ideas . . .
>
> *There's no such thing as 'feeling' or 'not feeling creative'.*
> *There's only feeling or not feeling lazy.*
>
> Jon Fox – Copywriter, BBH London

The development of the brief is reliant on a team of dynamic thinkers with the intellectual capacity to understand objectives and to interpret them in new ways. The story of the brief begins with the client. An account management team will start the process off by meeting the client marketing team to discuss and clarify the advertising objectives. However, before that meeting takes place the account management team will be very familiar with the client's business and product or service offers. If the advertising agency has worked with that client before, the team will already have a clear understanding of the business culture and products – in other words, the brand. If it is a new client, then the team will have done its homework and not just by taking a cursory glance at the client's website either. They will have visited the client's offices and spoken to the people responsible for marketing and developed an intuitive 'feel' for the brand language, tone of voice and business style. A trip to a factory that makes the client's products or the environment in which they are sold also provides some vital insights for the account management team to use within the creative brief. American companies in particular are extremely good at instilling a brand lifestyle into their employees, drawn largely from a customer-focused perspective that is sometimes lacking in the UK and other parts of the world. Their objective is to employ and train 'brand ambassadors'. Consider McDonald's as an example, though the organization is far from unique. Every aspect of its business oozes a brand culture: new staff or 'crew members' are trained the same way irrespective of the location of the restaurant in which they are to work. The way food is cooked, presented and delivered to customers is a well-defined model across the world. 'Crew members' are also instructed in what it means to work for McDonald's, how they should speak to each other and to customers, and in the philosophy of the McDonald's brand. An advertising agency must understand this business culture, so perhaps it is essential to be involved with their client's staff and products. Still using the example of McDonald's, an account management team should have experienced everything except work at a restaurant (though some may

have whilst studying!) – so actually that may be useful too. The first rule of advertising account management is simple – make sure you know, don't just think you know. This is an approach that you as students can use in your project work too. Throw yourself into the brand behind your brief. Consume the product, visit the outlets for that product, talk and listen to the people involved in selling that product in order to understand it as thoroughly as possible. I guarantee that a couple of hours spent 'living' the brand will be far more enlightening than reading their website and, guess what? You will produce better, more effective work too.

McDonald's instils a deep sense of brand loyalty and pride into its staff and customers. It also commissions some very clever creative to support that brand personality.

Image courtesy of DDB Sydney.

Right, back to the client meeting. Armed with a wide understanding of the client, its business and its products, the account management team will discuss and develop a client brief over the course of that meeting. This will define exactly what the client wishes to achieve from the expensive advertising campaign they are about to embark on. Following the briefing meeting the agency team should be able to answer three questions clearly and concisely. 'What does the client need to say?' 'How does the client need to say it?' And 'who does the client need to say it to?' Understanding fully the answers to these questions provides the basis for the creative brief. The team returns to the agency fully in tune with the client and where they want to go with their advertising campaign. Time to get the campaign and strategic planning process underway. Inevitably there will still be research to be undertaken – yes, the account team understands the client, its brand and its business, but there is more specific data to gather. Some of this may have come from the client; some may still

need to be researched. The following broad questions help the agency understand where the client is, relative to similar types of competitive business.

Where is the brand today?

Do similar brands sell more?
Who are they?
How much more do they sell?
How much do they spend on advertising?
Does it work?
Which media do they favour?
What do consumers believe about this brand?
How aware are they of this brand?
What makes this brand special?

Where would we like our brand to be tomorrow?

This is the fundamental basis of the creative brief. Fully appreciating the position of the brand and, most importantly, what consumers really believe about the brand. This goes back to knowing or thinking you know – clients are often poor at understanding clearly what consumers really feel, basing their opinions on what they feel about their brand themselves. The advertising agency should understand what the brand means to consumers, and if they can provide a new and alternative viewpoint, so much the better. This prompts the following questions:

Does the product and/or brand need explaining more clearly to consumers?
If consumers know what it is, do they also know what to do with it?
Do consumers remember the brand prior to purchasing it?
Do they only remember it when they see it?

It is important to have information available from previous campaigns to appreciate what prompted consumers to respond and where they responded less well. How well do they remember and/or recognize the brand?

Armed with all this research, the account management team will work closely with the account planning team to answer questions raised by the client's brief and to provide clear, succinct answers for the creative brief. At the top of the list will be identifying the target audience. In factual terms the consumer profile will be based on these factors:

Their age; e.g. 30–45
Their status and gender; e.g. married women
The job that they do
Where they live
Their lifestyle

Often within a creative brief this would be presented in a more descriptive, evocative way along the lines of: 'our target is a married woman with a growing family between the ages of 30 and 45. She works, as well as runs the home, so her time is at a premium. She and her friends are aware of the brand and are warm to its benefits. She understands what the brand means to her, but tends to buy a cheaper alternative.' Or maybe: 'the target is male between 18 and 25, fun loving, very sociable and enjoys his nightlife. He is single and therefore has money available for himself. He is aware of this brand and knows people that enjoy it. He is unclear how the brand will benefit him though.' The account planning team will need to have the clearest understanding possible of the target consumer. Not just the facts, but insights into their behaviour, activities and their social and buying habits. Good planners build up this knowledge from combinations of research and observation. The research helps them to appreciate exactly who the target consumer is in terms of age, gender, status and career. Observation provides the knowledge of their behaviour, language and stimulation. Magazines aimed at the target group offer some keys to their lifestyle and interests, and we discussed earlier the part that social networking sites can play. But there is also plain old being nosy: listening to people in shops or bars and other places frequented by the target group. Watching them individually and with friends. Don't get the wrong idea, I'm not talking about stalking here, just being aware of people and how they talk, look and act. For goodness sake don't start following anyone around! But heightened awareness of people, in all sorts of target groups, can again help you in your work as a student. So, to improve your planning skills, get busy reading magazines, sitting in coffee shops and bars or walking around town going into shops – life is tough, isn't it? The vital objective is experiencing the brand.

> When I'm struggling to have ideas . . .
>
> *I try a number of things . . . I get up from the desk and do something else or go somewhere completely unrelated to the job in hand. I have a walk; I go to see a movie or an exhibition. Making a cup of tea is a good one, tea seems to create clearer thinking . . . Or I have a shower. Bit hard to write things down though. Will have to turn the tiles into a whiteboard or something.*
>
> Mareka Carter – Art Director/Copywriter, BBH London

Next, the planning team will need to identify and clarify what makes this brand special and what sets it apart from its competitors. In advertising speak, this is known as the USP or Unique Selling Proposition. This is a simple concept that became an integral part of American advertising culture in the 1950s. In contemporary

advertising, the principle of defining a USP is less simple. Most brands in any given marketplace are worryingly similar in their quality and their factual benefits. The individual uniqueness of brands is more closely aligned to their personalities and language. Going back to burgers for a moment, consider the difference between the two major players, McDonald's and Burger King. McDonald's tends to present itself as a global brand that cares about the quality of its food and retail environment; Burger King tends to feel more *risqué* and likes to convey a sense of mischievous fun. Just grab a pencil here and make a quick list for yourselves of five keywords that reflect each brand individually. Do the same for Coca-Cola and Pepsi, Nike and Adidas or Levi's and Wrangler. Each of these global brands has a unique personality that must be retained yet also developed in new ways. The idea of USP has evolved into a more emotional buying process rather than one based wholly on product benefits. Some agencies now use the term ESP – Emotional Selling Proposition (as distinct from extrasensory perception, though the two may be related). I am willing to bet that the quick lists you scribbled down just now are much more inclined towards ESP than USP. It would be correct to say that during the past 50 years of advertising, facts have been superseded by emotion. No longer do consumers completely base their buying decisions on whether, say, a car does 10 miles to the gallon more than a rival brand, they buy into the sense of aspiration and emotional pleasure a car gives them. A kind of wow factor. Consumers are no longer just surprised or impressed by service intervals, driver comfort or suspension types, they want features to suggest that the brand fits in with their lifestyle and emotional expectations. I am a sucker for 1960s British cars; not necessarily sporty jobs either. On my office wall I have an advertisement for Triumph Herald created I guess in the mid-1960s. The headline states, 'If the Triumph Herald wasn't beautiful it would sell on its cleverness alone. Here's why.' The emotional trigger is still evident from the image of a young family enjoying the freedom of a car with a fold-down roof, yet the copy focuses on factual benefits like turning circle, servicing, comfort, safety and cost. All these are factors that are still important to modern car brands – yet somehow consumers now wish to be sold more of a dream. Gone are the days when advertising car brands relied solely on sexy images of sleek, shiny vehicles cruising around hairpin bends on South African mountain ranges. Recent campaign themes created by Ogilvy & Mather for Ford Focus (one of the UK's best-selling new cars) are based around musicians playing instruments made from parts of the car. In one commercial, a specially composed piece of music called 'Ode to the New Ford' by Craig Richey features, among other instruments, a 'clutch' guitar, a suspension-mount violin and a transmission-case cello. The orchestra and the message builds up to the appearance of the car itself and the closing line: 'The new Ford Focus – beautifully arranged'. The Ford brand statement 'Feel the Difference' appears at the end to reinforce the message that the brand is about style, entertainment and feeling good about oneself while driving it. Yes, this style of car advertising nods towards the work Wieden+Kennedy did for Honda, but it is asking the consumer for an involved

emotional response based on being sufficiently engaged to remember Ford Focus and to trust the Ford brand. Long before the creative team devised the concept of car-part musical instruments, the planning team will have 'got inside the head' of mid-priced car consumers to understand what it is they want from car brands.

The advertising brief is taking shape now. It includes a definition of the target audience, and the planning team has created the proposition. This is a clear snapshot of what the consumer should believe when they see the advertising. That belief is of vital importance, and as such the proposition should be absolutely crystal clear. One of my favourite examples of an astoundingly simple strategic proposition that takes a brand to a new place for consumers is Milky Way. Commercials for this brand have not necessarily been particularly inspirational or creatively challenging but a lightweight chocolate bar without very much to say was reinvented in the 1970s as being the 'sweet you can eat between meals without ruining your appetite'. Suddenly the advertising message had a blindingly clear sense of direction, and parents of young children easily bought into the proposition, and thus, Milky Way was established as the treat of choice for the walk home from school. A proposition that cuts right through the clutter and ever-present wallpaper of advertising messages will give the advertising the means to be successful. In creating or understanding the proposition built into an advertising brief, that degree of simplicity and clarity will work every time. Easier said than done I know, but try it. For every piece of advertising you see today; write down what you think the proposition is as clearly and in as few words as possible. By focusing on the importance of what you want your target audience to believe, your advertising work will take on a new clarity and provide a platform for stronger creative thinking. Now go into the kitchen and find three eggs. Pick one up and toss it in the air and catch it – easy unless you have been drinking. Now do it with two – not quite so easy because you have to look at two eggs at once. Now try it with the third – unless you have been to a circus skills workshop the floor is looking a bit of a mess and I think you probably ended up dropping all three. If you held on to one was it the right one? Proposition is the same process. Give consumers too many messages to absorb and they will either take in the wrong one or ignore them all. Advertising works so much better when consumers are clear in what they need to believe.

The brief so far contains some emotive statements about people and brands, but there needs to be some clarification. The advertising created from the brief needs to leave a persuasive thought in consumers' minds, but it is unreasonable to expect them to believe in a proposition without supporting it in different ways. Persil advertising might have aimed to leave people believing that it washes whiter – but they will not have been convinced without visual comparisons of dirty school shirts washed in Persil and in lesser detergents. British television presenter (of *Big Brother* fame) Davina McCall may try to convince consumers that her preferred shampoo brand leaves her hair bouncier and grey-hair free. Without being seen to telephone her Mum, shake her head around a lot and talk through the 'science bit', consumers

Ogilvy & Mather's inventive combination of sounds and images continues to move the car advertising genre forward.

Image courtesy of Ogilvy & Mather.

would be disbelieving. The tightly focused propositions come through loud and clear, but facts and figures or popularity referrals from other consumers have a part to play too. '8 out of 10 owners said their cats preferred it' didn't they? Test that proposition by naming the brand! The creative challenge is to use supporting benefits and motivations in an expressive, exciting way. The planning and account management teams will also need the creative brief to pass on some notes about tone of voice. In other words, the mood the campaign should give out. Should it be funny, confident or serious? Should the campaign entertain or warn of dangers? Should it be intellectual, ironic or direct? Tone of voice is a subtle art and should be handled with care creatively to get across exactly the right connection with a consumer. Think about the tone of voice used by Cillit Bang advertising and its Barry Scott character. Or commercials warning of the dangers of drinking and driving or speeding. How do cereal brands aimed at young children communicate? Think 'I'd rather have a bowl of Coco Pops' here. Now imagine if the loud bloke shouting in Cillit Bang commercials was voicing a 'slow down near schools' campaign, the results would be disastrous. Again, to sharpen your skills think of appropriate adjectives to describe the tone of voice in a selection of advertising you've seen recently. How

Love it or hate it, Cillit Bang commercials have made Barry Scott a cult celebrity and built a strong brand. His and the brand's image have been hijacked for a number of online parodies. This image advertises a viral video compilation.

Image origin unknown.

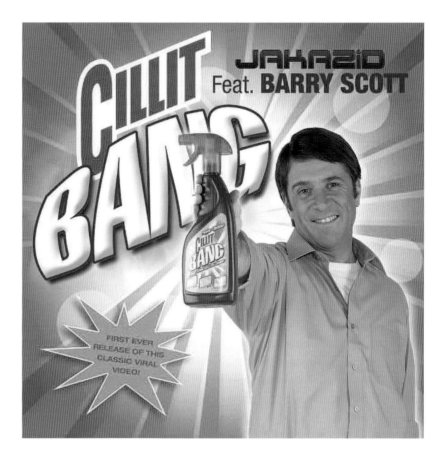

96

would you describe the tone of voice advertising for Apple iPhone uses, or T-Mobile, or BMW cars? Think of the advertising language brands use and how consumers might translate it.

There are quite a few boxes ticked in writing the creative brief now, the planning team have really nailed the 'who are we talking to', 'what are we saying' and 'how are we saying it' parts, now comes 'where do we say it?' Which are the most appropriate types of media to get our message across? In getting this far into this book, your understanding of advertising media and what it can achieve should be pretty good. So without covering that ground again, the account planners in conjunction with the media planners will identify the most appropriate media combinations to effectively deliver the client's objectives to as wide a consumer base as possible. It is necessary to communicate this in as full a way as possible to enable the creative teams to devise concepts that will communicate across all the platforms the brief specifies. With subtle differences and changes of emphasis, this process of writing a creative brief is much the same with every agency. It is a tried, tested and comfortable formula yet it is an extremely effective one. Account management teams work well with clients, account planning teams are in charge of the briefing process and creative teams make the whole thing explode from screens, posters and publications with as much dynamism and excitement as possible. Do not however be fooled into thinking any agency team is more important than another is; each team takes charge of their domain with enthusiasm, commitment and creativity. Actually, that may have just answered my big question at the start of this chapter – those three qualities are what I look for in an advertising student – enthusiasm, commitment and creativity.

> When I'm struggling to have ideas . . .
>
> *Go for a run, talk to people who don't work in advertising, talk to planners, colleagues, then if it doesn't happen stand back and sweat a bit. I find that the best ideas come when I'm relaxed. Stressing over not having an idea is pointless and unproductive.*
>
> Rob Ellis – Art Director, Agency Republic

The creative process or the arty bit

It's a good day in the creative studio – a new brief has been promised. It doesn't altogether matter what the brief is; all briefs are exciting, it is just the ideas that can sometimes be dull. How many times have I had to say that to groups of students when they whinge about a brief they don't happen to like? How does it go? Sorry my ideas are late, few and far between or totally uninspiring – I didn't like the brief.

Oh, I'm sorry, I'll try and pick something you like next time. Will I heck! I am an easy-going kind of guy who tolerates most student excuses with a wry 'heard that one before' smile, but using the brief as a smokescreen for dullness bugs me, big time. Needless to say there are always very good reasons why students create boring concepts – I believe all of them are directly linked to a lack of research and not taking the trouble to get inside the strategy. It is outside the 'comfort zone' of student experience, so therefore it must be a boring brief. Wise up brothers and sisters – creative teams have found themselves looking for new jobs for lesser offences. If you don't know, find out, shock horror, you might even learn something. I recently introduced a student competition brief to a second-year group. The brief was for a leading financial newspaper and the proposition was based on it being the leading source of information for business, politics and sociology students – all delivered online. I told my student group that I didn't believe they knew enough to tackle this brief and challenged them to take my current affairs quiz. All of them had the same 28 questions: the highest score was 12 and the average score 8. The scores were immaterial, it was not about exposing weakness, it was about instilling a mindset into those students that they had to research and understand more about the newspaper and its readers. On the whole the resulting creative work was excellent and the students dreamed up all sorts of research techniques to use – from face-to-face interviews to Facebook forums.

> When I'm struggling to have ideas . . .
>
> *I try to switch off by doing something completely different; best is probably doing something physical I reckon, like walking, cycling, running, swimming etc. And if the timing is ridiculously tight, I write or draw all the first easy and stupid ideas that come, to clear my brain, and then I panic.*
>
> Damien Bellon – Creative, Mother

Meanwhile back in the creative studio, the team are discussing the new brief with an account manager and a planner eagerly finding out as much as they can about the objectives of the brief. Here are the highlights:

Background about the client and product
Some insights into the target audience
The advertising proposition and message
The benefits of the product
The media plan
The deadline and other timescales

In spite of having no interest at all in insurance for the over fifties / soft toilet tissue / dog food / electric cars / feminine hygiene or any other seemingly uninspiring product, the creatives are eager to start work. So, what happens next? Initially, the relationship and empathy the team have with each other allow them to begin a conversation about the brief and to scribble down thoughts and ideas. Hold it there. Two things came out of that throwaway sentence you should know about. The best creative teams are not necessarily best mates or drinking buddies – the connection is less obvious than that. Mentally and intellectually they are on the same wavelength (or planet!). Their individual skills of being a sharp writer and visual thinker unite to send creative sparks flying – the brainstorm conversations are of the 'supposing we did this' and 'yeah, but how about if we then did this' variety. No magic formula exists to create a creative team, though – opposites are just as likely to attract. One loud, one quiet. One outrageous, yet the other restrained. Whatever, it's a deeply personal thing – trying creative partners for size and testing the chemistry is a good place to be, especially when you are still studying. Somehow, good teams gel together and can quickly get to the point of sharing ideas. All of them need to be explored on paper and verbally – don't disrupt the flow with complex spider diagrams and flow charts; the time spent drawing these is dragging you away from having more ideas. That is the name of the game, ideas and plenty of them. Some good, some dull and some just plain awful but all are useful in the search for the BIG idea.

> When I'm struggling to have ideas . . .
>
> *Keep thinking, it'll come eventually. A very clever teacher of mine once told me, if someone asked you to come up with a great idea whilst pointing a loaded gun at your head you would, wouldn't you? You would, so you should. Simple.*
>
> Stuart Outhwaite – Creative, Mother

Have you got what it takes to be an advertising creative? Who knows and what does it take? Surprise, surprise, I've a few thoughts. These are not might bes or maybes in my opinion, these are must bes. Chances are you will have been creative for as long as you can remember, spending every day seemingly bursting with ideas. Probably, all those ideas will have had little focus other than finding new ways to express them. For some of you a pencil will have been an extension of your hand. You have always drawn – funny little cartoons to delight your family or portraits that were not always as flattering as they might have liked. Art lessons were the highlight of the week – drawing flowers or shiny kettles, painting from imagination in a number of styles, carving out potatoes to print with and shaping wet, slippery clay into fabulous shapes. Chalk, crayons, felt pens, big fat paint brushes – they were all fair game as you

explored new ways of putting your ideas into practice. Art is not a prerequisite for advertising creatives, though. Many of you were and still are inspired by technology to find outlets for your creativity. Think back to pestering your parents to borrow the digital camera or video camera to take pictures or make quirky little films or animations. Others of you may have performed – dance, drama and music are all about creative expression too. A few of you may even have found joy in creative writing – stories or poetry. The link is finding a home for your endless flow of ideas and schemes. The portfolios brought to interviews for places on my course have included all these media and more besides. One guy brought in a dummy copy of the weekly music magazine *NME* with his own band featured visually and in words. Another arrived with a single sheet of paper and read aloud his words. A young girl showed me a portfolio filled with images of body art and extreme make-up. Yet all of them were highly creative and expressive in their own way. There is no single path that prospective creatives must take prior to a university course in creative advertising. However, all the creatives I have ever met or taught have both exciting and excited minds. They are ideas people who are naturally inquisitive and with an urge to explore and develop ideas. Advertising gives their instinctive imaginations a focus and an outlet.

The best advertising creatives are also risk-takers. They take chances with their time to bring ideas to a conclusion – in some cases ideas that others find misinformed or just plain ridiculous. Why have five ideas when you can have hundreds or thousands? Advertising is a breeding ground for experimentation and its best thinkers have lost their fear of being wrong. Being told that an idea 'can't be done' is a challenge for idea people – the correct response is not 'ok, I'll do something dull instead' it is 'ok, I'm going to try it anyway'. If it works you are a genius, if it goes wrong well hey, there's always next time. The biggest mistake new students make in my opinion is being overly conservative – trying to invent advertising ideas that look like everyone else's or that look like something else they have seen. Creative teaching at its best allows opportunities to push the limits of a brief and exceed personal boundaries and if the end result is miles adrift then so what? Learn why it doesn't work and move on to the next idea, knowing this time you are going to nail it. For every clutch of ideas you have today, if only one is a good one then you are well on your way.

The least creative state of mind that it is possible to get into is one where people become precious and defensive about an idea. It may be a good idea, it may not – but being mentally unable to develop and explore other ideas does the damage. The idea is stuck in a big hole and can't get out because the brain has shut down and won't let it escape. Keep asking questions of your ideas – now, that is a much better place to be. Continue to prod an idea that seems comfortable or workable. Go back and explore the rubbish ideas to see whether there is anything good in them after all. Most of all, being so annoyingly inquisitive that you cannot help but keep turning an idea around, over and upside down to find a different way of expressing it is a

Advertising agencies are stimulating, creative environments in which to work. This is the inside of the Rain Agency. . .

Image courtesy of Rain Agency.

. . . and this is Wieden+Kennedy, London.

Image courtesy of Wieden+Kennedy.

her or their head. The planners have been devilishly cunning with their assessment of the target audience and wonderfully insightful with the advertising proposition. The media guys have come up with an exciting plan of attack. Now it's time for the creatives to get involved. The stage has been set for some big ideas to perform on it. Advertising's best campaigns have started with a strategy, not a creative idea. So work from it. The art director and copywriter complement each other perfectly and because they have a real chemistry between them and are skilled at concluding ideas visually and with words. It is a two-way process – the headline completes the thinking started by the visual and/or the other way around. Staring at an image for hours and struggling to write a headline is an advertising campaign well on its way to failure. Similarly, searching high and low for an image to complement a great headline will end in the same way. Exploring visuals and headlines that extend, expand and then clarify the idea – now that is much better. That is the way art directors and copywriters work together. It is immaterial who has the idea or comes up with the headline or visual – they are a team who can shape each other's thoughts into an advertising concept. You will be familiar with the phrase 'quality not quantity'. Not true for a creative team – here is where it is necessary to have an almost endless stream of ideas. In executing the creative brief the art director and copywriter will not waste time and energy early in the thinking process judging and evaluating their first three ideas, they will just keep right on going. There's an idea, good, let's have another and another. That's a mad idea, fantastic, let's get madder. Hey, that's a great idea but supposing we did this as well. The creative team always wants more and always wants better. Easy to see now why advertising is not an environment for isolated solo thinking. A collection of ideas people allows interesting or good ideas to become great and even brilliant. Even at a time when they both jump up and run around the room shouting that's it – there is still likely to be something better. So they keep going, quickly sketching out seeds of ideas that can grow and grow. But an experienced creative team knows when the ideas have dried up and when to take stock. They may have a layout pad filled with ideas and directions, but at some point they will step back and weigh up the ideas against the brief. If we accept that the most important pieces of equipment are a pen and a pad, then the next most valuable is the wastebin. Does the proposition shine through that idea loudly and very clearly? No? In the bin then. It's a great idea but will the client be prepared to spend 10 times more than the budget? No? In the bin then. That's really clever, but is it just too complicated? In the bin then? Will this idea surprise the audience and make them look or think twice? Good, worth coming back to. Has this idea taken the proposition and presented it in a completely new way? Yes. Take another look. This idea made us laugh, but will consumers laugh too? Ok, another one to come back to. And so it goes. Some ideas are going nowhere, some are interesting but not right for the brief so it can be saved for another day, other ideas look like they have real possibilities. The creative team may at this stage say, 'it's been a good day, let's have a look at the best ideas again in the morning to see

if they still stand up'. After all that mentally draining concentration and creativity it is all too easy to lose sight of the real objective, so returning to ideas fresh and with an open mind can offer a better test of their value. This is a challenging exercise. Recognizing that out of 100 ideas, 80 or 90 will be rubbish, is a hard skill to develop. The key to this is knowing how far to go before stopping. Sometimes the initial rush of ideas are of the clichéd, overfamiliar, seen it before, childish wordplays or crap joke variety. Creatives who think this is the right place to stop will be responsible for cheesy uninspiring ads. Creatives who take a break, come back stimulated and with new inspiration will start again at this point. They will look for different directions and reinterpret the brief from other perspectives and always remember that the big idea needs to connect with an individual not a faceless mass, so how can it reach them? To search for new ideas, it is usually best not to follow the rules and conventions associated with the brand being advertised. Remember *Resist the Usual?* Reinventing or replicating existing advertising no matter how many awards it has won or how many people talked about it is a bad idea. Don't do it. Be inspired by the simplicity, cleverness or stunning visuals contained in your favourite campaigns, but don't retread the same ground. Strive for an idea that has never been done before. The creative team attempts to achieve that with every brief it is faced with, but probably doesn't always succeed. Creativity is a word so overused in advertising that its true meaning has become clouded or obscured. Creativity is a word that describes the advertising process today – but if you go back to the simple definition of the word it means simply *to bring something into being that has never been seen or done before.* The title of 'advertising creative' is quite something to live up to.

The first idea-generating stage is now over. The creative team have ruthlessly culled their pad down into maybe six ideas they believe will deliver the strategy in different but effective ways. Time to go public. Every advertising agency has a creative director and many have more than one. This person will have a wealth of advertising experience and started out as a junior art director or copywriter. Having worked for many different clients and typically several different agencies, the creative director now has total responsibility for the advertising agency's creative output. The final pieces of advertising are in many ways the public face of the agency, this is the work consumers see and the work that clients judge it on. You are only as good as your last ad is a familiar adage and that is one hell of a responsibility. The creative director has the final say on the ideas the client sees. The creative team will sit down with the appropriate creative director and talk through the ideas they have. If you are a creative advertising student you will already have experience of this – your tutors take on something of this role when evaluating your ideas. During this meeting the creative director may throw out ideas that he or she feels are not strong enough or appropriate enough to deliver the objective of the brief. At the same time, the best ideas will be met with warm encouragement and suggestions on how to nurture and develop the idea to deliver the proposition in the most effective way. Whatever happens, there will be more work for the creatives to do.

Raw conceptual ideas are the starting point for emotionally charged, tight communication pieces. The creative team will need to explore how the idea may work across the range of media suggested by the brief – it will need to be 'campaignable' and deliver its message in a variety of ways. The brief may require a TV commercial and three separate posters – therefore the idea will need to be fluid and flexible enough to convey the same proposition with different visuals and headlines. Digital media may demand more than just uploading the commercial to YouTube; how will the campaign translate onto Facebook or an interactive website? If the idea won't work beyond just a TV execution it might have to be shelved. The creative director will guide the team towards honing the idea into a message that hits what is known as 'the sweet spot'. This falls halfway between the strategy and the execution. Ideas that just address the needs of the strategy are likely to be dull; equally, brilliant concepts that look exciting but don't drive home their message are irrelevant. Ideas that land smack in the middle where strategies and wild ideas overlap are winners. Advertising never stops attempting to reach real people, and the creative quest is to find the message that connects and switches on their interest. Beauty products aren't all about changing hair colours or having redder lips, they are about giving people more ways to feel good about themselves. An effective advertising campaign may just be about finding a human angle that consumers will believe in. Then again it may not – it may be about presenting consumers with a completely new way of using a product so that they now believe a product they thought had no use for in fact would be extremely useful. Perhaps suggesting to them that their lives are incomplete without owning a product is a better direction. And encouraging consumers to buy into the idea that brands and their lifestyle are made for each other – everyone wanting this way of life must have this brand. Whatever – you must be getting the point by now. *Find something new to say.* Don't be a slave to fashion and trend. Make brands desirable, attractive and very special in the minds of consumers.

The idea battleground

Great ideas do not come cheap. The creative team has worked for days and nights to present a series of killer concepts to the creative director. Then, they've worked for more days and nights to shape and form the best of these into a sharply focused set of visuals or scamps using a big black marker pen and a piece of paper. Usually right about now, the creative flow comes crashing down for students. But I can't draw, I hear you cry. I don't care, I cry back. This is an issue that is almost guaranteed to bring on a massive attack of creative block. Just when the idea is starting to flow and fly off at exciting tangents, students begin to get hung up about the marks they are making on pieces of paper. Brains and pens start to fiddle around with overcomplicated drawings that attempt to include every last detail of the image. Stop it now. All the time you are spending filling A3 sheets of paper with single idea executions would be better spent thinking of newer and better ideas. Write in the headline, draw out the logo and sketch out the visual with as few lines and marks as you possibly can. That's better – drawn up quickly and cleanly with the minimum of fuss and time. Tutors and creative directors aren't complete half-wits you know, they want to see a big idea shining through from a page, not a work of art. Raphael or Michelangelo were gifted draughtsmen, but all that shading and subtlety would make them hopeless art directors. An advertising course will teach you how to make effective marks on paper to communicate your idea, so stop worrying about it. If the worst comes to the worst, you can always write a little caption next to your unintelligible squiggle.

Having said all that, the jury is out at advertising agencies in terms of how to present ideas to clients for the first time. There are factors that influence the decision, though. A visually literate client, used to advertising concepts, with which an agency has a long relationship, will be more than happy to evaluate ideas from simple line drawings. When an agency is pitching ideas to a new client, competitively with other agencies, the visualizing may be more developed. There still exist in advertising's underworld, people who are skilled illustrators who can craft an advertising visual from a box of coloured marker pens creating highly coloured, effective representations of the campaign. Sadly, from a hand skill point of view, they are a dying breed. More common would be creating finished visuals for client presentation using Apple Mac software – Adobe InDesign, Illustrator and Photoshop (with QuarkXPress still in the mix too). Sometimes imagery may be visualized using photographs or illustrations from a picture library or from digital camera shots and even marker drawings scanned in. The visuals here represent the advertising concept in a more finished state. This can be dangerous with clients, though. It is not unheard of for

strong concepts to be rejected on points of detail like the colour of a model's hair or the shade of yellow used and so on. Sometimes clients just cannot see past the execution. Equally, the client's immediate acceptance of a visual 'just as it is' limits the opportunity for an art director to shape and craft the concept beyond the presentation meeting. The decision on whether to show clients roughs or finished visuals is a swings and roundabouts one, but in general getting initial concepts across the boardroom table is often best done with simple scamps to start with. It is always best whilst you are a student.

Back to the brief. The big idea is standing proud on a table in front of the client for the first time. The agency will have sent a team to talk it up: an account management team with a client services director who looks after this brand's business. Sometimes a planner will be present too; the creative director could well be there and maybe the creative team as well. The concept is good and the agency has faith in its ability to achieve the client's objectives. In making a creative presentation, belief is a vital component and has a habit of being infectious. If the client sees the agency getting excited about the possibilities of the campaign then it rubs off on the marketing team present. The agency will communicate the idea eloquently, clearly and with conviction. Those of you who see yourselves as account managers need to develop a presentation style that comes across as being warm, friendly, passionate and accessible. Clients hire advertising agencies because they have produced innovative work that they believe will benefit their businesses. They also want to work with people they like and to strike up a good relationship with them. People skills are a huge part of account management. To see how it is possible to capture attention, sell ideas and build warmth and respect track down Barack Obama's presidential acceptance speech on the internet: it is spellbinding. Whilst

you don't need to be Barack Obama to sell an advertising idea, the ability to communicate with people in a tone that captivates them is a real bonus for a top-level account manager or client services director. Three things are going to happen before the end of the meeting: the client could be bowled over by the ideas being discussed and be eager to see how the campaign will be developed. Option two is possibly the worst outcome: the client will be only lukewarm on the idea and ask to see more ideas. Outright rejection is better in some ways, because at least everyone knows that they need to start over. Over the years I have encountered all sorts of clients in many types of business, but in my experience they fall into only three categories. The first client is open-minded and willing to be guided by the agency – these are great to work with. The second is not a natural decision-maker and says they don't know what they want until they see it and even then they still don't quite get excited by anything. The third has the notion that they could do this themselves if only they had time. Very difficult customers, because it is rarely easy to get inside their heads to see what they really respond to.

In the aftermath of presenting creative work, there will always be more work to do. Assuming that the client is pleased with the concept and suggested a few developments, the agency now needs to bring the raw concept to life. The creative team has to really focus to expand the idea into the required media environments, sustaining the strength of the idea and clearly delivering the proposition. The team will regularly discuss new idea developments with the creative director until the concept is absolutely spot-on.

Ideas that work across different media campaigns are a very tough call for aspiring creatives. Most advertising students I have had the pleasure to meet can, when pushed hard, at the end of their final year put together a decent book of work and a graduating exhibition. So what is it that separates out the truly talented with a bright future and wins them placements or internships at swish advertising agencies? Campaign thinking, that's what. A great idea executed as a one-off poster is not a campaign. A couple of loose executions tied together by a logo or an idea that just replaces the one image for another of similar type is also not a campaign. One idea drawn up as two posters is not a campaign either; it's a coincidence. A big, butt-kicking idea that is equally at home on TV, across billboards, online and in magazines – now there is a campaign. To be taken seriously by creative directors your work needs to reflect this. Modern advertising hijacks the media in as many ways as it can – if your work is a collection of fun, ambient one-off stunts or all posters or internet-based, your chances will disappear in an instant. Wielding a great idea in front of media-savvy modern consumers is gold dust to creative directors. Work on your campaign technique. If the brief says create ideas using a media platform of your choice, don't stick with a storyboard or a poster – go broad here. Creative advertising students adore ambient ideas, some of which are absolutely brilliant. But mention the word strategy and their eyes glaze over. The single most brilliant ambient idea ever invented is not an advertising campaign, it might be a small part

of one but it happens and it is gone. If it is only organized in central London a few thousand people will have seen it at best. Which is fine, but what about consumers across the rest of the UK or the world?

It is not my intention to present my words and thoughts to you as a complete 'how to do advertising' manual. Some very good books on that subject already exist. Besides, you have a good team of tutors working with you to do that job. My ultimate goal is to highlight possibilities, expand your range of thinking and to suggest alternative ways of approaching advertising problems. To do this it is essential to understand strategy and the way in which agencies work with clients; exploring the creative use of media is equally important. But it still all hinges on the relationship between all of these factors and a big idea. That is how the advertising industry works and that is how you should work too. It does not matter if your study course and career aims are to work in account management, planning, the creative department or even in production – you all need to have as full an understanding of the entire process as possible to improve your chances.

I have mentioned production here. So let's go back to the agency to have a quick look at how our campaign is developing. The creative team have moved on now, the big ideas the client loved so much are developed and expanded to encompass all media factors. The account management and planning teams are satisfied that all the strategic objectives have been met – so what happens next? The art director and the copywriter bring their individual skills into play here (although they are a team and will still bounce their ideas off each other). The writer must now shape the copy. It is obvious that the headlines are of major importance here – the reader or viewer will see and respond to this first, along with the imagery. Supporting copy is the last thing they read – but only if they have been sufficiently drawn in by the headline and imagery. Headlines are not written to provide a completely separate or irrelevant message, they are crafted to complement and reinforce the messages delivered by the imagery. Both carry equal weight in attracting the consumer's attention. The headline may suggest a new dimension to the imagery or offer consumers a different, unexpected meaning to it. Language and tone of voice must be absolutely appropriate to the target audience – no point in writing a headline in a 'texting' style or based around urban-street slang for an audience of over fifties looking for retirement plans. All the irony, colloquial phraseology and clever wit in the world counts for nothing if consumers 'don't get it'. The combination of headlines and imagery closes the loop in the audience's mind. They should not need to read the whole ad or watch the whole commercial to understand the proposition – better if they do, but hey, that's consumers for you. Writing styles have changed considerably in advertising since the heyday of the Madison Avenue pioneers. Then, long descriptive copy was the norm, with imagery used to support the narrative. In keeping with consumers' 'rapid absorption' mindset of the past decade or so, copy is shorter and of the more instant-impact variety. The way in which art directors and copywriters work together as a single creative unit is borne out by modern advertising campaigns that often use no more than three words on a poster. Conversely, revisit some of the outdoor advertising for *The Economist*, which brilliantly uses copy in conjunction with a simple, plain red background colour. I am open to being shot at here by copywriters everywhere, but I would suggest that direct mail provides the opportunity to write long copy more so than any other advertising media. Once again, some extremely talented copywriters have written some illuminating books on writing for advertising and I'm not here to tell you everything there is to know about writing great copy. In campaign terms, the writer will develop the headline and proposition into persuasive, motivating copy or dialogue to grow the message in the minds of the target audience.

> I don't know the rules of grammar . . . If you're trying to persuade people to do something, or buy something, it seems to me you should use their language, the language they use every day, the language in which they think. We try to write in the vernacular.
>
> **David Ogilvy**

Meanwhile, the art direction of the campaign needs similarly careful attention. Taking the 'still' media first – posters, press advertisements or internet banner advertising – the creative team needs to visually interpret their ideas. Sometimes this might be done by selecting and purchasing images from Image Libraries. Photographers and illustrators are able to sell pictures to libraries, which in turn charge for their use, depending on the media to be used. It is rare for a high-level outdoor and press campaign to use 'stock' images to front the idea; however, in publishing and in the design of company brochures they are used frequently. A direct mail campaign may also feature library images within inserts and leaflets. The advantage of library images is that they are cheaper than commissioning photographers and illustrators; and if the right image can be sourced, then why not? The main disadvantage is that there is a real danger of imagery being used on someone else's campaign at the same time. I once worked with an agency on a high-profile direct mail campaign for a major financial institution. Particular library images of a young, slightly quirky girl provided the visual cornerstone of the idea – unfortunately the girl also featured heavily in a press and television campaign for a furniture retailer at the same time. This diluted the effectiveness of my imagery and created confusion in the minds of the target audience. Ouch.

So, the creative team may have the budget available to commission original images. The style and content of the image will be very clear in their minds. Developing the idea on paper will have involved them discussing and creating in their heads a visual style for the advertising. To capture that perfectly, they will look at the portfolios and websites of a number of photographers and/or illustrators to find someone whose style, technique and creativity matches exactly the concept. A note here to any photographers and illustrators reading this who want to work in advertising – make sure advertising agencies know you are out there. Send the creatives postcards that show your work off and advertise your website, or at the very least make sure they can find your website easily based on the kind of search keywords they may use. 'Advertising photography' or 'illustration' is going to deliver millions of results. Make sure they can get to you easily if you specialize in photographing people, location or still life. Illustrators – make sure your style and the media you use are found. Once the creatives have narrowed their search to a shortlist of image-makers who can deliver their concept, they will involve the rest of the campaign team in making a final choice. For a photographic shoot it will then be necessary to find the right locations – there are specialized location finders who help with this. Any models required will need to be selected as well; most have agents, and the creatives will describe exactly the look they need and agents will send selections of suitable people. The shots will also need to be 'dressed' – so the correct props will need to be found under the direction of the creative team and also the clothing the models will be wearing. It may be necessary to bring in other creative specialists too – make-up artists, for example, or people who can make food look enticing. My wife once painted children's faces at summer events – one weekend a passing art director hired her to paint designs onto models' faces for a photo shoot the following week.

The advertising concepts may be delivered across online platforms, so the creatives will need to work closely with designers and programmers to ensure the campaign runs exactly as they envisaged. Print campaigns also require creatives to be involved with graphic designers. In both of these instances it is likely that the creative team will be briefing and crafting their concepts with the agency's own studio teams. Welcome to yet another world. The words studio, madness and very late nights are closely entwined. Typically these are the people at the sharp end of the agency with whom the creative buck often stops. Advertising spaces – whether online, on outdoor posters or in the press – have deadlines; miss those deadlines and the agency ends up quite literally paying for blank spaces. Advertising studio designers thrive on pressure. A production manager or 'traffic' manager usually oversees the whole show; they are skilled designers by profession too. Most studio managers I've met are gluttons for punishment – they will fend off screaming account managers, compromise with overambitious creatives and organize advertising reproduction and print suppliers. The late-night pizza-delivery industry relies on studio managers for much of their nocturnal business! I am convinced these guys have no homes and bunk down alongside their Apple Macs. In all seriousness, the studio is where concepts come to life. Studio designers will spend time with creatives developing styles and layouts – and discussing image manipulation, retouching, colour and typefaces with knowledge and confidence. Some creatives underestimate the role of designers – feeling they are there merely to do their bidding. If any of you ever find yourselves adopting the same bad attitude, stop it. The studio people are as skilled as you, as highly trained as you and are as instrumental in achieving a campaign look. Their quality standards are high, they are excellent creative designers and they know Apple Mac creative software inside out. Respect is definitely due.

Of course, if the ideas are to be produced for TV or digital video then the creatives need to work alongside some serious production heavyweights. Every commercial needs a director – some respected movie directors have made commercials – Ridley Scott, Julien Temple and Tony Kaye for starters. That reminds me, track down Tony Kaye's 1990s commercial for Dunlop tyres on YouTube. It is a creative and visual epic bolted down by the Velvet Underground's 'Venus in Furs' as a soundtrack. Stunning. Directors of music videos have often crossed over into advertising and vice versa. Even British comedy star Mel Smith has now become better known in advertising circles as a director of commercials. The agency creative team will share and develop ideas with their chosen director; as with photographers and illustrators, this is a two-way process. The team will consider very carefully their choice of director – he or she will have been commissioned for the creative input they can bring to the advertising as well, so once again the pool of ideas gets deeper. The director's production team will provide camera crews and a sound team – but as with a photographic shoot the agency will need to be involved in casting the commercial. Actors will be selected in much the same way as models to achieve the look and style the concept depends on. Bartle Bogle Hegarty made a commercial for Levi's in the early 1990s which starred an up-and-coming actor called Brad Pitt. Some of you may have heard of him . . . Of course, celebrities have featured in many advertising campaigns – David Beckham has been the face of Vodafone, Gillette and Police sunglasses. A whole host of sports stars have advertised a diverse range of brands too. Gary Lineker featured in Walkers Crisps ads for many years and Nike has regularly crammed sporting royalty into its brand-awareness campaigns. Pepsi-Cola counted Michael Jackson among its more famous celebrity endorsers; in fact, brands all over the world have rushed to feature the face of whoever is currently 'in'. This can backfire. When British supermodel Kate Moss was reported as being involved in drug taking in a number of press stories, she was dropped by a clothing brand. However, a cosmetics brand considered that she still communicated well with their target audiences. The relationship between celebrity and advertising will always remain, but it is subjective. Actors, sports stars, musicians and other media celebrities will always be in demand to act in commercials, be photographed for campaigns and to provide voice-overs. For consumers, the presence of people they admire in advertising messages can provide persuasive endorsement for brands and their products.

In detailing the progression of an advertising brief through an agency I have attempted to offer an overview of how people, with their individual skills and talents, can interact to produce effective advertising. Before I move on to look at the jobs they do in more detail, I will leave you with a single thought. To work in advertising demands a myriad personal skills – the most successful creative people have more than just skills. They study life. There is nothing more vital in creative thinking than

Tony Kaye created stunning visual imagery for this surreal campaign for Dunlop tyres.

Image courtesy of Tony Kaye Films.

being stimulated by experiences. Watch, read, talk, listen and learn. Being articulate, dynamic and having a broad range of social and cultural references to draw upon will make you and your work more interesting. That will take you a long way on your journey towards a fulfilling career in advertising.

David Beckham has featured as the face of several brands.

Some interesting references

In previous chapters I have ended by offering websites, books, magazines and other reference points to expand your minds and answer more of your questions. This chapter is different. My main message is just to soak up all the culture you can. That is an ambiguous statement I know. Do it all. Follow these extremes:

- Visit Tate Modern and your local supermarket.
- Watch any of the *High School Musical* movies and European art films.
- Read celebrity gossip magazines and the advertising, marketing and PR trade press.
- Watch soap operas and political debates on television.
- Have a drink (sensibly of course) in backstreet pubs and expensive bars.
- Read all the time – from blockbusting novels to Franz Kafka.

- Observe people, from young children to the most senior of citizens.
- Pack a lunch, switch your phone off and spend days at a time in your library and learning centre. Make it your mission to watch all the DVDs on the shelf, look through every design and advertising book regularly, read every newspaper and magazine, track down all the material you can find about popular culture. Look at the work of every artist, photographer and designer you come across. Think fashion, interiors, architecture, graphics, sculpture, painting, reportage. In simple terms – treat your brain as a giant scrapbook – store everything you see away as a possible starting point for an advertising strategy or concept.

But please, do not use any of the above as an internet keyword. Get away from Google and see and experience everything in context. You will be amazed at what you find. Experience the joy of life and all its quirks, culture and diversity.

Finally for me, but as a starting point for you, read Edward de Bono's *Lateral Thinking* for some radically different ways of solving problems creatively. Try Hermann Vaske's *Standing on the Shoulders of Giants* too.

Many a small thing has been made large by the right kind of advertising.

Mark Twain

6 Time to get real – getting a job with an advertising agency

Most students I know stay awake all night for a variety of reasons I am not going to discuss here. But as they near the end of their courses, the thought of getting a job is instant insomnia. That peculiar mix of hyper-excitement at the thought of finally getting out there and the paranoia and black depression of 'aah, what am I going to do?' is invigorating yet daunting. Students love being students; the lifestyle, the experimentation and above all the learning process are fondly remembered forever. I have been there, but more importantly, so have most of the people you will ultimately work with and be interviewed by. That thought provides a glimmer of hope. Advertising agencies are notorious among students and graduates for not replying to letters, phone calls or emails. Somehow, though, advertising people are sympathetic towards new talent struggling for its first break. That is because for many it is an all too recent memory – don't forget that. Your struggle is not unique, the recipients of your pleas for work have gone through much the same.

Before I share some ideas, thoughts and advice with you on how to get through the door, let me shatter a few illusions. Sorry, but advertising attracts more than its quota of urban myths. Students are often under the misapprehension that advertising only has room for superconfident, egotistical, movers and shakers who seem to know everything. Any of you reading this, who think that this sounds like you, forget it. Give up all hope now of ever getting a job in advertising. Those of you who are convinced that one day you will be successful and are eager to learn all the ways needed to achieve your personal interpretation of success will get a job. I have mentioned many times that employers welcome articulate communicators and I stand by that. But if your idea of being able to talk clearly and concisely is to prattle on about how great you are and how much you know about advertising then, once again, forget it. I know you've seen and heard the founders of international super-agencies coming across all arrogant and full of their own egos (apologies to any super-agency founders reading this, but you know what I mean), but remember, you don't own a massive advertising agency. At best, you are the owner of a promising portfolio. One of my favourite quotes on this theme comes from Dave Trott in his downloadable blog *How to get your first job in advertising.* In it he says:

> Unless you realize that you do not, at present, know any more about advertising than your mother, you are no use to a good agency. In fact, your mother may be more useful because she at least buys most of the products that agencies are trying to sell.

A series of awareness-raising press advertisements and posters for Defra.

Images courtesy of CST.

You can access a copy of Dave's words of wisdom at www.cstadvertising.com and download a PDF version to read at no cost! The site also features an on-going blog which offers continual and updated thoughts from one of advertising's wisest practitioners.

Copywriter Jaimin is 24 and born in London, Waldemar is 26 and from Kazakhstan – he's the art director. They met at university in Buckinghamshire and are currently chasing their advertising big break. They have documented a meeting with Dave Trott on their blog at: http://creativeinlondon.blogspot.com/2009/02/dave-trott.html. Here's what they have to say:

> Yesterday we went to see Dave Trott, creative director at CST. We knew it would be interesting to talk to him and show him our work – and it was a brilliant session indeed. Dave certainly knows how to be a brand himself. He compares getting a job to selling a product – of course he's right, we are the most important product we'll ever sell. It's about researching the market (creative directors) and looking into the product (the creative team) and matching those two together. We like the fact that the whole topic was more how to get the job rather than the work. In fact, we spend two hours with Dave, and he didn't even look at our book.
>
> There were lots of nuggets we took away from this meeting, lessons you won't find on his blog. A lot to take in, and a great deal to talk about. Perfect to kick the January blues in the ass and rock on. Thanks Dave.

The myth that makes me laugh most is the insane idea some people have that advertising is the doorway to a world of expensive champagne, foreign beaches, supermodels and glamour. Sorry guys, you are confusing advertising with football players in the English Premiership. One day, when you have built up years of experience and a reputation to match you may get to go on a film or photo shoot in a tropical location – but you will be working so hard you probably won't see daylight. I have art directed many photo shoots – most were in hot, sweaty studios on industrial estates. Though I did once go on a shoot for Volkswagen to South Wales – my boss saved the ten-day trip to northern Spain for himself! Advertising is all the fun you will ever need, but Hollywood it certainly isn't.

So why are you at college or university? Stupid question you might say, you are there to learn and to equip yourself to work in advertising, marketing or PR doing whatever job you've trained for. Actually, I am going to argue with you there. Even though I am a university advertising tutor, I would say that I cannot teach any advertising student how to *work* as a creative or account executive or planner etc. The best I can hope for is to teach you how to learn – to be receptive, alert and willing. After a three-year degree course you will hopefully find yourself in a job – and then you need to start learning all over again. A graduate fresh out of college or university will need a considerable period of encouragement, nurturing and guiding to become a fully contributing member of an agency team. During that time, experience, knowledge and confidence will grow and grow. As a tutor, I like to startle and shake my students out of their comfortable bubbles. Nothing I say has any greater impact than my comments about their future qualifications – their degree in Advertising (BA Hons). I am not being horrible for the sake of it. Doing the hat and gown thing on Graduation Day, with all your friends and family congratulating you, is a fine thing. And boy will you all feel pleased with yourselves too when you are clutching your degree certificate. The official line goes something like – having a degree will open many doors for you. Yeah right. Ok, if you are a business type or a would-be politician then an Oxbridge degree will get you ahead in life. But a degree in the advertising world is maybe not such a magic wand. Sure, it will tap politely at the door for you, but it will not kick it open all that far. Your qualifications look great on your cv and are an indication of your learning and commitment, but on their own they don't cut it. Right, dry your eyes, I'm not suggesting your education is pointless – if it was I'd be out of a job – it's just that the creative industries don't offer jobs simply because you have got letters after your name.

This is blunt but true in my experience, but stay with me on this, I'm trying to explain. We need to start talking about getting a job here. Assuming for a moment that you are a fledgling advertising creative, though the same rules apply for most agency positions, how do you attract the attention of a creative director? Here's a quick quiz; you decide the answers:

What will the creative director say?

1. 'I've got a degree in Creative Advertising.'

Will he or she say?

a. So what.
b. You've got the job.

2. 'I've got a degree in Creative Advertising, would you give me a job?'

Will he or she say?

a. Go away.
b. You've got the job.

3. 'I've got a degree in Creative Advertising and an amazing portfolio.'

Will he or she say?

a. Go away.
b. You've got the job.

4. 'I've got a degree in Creative Advertising, would you please review my portfolio?'

Will he or she say (sometimes)?

a. Ok.
b. Yes.

I know that is woefully simplistic, but there is a lot of truth in those questions and answers. Asking advertising agencies for advice, help, opinion and guidance is likely to be a whole lot more successful than endlessly pestering for a job because you think you are God's gift to advertising. It is likely to be that the agencies you approach won't give you a job simply because they don't have one to give you. They work hard to ensure that they have a lean, tightly organized team of people making campaigns happen – jobs are in restricted supply. Of course, though, any advice and guidance you can gather from advertising people will be hugely beneficial to you the next time you are attempting to sell your skills. Maybe, just maybe, if what you show and what you say is sufficiently exciting and perhaps even different they will offer the glimmer of a chance by taking you on a placement. More about placements later.

How to get that elusive first job

You should by now have a working knowledge of how advertising agencies operate and types of jobs that are potentially available to you. With the help of some people who have established themselves in advertising, I am now going to look at their roles in more detail and offer some insights into how to get jobs like theirs. In his foreword to this book, Trevor Beattie makes a very insightful observation. He suggests that focusing on getting a job is a much better way of using your time than trying to predetermine where that job should be. This is a worryingly common error that students make. Typically, talented young creative people make a mental list of the very biggest and best-known agencies that enter their radar, then they attempt to make contact with them. The reality is this. Your advertising course is likely to have over 30 students on it. So will every other advertising course. It is also likely that in organizing work-experience programmes, or trying to find placements and full-time jobs, many of those students will make applications to the same relatively small number of advertising agencies. Just consider that for a moment and, in your heads, flip the scenario over. Imagine you are in a senior position at a very well-known advertising agency. Every summer you could probably expect to receive dozens of letters, gimmicky mail pieces, emails and telephone calls from advertising students across the world, all of whom have similar experiences, portfolios and future qualifications. Is it any wonder that replies are at a premium? Hundreds of students queuing impatiently to chase down a handful of possible jobs – not going to work

is it? Agencies in general have their own, very specific ways of recruiting new blood. Usually those ways don't involve replying to cold contacts. Here comes that black cloud of depression again. Try to take some heart from the fact that although getting your first job will be the most draining, disheartening experience of your career, the second job you try to get will be an awful lot easier. Armed as you will be with a commercial portfolio of campaigns and agency experience.

It is not all bad news, though. I have said before that advertising relies on, and is sustained by, a fresh pool of talent to pick from every year. Agencies do want you and do want to hear about you, but there are better ways of attracting their attention. So how do you get started? Employ some research and strategy – now doesn't that sound like a familiar mantra? Create for yourself a hit list of advertising agencies that feel to you like they may want to hear from you. Perhaps be focused to start with and settle on a short list of 20. There are hundreds more, so if that list yields nothing, create another and another as required. Absolutely do not simply pick the top 20 agencies published by some trade publication or other – that is what everyone else could be doing, remember? New York, London or Tokyo's finest are inundated, so be more creative. Every reasonably sized city has practising advertising agencies and damned good ones too. Don't confine your list to agencies you have heard of – you will struggle to reach 20 and once again they will be on the same list as everyone else. Instead, visit websites of agencies and see exactly what they do and who they do it for. It is not just the Saatchi & Saatchi, BBH, Abbot Mead Vickers and Ogilvys of this world that produce spectacular advertising for household-name clients. I guarantee that you will be absolutely amazed at the work being produced out there by a huge range of agencies.

Now decide whether to approach them or not and base that choice on your instinct. Does the work and 'feel' of the agency attract you? If so, most usefully, does their website have a careers or graduates page? If it does, you now have a point of entry. Chances are that page will say something like, 'we are always on the look out for new talent and we want to hear from you'. There may be specific vacancies advertised – these are unlikely to be suitable for new graduates – or simply a statement along the lines of 'get in touch with your cv and tell us what you can do'. My rule of thumb is normally to base the 'tell us what you can do' bit around what they say about themselves. Have you produced any project work for the same market sector as one of their clients? Are you particularly good at, or excited by, any specific advertising areas that they are involved in? Digital or direct marketing for example. Consider the 'tone of voice' of the agency – are they fun and funky or calm and businesslike? Write your response in a similar, appropriate tone. By all means write with conviction and sell yourself – clever forms of words can sometimes be effective at attracting attention too. But be careful – you don't know the person you are writing your email to, so your idea of hilarious repartee may not be theirs. Don't forget the basics either; have you spelled the person's name correctly, have you checked your email thoroughly for spelling and grammar, have you been completely honest? You are also not emailing a friend, so text lingo and email abbreviations are a definite no-go area. If you are completely convinced that your response is as good as it can be, then hit send and wait. You may wait forever and get no response, you may get a short message saying sorry we have no opportunities right now, or you may get the chance to go along to see them and talk and show your work.

Keep searching and keep replying via the careers pages – sooner or later you will have covered plenty of agencies. I make no apology for repeating myself now – don't ignore any interesting agency just because they are small, not in New York or London or wherever and you haven't heard their name before. That may just cost you your perfect first job. The job is what you need, not a familiar name above a swanky reception area. That does not mean you should aspire to a low-level rubbish job, it means that your limited knowledge of any particular advertising agency should not hold you back. A few years ago a talented student with all the right attributes to become a successful creative sent back an email to us after he had graduated. He said that he had been offered a placement at a London agency but he hadn't heard of them and he was unsure as to whether to accept it or not. Obviously, the response of myself and my colleagues was: don't be a fool, check it out and if it doesn't work out you will at least have gained some valuable experience and some relevant portfolio work. The agency was Iris – one of London's fastest-growing integrated agencies – and the last I heard, he was still there enjoying life as a middleweight creative working on some of the most exciting advertising briefs around. He could so easily have screwed up and so could you.

There are other ways in which you can be proactive and increase your contacts list. The advertising network is another way to break in. Graduating students on my course always exhibit their work at D&AD's *New Blood* exhibition in London, several have met and spoken with agency creatives visiting the exhibition and been offered the chance to present their portfolios – this has sometimes led to placements and job opportunities. Good advertising courses have strong links with the industry too – you may already have met and presented work to people from agencies. Impress them with your work and ask if you may contact them to present a full portfolio at a later date – once again I know students who have gained placements and jobs by doing this. Perhaps you might consider getting involved with D&AD creative workshops that put students in direct contact with *real* advertising people. The workshops take the form of a weekly evening creative session for around seven weeks. The sessions are hosted by leading agency creatives and involve challenging 'live briefs' that explore student responses to creative problem solving. Creatives also share their own experiences, work and insights into the latest industry trends. There are three workshop groups currently offered by D&AD. The Advertising Workshops explore creative solutions across television, poster and print. The Integrated Workshops develop the student's ability to carry a campaign concept through a range of media, and Digital Workshops favour creative thinking for digital

and online platforms. However, with only around 20 places available at a time the selection process is tough – but give it a go. When you register you will be sent a creative brief to be judged by the creatives who set it. If they like what you do, you're in. If you are talented, committed and serious about improving your creative thinking and understanding the industry better, you are in with a chance of getting on one. The workshops are held at agency premises in London, Manchester, Leeds, Glasgow and Edinburgh. At the end you will have some serious learning under your belt, have met some new people from the industry and bolstered your creative portfolio with some *real live* work.

As you broaden your network of contacts you will find that advertising is a surprisingly small world – if one agency can't help they may well suggest another who might. Keep your ear to the ground – people in advertising know what is going on and are full of suggestions as to where you might try next. Involve yourself in the advertising *scene* and who knows what you may find out. Lastly, keep your eyes on the recruitment advertisements in the advertising trade press and on job websites. But be warned: I recently heard someone say that only around 20 per cent of advertising vacancies ever get formally advertised. So don't miss out on the hidden 80 per cent.

What about recruitment agencies?

There is one more avenue to explore and keep an eye on. For some reason the creative industries are remarkably secretive about the staff they need, and avoid going too public. There are exceptions to this – Iris once parked a van with a large hoarding outside the larger London advertising agencies. The hoarding invited creatives to apply for one of 22 positions at all levels. Cheeky, but effective – their website got an extra 100,000 hits in a week. Anyway, to preserve anonymity, a large number of jobs across all advertising agency roles are often filled and advertised by specialist recruitment agencies, and there are plenty dedicated exclusively to jobs in advertising, design and media. Besides the obvious fact that recruitment firms have real jobs waiting to be filled, they can be extremely beneficial to graduates as a learning experience. Recruitment consultants are specialists who have an extensive understanding of their particular sectors. The larger firms have people dedicated to specific roles, for example creatives, account management, designers or strategists. That reminds me, whilst you are on your job hunt you may come across the term 'suits'. Advertising agencies often use this as a friendly generic description of account management, planning and client services staff. So if an agency or recruitment website has a contact name for creatives and one for 'suits', remember which you aspire to be. The general *modus operandi* of a recruitment agency is this. An advertising agency will brief them as to their people requirements. This will indicate the job function, the level of experience they require, their type of agency and status and the kind of money they will pay. So it may read something like this:

Junior/Middleweight/Senior Art Director to work on international brands for respected London digital agency.

Applicants must have worked in a busy agency environment.

Graduates welcome too.

Salary up to 25k/35k/45k (or whatever).

The recruitment agency will never say who their client is in their advertising, and to apply you will need to contact them directly. Alternatively, you can register with a number of recruitment agencies and have them let you know when a suitable position arises. Either way, the first interview will be with a recruitment consultant who will be sufficiently experienced to assess your personality, talents and portfolio before they decide whether or not to put your profile forward to their client. At which point the agency that has the vacancy will decide whether to interview you themselves (or not). It is a relatively straightforward process, and I have been interviewed for more than one position myself through a recruitment agency. As a graduate, these guys know their stuff and have their fingers on the jobs pulse, so they can be a useful source of advice in terms of opinions on your portfolio and in helping you with interview techniques.

Selina Hull (BA (Hons), MISTD) is Junior Creative Consultant at Periscope, Creative Recruitment LLP. Not only that, but she is a relatively recent graduate too. Here's what she has to say about the role a recruitment agency can play in helping graduates get started:

I am the freshest recruit to join Periscope, and a BA (Hons) Graphic Design and Typography graduate. I studied and graduated from the University of Lincoln, and left with a 1st class degree. Like most design graduates, I embarked on my rounds of work placements. The good thing about doing work placements is that you not only get a feel for the real design business and studio environment – but it's a great opportunity to figure out what does and doesn't suit you (you can learn just as much from the wrongs as the rights). I took various placements: a packaging design studio (Lewis Moberly), to an integrated agency, a small branding studio . . .

After doing my fair share of work placements in London design studios, it dawned on me that I was more interested in the people that create the work than creating it myself. A very short stint recruiting in an entirely different sector gave me the basic grounding to join Periscope, and I joined as a Resourcer – responsible for sourcing creative talent from identity, branding, packaging designers right through to all things digital, and everything in-between. With my ear to the ground and my eyes on greater things, I was quickly nurtured and trained as a Junior Creative Consultant. I now work with graduates and rising junior-level designers, helping them get a foot in at the right agency.

I love the buzz of the design industry. My heart is very much in design, and inspiration comes from seeing great work, great ideas and great talent, and discovering how and where to place them. There are so many interesting people in this industry, and although we recruit for a niche sector (branding), design as a whole is very broad – and attracts people from every corner of the world, and every area of creativity. To do what I do, you need a 'go-getter' attitude, a keen eye for talent and appreciation of design, coupled with great people skills. I talk to a variety of people all day every day, from corporate clients, to laid-back creatives – and it's up to me to speak to them in the appropriate manner.

When preparing portfolios, a graduate should bear in mind that they are designers, and studios/agencies will expect to see this. Not only in the work that they've produced at university, but all the way throughout. Take some pride in how you present your portfolio (don't turn up with a shabby-looking folder), to the way you've written your cv (think about the format, typography). Attention to detail does not just apply to margins in *InDesign*, it applies to your spelling also. Spelling mistakes stand out, and make you look lazy – neither are they expected at graduate level. Keep it to a few key projects – they simply won't have the time to spend hours trawling through an entire portfolio, they'll just want to see your best work. About five to six key projects are ideal – you need to make an impression, so ensure it's your best work. As a general rule of thumb, we say dazzle them with the first and last two projects, so you start and end the interview on a high note. Also, at this stage in your career, many studios are interested in seeing your developmental work, i.e. sketch books, etc., and so take one or two along with you. It gives them an idea of how you develop your ideas.

Before you even think about interviews, research, research, research the studio/agency, long before you even approach them. Research the work they produce, how and when the studio was formed, how large they are, their ranking within the industry, the name of the creative director – you don't want to get caught out once you land an interview. Don't just rely on their website; look at articles within industry press.

Have a thorough understanding of your own portfolio – that may sound silly, but you would be surprised how many designers are unable to talk through/ explain the work in their portfolio. Practise, keep it simple and concise; good design will do most of the talking anyway. And don't forget, you are presenting your work to them – make sure you position your portfolio so they have a clear view. It's always good to have some questions of your own to ask towards the end of the interview. It demonstrates that you are interested in the studio/ agency and the way they work. And of course, basic interview etiquette:

- Smile – when you walk in. Shake the interviewer's hand. When you're answering a question – look them in the eye. Be articulate. Do not be overconfident, arrogant or brash.

- The design industry is not a classically formal environment; it is more relaxed than most. So unless otherwise requested, you probably won't need to turn up suited and booted, but think smart-casual.

Talking about us as a recruitment agency now, we do have to be selective with the graduates that we decide to take on. We review all the cvs and portfolios that are sent through us at the time they are sent – regardless of whether or not there is an active job advertised. If we are impressed, or think that we will be able to help them now or even later down the line, then we give them a call and invite them in to meet with us. We ask them to bring themselves along with their portfolio for a chat. Call it quality control, call it what you like, but we believe very much in getting to know our candidates – finding out what makes them tick, what inspires and motivates them, their future aspirations – this helps us get an idea of where in the industry they'd be best placed, and how we can help them. We keep it informal and relaxed at this stage, but we expect to see their presentation skills, and get an idea of how they will perform in a real interview. We then give our feedback as to where they can improve – whether it's the layout of their portfolio, the projects that they've included or the way they tackle questions. If we feel we can represent them, we will put together a 'plan of attack' – we discuss studios and industry figures that we will approach on their behalf. After discussion and with approval, we begin to introduce their details to people in the industry. A positive response results in a call for an interview. We mentor them through the interview process; we're best placed to give advice, as we know the studios and interviewers well. We also do the behind-the-scenes negotiations of freelance and permanent salaries, which takes the stress out of the process for them. The great thing about being represented by a creative-industry recruiter like Periscope is that we have industry knowledge and muscle – we talk directly to the decision-makers, and have access to the heavy-hitters in the business. The candidate also comes away with great advice, and a constant mentor throughout the job-seeking process.

Creative cvs and portfolios should be love at first sight – and the good ones always are. Bear in mind we do have to be very selective about whom we choose to represent. We receive hundreds of applicants for any one job. So it's that needle in a haystack feeling, and gratification I get from finding the perfect candidate or selection of candidates to put forward to a studio for a particular role that gives me my biggest buzz. Of course the cherry on the top is when they finally land the job, knowing that you've helped someone take another step in their career and helped a studio find great talent.

For me, the most important factor for graduates is enthusiasm – if they don't get this across in a covering letter/cv, and ultimately in the interview, then they will most likely not get the job. The reality is that there are thousands of design and creative graduates coming out of universities now, and they have to stand out. They must possess a tireless drive (do not give up) – be aware that there are lots of graduates going after the same jobs, so there *will* be disappointment along the way: they will need a thick skin. Stick at it, be persistent and things will happen for you eventually. When you do land a role, be realistic and expect to start at the bottom – you won't be working on the best projects, and you will be expected to work hard to prove yourself. And finally, network constantly. Keep up to date with what's going on within the industry, and keep in touch with key people you meet – you never know where your paths may cross in the future.

Student creative-advertising portfolio.

How do creatives work?

Some horror stories

You are a talented and enthusiastic art director or copywriter either flying solo or as part of a two-person creative team. Doesn't matter, the game works in the same way. The process of getting your first job is horribly subjective and will be a roller-coaster ride of extreme highs and desperate lows. It will test your mental strength to the limit, your head will spin from advice and confusion, and self-doubt will be the norm. Roll with it guys – I still cringe with the pain but you have my assurance it is worth it in the end. Before I talk about you and your portfolio I am going to try and make you feel better with some of my own hideous interview experiences. You are not alone!

My very first interview was a disaster. I arrived at the appointed time and the receptionist was lovely, making me coffee and trying to put me at my ease. Some hope. If a double-decker bus had crashed through the door and crushed the life out of me at that moment, I would have been much happier. I was fidgeting uncomfortably on a fat leather chair that made farty noises every time I moved and was almost overwhelmed by a vast triffid-like pot plant intent on strangling me if I relaxed for a second. Anyway, the receptionist phoned the creative department to say I was there, 'Someone will be with you soon,' she said. Five minutes later and 'Sorry, but the creative director has been delayed, a senior art director will see you instead.' Fine I thought. Ten more minutes gone and 'Sorry, it is so busy this morning, an art director will see you shortly.' By now, I had been twitching away for 30 minutes. Finally, a creative guy flew down the stairs, sat in front of me and said, 'Show me your book.' Honestly, the guy was barely older than me. There I was, my career resting in the hands of a bloody junior art director. He leafed carelessly through my portfolio, grunted a grudging 'thanks' and shot back upstairs. I sat there like a lemon wondering whether to leave or not. Finally, the receptionist phoned up to see if they had finished with me. They had, and I was finished with them. Extreme rudeness was my first exposure to the real world of advertising. They simply could not be bothered to see me. Thankfully they are not all like that.

Another time, I had a great interview with a creative director who said, 'We'd like to see you again. I'll arrange for you to meet our Head of Art in one of our other offices – I think you'll fit in well there.' I was delighted, he liked me, I liked him, the signs pointed to me being on my way to a great job. Oh no. Off I went to the other office to be met by the most dislikeable person ever. I am an easy-going guy who gets on with almost everyone on some level or other. Not that day – this fellow took an immediate dislike to me and I to him. Personal chemistry blew that one for me. He didn't need to look at my portfolio really; I was not going to get the job no matter how good he thought it was.

The worst experience of all came later in my career, though. This time we were talking Senior Art Director position. I went to a small, but very dynamic and very ethical advertising agency that excited me hugely. I met all the management team there; the whole personal chemistry thing was working perfectly here. They said come back and meet our creative director; he's away on business today. I did and that went incredibly well too. 'I think we are going to work very well together,' he said and I agreed. Sorted, this was just the job I was after at that point in my career. There was a week or so delay while they sorted out the money and, after a little negotiation, I verbally agreed to take the job. Good they said, we will confirm it all in writing and then we can talk about when you can start. One week later, still no letter. I decided to call them at the end of that week to see what was happening. The night before I was planning to phone I read a story in my local newspaper. A man had been found hanging in a tree in a remote wood, with a suicide note at his feet. Sadly, it was my new creative director, who had got into severe financial difficulty

involving the agency and had taken his own life. Fifteen years on and this story still upsets me. Shortly after, the agency went out of business. The moral of these three stories? There is no easy way!

Student creative-advertising portfolio.

Creative placement schemes

Would-be advertising creatives must also be prepared to face the challenges presented to them by the creative placement schemes operated by various agencies. As Trevor Beattie says, no one has really come up with a less daunting or more practical system to assess creative talent in a working environment. The way it operates differs from agency to agency, but the principle is, if your sparkling personality and killer portfolio excite the creative director sufficiently you may be offered the chance of a 'trial'. That can vary in duration from a month to three or even six months, and even that can be extended at the discretion of the agency. The pay ranges from absolutely nothing through to living expenses or a modest salary. At the end of the placement you may be hired permanently or just simply have to move on to another placement. On the positive side, aspiring creatives learn their craft 'on-the-job', receive some invaluable mentoring from established creative teams and once again add some new campaigns to their portfolios. The agency has the opportunity to assess how new blood responds to pressure, develops creative thinking techniques and fits in with the existing teams. In other words, answers the question, 'Your portfolio is good, but can you cut it in an agency environment?' On the negative side, graduates go through months of uncertainty for very little financial

reward without knowing whether there is a job at the end of it. D&AD also runs a graduate placement scheme for students who have been commended through the D&AD Student Awards, D&AD Best New Blood, D&AD talentpool, Portfolio Surgeries and Advertising Workshops. D&AD Award-winning graduates can showcase up to six projects and six images on the D&AD talentpool, a web-based showcase that provides a start for recognized emerging talent in the industry. This online recruitment service has more than 45,000 registered users and connects graduates and employers. The networking and matchmaking service also helps those seeking a creative partner. There is plenty of other practical help and guidance on the D&AD website at www.dandad.org.

Clearly, to a creative looking for a first placement or permanent position the portfolio is the most important weapon in their arsenal. It is important to look at that more closely later, but let's hear from some people who have been there, done it and are now proudly wearing their 'established creative' T-shirts.

Student creative-advertising portfolio.

How Lucy and Darren got to Wieden+Kennedy

The following case study appears in its original form on www.prospects.ac.uk, a website dedicated to offering careers guidance to all types of students. It was sourced by Alison Zorraquin of AGCAS on 1 June 2007 and I have paraphrased it here to help you understand the value of placements and the process that graduating creatives usually need to go through.

After studying a Graphic Design with Animation and Advertising course at college, Lucy realized that life as an art director was her destiny, so she took an Advertising Diploma to sharpen her creative skills. Lucy has worked with her copywriting partner, Darren, since they met at college over ten years ago. Even though they graduated as one of the top four teams of the year, it was two years before they were permanently hired. In the first year they had paid placements at several top agencies. However, subsequent placements were harder to come by and there was a significant time gap between the placements they had completed and the next two they had lined up. However, on the back of their placement portfolio they had the good fortune to be offered three positions at smaller agencies and opted to accept the chance at a new start-up agency, Malcolm Moore Deakin Blayze. Lucy and Darren currently work for Wieden+Kennedy in London for clients such as Nike, Honda, Nokia and *The Guardian* newspaper. Both however say that their roles are changing rapidly and that they are increasingly involved in creative projects for different types of clients and media. Their present jobs involve them in concept development, client presentations, briefing and art directing photographers, working with designers and mentoring placement creative teams. The importance of a strong portfolio to students cannot be stressed strongly enough by Lucy, and she has the following advice on creating a book that will really stand out:

- Creatives have limited time to look at work, so make the most of the chances you get. A balanced portfolio will have seven to nine campaigns and some other smaller ideas.
- Demonstrate a range of 'tones of voice'. No one gets hired if they can only communicate in one way.
- Show you can develop strategies as well as creative executions.
- Listen to advice and make notes.
- Include work that goes beyond advertising – a short film, a product range or a T-shirt – but keep it relevant to a target audience.
- Be open to thinking that is bigger than just advertisements. Think about business problems and how you might solve them.
- Keep the product range varied. Some big, some small, some expensive, some throwaway, some for adults, some for children. Make sure they are everyday products – walk around the supermarket for ideas.
- A warning. Advertising is a small world. Annoy people and others will hear about it.
- If after a placement you have a good relationship with a creative team go back to them with more work. Make more contacts and they may recommend you to others.

Student creative-advertising portfolio.

David Sloly, Mason Zimbler

David Sloly is creative director at Mason Zimbler, an integrated agency with offices in Reading and Bristol, UK, and Austin, Texas, USA. Their work is based across digital, advertising, direct marketing, branding and sales promotion disciplines. David himself has a broad range of experiences, including (in his own words) entrepreneur, sales executive, traveller, writer, broadcaster, advertiser, producer and creative director. He does the job he does because 'it's difficult and therefore works my brain hard enough to keep me occupied'. His role as creative director at a busy agency is demanding and he lists the following as the skills he needs to do his job effectively: 'Kindness, firmness, smart thinking, the ability to play dumb, understanding and pushiness, people skills, negotiation skills, the ability to listen and communicate clearly, be happy even when things are not so good, appear angry when in fact things are not so bad. The ability to tell the truth when the truth will hurt and to tell a white lie when the truth will hurt too much. Come up with ideas in a split second and be able to take a week to solve a problem. To control frustration and yet say when you are expecting more. Like all people and their personal quirks. Know when to put people together and pull them apart. Be able to praise people and be able to discipline that same person without it ever being personal. That said, I need to be able to be personal and professional in the correct amount at the correct time. You must be creative in ways you never imagined possible. Finally, you must gain the respect of your staff by being a great leader.' He numbers winning new business pitches and seeing his staff achieve as the biggest buzz his job offers. 'Life skills, creative skills, people skills and an amazing can do attitude I believe are what graduates need most to get a job in an agency.'

Student creative-advertising portfolio.

Rob Ellis, Agency Republic

Rob Ellis is an art director at Agency Republic, a London agency specializing in creative, strategy and media planning for digital advertising. Their client list is internationally recognized. He graduated from university in 2003 and spent four years on placement at Wieden+Kennedy, Rainey Kelly, TBWA, Karmarama, Mother, Naked, CHI, DDB and JWT. With a striking portfolio and the experience gained from such a wide range of placements, Rob then worked freelance for two years at Agency Republic, AKQA, RGA, St. Lukes and Work Club. While at Agency Republic he helped them win several new business pitches. In case that wasn't enough, he set up Please Yourself Ltd with a copywriting partner, Nick Horne, creating artworks in their spare time before taking a camper van called the *Pleasure Bus* on tour around the country peddling their wares. Five years after leaving university he was offered and accepted a position as an art director at Agency Republic. Rob does what he does because, 'I like problem solving and creating interesting, innovative and engaging work for myself, for my company and its clients – in fact, effective digital campaigns that engage and excite audiences. The skills I need for my job are art direction, concepting, being able to work in a team, problem solving, drawing, strong knowledge of strategy, interactive capabilities and technology, photography, illustration, typography, direction, innovation, energy, balls! I think graduates need all of the above with bags of energy and plenty of willingness to work into the early hours. Seeing a project go live and people engaging with it (not just people who work in advertising) gives me a massive thrill.'

The following brief/follow-up case study gives an insight into the type of work Rob and Agency Republic are involved in.

The Killzone 2 webgame

Battle the Helghast across the entire World Wide Web. Create your squad. Hunt down and destroy the enemy. Leave a trail of destruction wherever you browse.

It's World Wide War.

Brief

Create buzz and excitement around the release of *Killzone 2* and communicate the game's key features – more enemies, more hostile environments and more life or death moments.

Strategy

To cut through the clutter of generic 'first-person shooter' advertising online and engage with an active gaming community we decided to provide gamers with a truly unique and interactive experience. Using actual assets and 3D models from the game to ensure authenticity, we created the *Killzone 2* webgame – the first ever internet-wide shoot 'em up. Registering at www.killzonewebgame.com allowed users to download a browser plug-in that turned the entire web into a virtual battleground with enemies from the game liable to strike at any time. Once attacked, the user's cursor turned into a crosshair allowing them to rid the internet of the hostile Helghast. A competitive element and a squad play option allowing you to recruit your friends to play as a team and fight together in real-time, encouraged users to spread the webgame among their peers and ensure broader amplification of the campaign given the limited paid-for media support. Instead of using any paid-for advertising, the webgame was initially seeded to our primary audience through non-paid-for blogging channels before a paid-for viral seeding plan of the promotional video extended the reach of the campaign to a more mainstream gaming audience.

Execution

http://www.biginteractiveideas.com/figaro_killzone/

Results

In just three weeks . . .

- Over 120,000 people visited the site (30,000 before any paid-for seeding started).
- Over 14,000 people registered to play the game and more than 80,000 battles were fought (25,000 battles before any paid-for seeding started).
- Our webgame video was seen by more than 250,000 people.

SITE STATS SOURCE: GOOGLE ANALYTICS

Blogs and forums across the web discussed the webgame and a significant amount of free online PR and coverage was generated maximizing the buzz and awareness amongst our target audiences around the game's launch – http://tinyurl.com/d6fagm.

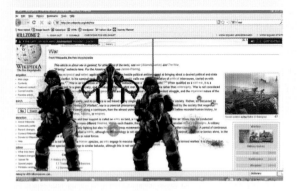

Screenshots from Agency Republic's digital campaign for *Killzone 2*.

Images courtesy of Agency Republic.

Paul Graham, Anomaly

In each of the (portfolio) reviews with superiors I have had in my time, I have always wanted to know what I was woeful at rather than what I was great at. Each time I vowed to be the best at each of those things by the time my next review came round, and each time I was. I doubt myself every day. I fail at something every day. I worry about whether something was good enough, or wide of the mark, every hour of every day. I constantly question whether there's a better way to think about a problem. Nothing's ever good enough is it? There could always be another viewpoint, a better answer I haven't considered, couldn't there? And that's ok.

I like graduates to scare the living daylights out of me, by knowing something I don't, by having opinions I've barely begun to get my head around. Good people surround themselves with good people. Great people surround themselves with people far better than them. I thrive by having bright people around me, changing how I think of the world, challenging what the right next step is. My gut reaction to something is generally good with the right provocation. But I need that provocation from others.

How should students approach me? A witty email will sit with the hundred other witty emails, until I finally get to it after all the important work emails of the day (or week). But then, a 'wacky attack' is likely to leave me thinking you're weird, unsurprisingly. Which means I'll probably ignore it, or depending on quite how strange it was, I might even scream like a girl and run in the other direction. So what do you do? Think about what is important to me, what is important to Anomaly, and let that be the thing. Be that thing more so than any other person in the world. And then get in touch. By then I'll be listening.

Paul Graham – founding Partner, Anomaly London

The Portfolio–your biggest asset

I hope you are feeling suitably positive and electrified by now. The prospect of working as an advertising creative, well, life couldn't get much better could it? Of course it is hard to break in, soul-destroying at times, but feel like you can do it. Lucy, Darren, Rob, Paul and hundreds of other graduates have. Be prepared to take risks and be flexible too – not just in the kind of agency you may work for but in its location too. As an extreme example, Niall Cook and Ant Morris are a couple of likely lads armed with the gift of the gab and a great portfolio who graduated from the course I teach on in 2008. After using up plenty of shoe leather in London, they decided to broaden their horizons and their minds by travelling around India for a while. They didn't forget to pack their portfolio though, and after seeking out a couple of placements they arrived in Mumbai. One placement later and they are still there – as a creative team at Saatchi & Saatchi. The fact that these two guys felt that their portfolio was the most important piece of luggage they had is indicative of the relationship creatives have with their work. Advertising portfolios are an extension of a creative's soul; they are a window into their creative minds and thinking. Yours will be just the same. Lucy at Wieden+Kennedy has given a pretty comprehensive overview of how a good portfolio should be. I will add just a few further pieces of basic advice to her list.

As you near graduation and your final year exhibition you will (hopefully) receive a head-spinning, lorry load of portfolio advice from your tutors and other creatives connected with your course. That will start you off nicely, but don't think you've done it. Once the university door has shut on you for the last time you need to show it to as many people as you can – creative directors if possible, creative teams at agencies for sure and maybe some recruitment consultants too. Their opinions, guidance and advice are vital to the fluid development of your portfolio. Ultimately, of course, the final decision on its content rests with you but that should be based on what the voices of experience have told you. Start your portfolio with a bang and finish with a bigger one and use your research wisely. If you are meeting creatives to show what you can do, find as much as you can about the kind of clients their agency has and the type of briefs they work on. Tailor your portfolio to suit. It may well only have eight campaigns and four small creative pieces in it, but your stockpile of work needs to be larger than that to allow you to target the book to the agency you are presenting it to. Get them interested when you open it and blow them away as you close it. Make sure you learn all you can in the short time you will have to get your ideas across. Don't bore and irritate creatives by laboriously explaining every nuance of your concepts – this is advertising, if they don't *get* your work quickly then you have problems. Big ones. You shouldn't need to bang on about what you have done and why. By all means introduce each piece and be prepared to answer questions about it, but really, let your work speak for itself.

Consider as well the possibility of uploading your portfolio work to a website. You could design and create your own site if you have the skill. Your Facebook page could act as your portfolio too. A word of advice here though – dedicate the page and its images to your work and your work only. Keep your professional aspirations and social life totally separate. No creative director wants to stumble through pictures of your drunken birthday party or you showing off your knickers or tattoos to find your work. Dedicate the words and pictures to impressing 'visiting' creatives. Alternatively you can use an online portfolio site which markets itself to creatives in the industry to demonstrate your capabilities. I've listed the URLs for some at the end of the chapter.

The work in your physical portfolio should be handled like an antique painting – it should be clean, neat and simple, and mounted in a way that stops it falling all over the floor as you open your case. If you have visuals prepared using a computer, print them on good-quality paper at the highest resolution you can, and mount them squarely on the page with edges cut perfectly straight. If you have marker scamps, make sure they are crisp not messy – don't worry about how well you have drawn them. You are hoping to be paid to think, not draw. Above everything else, ask the right questions – these should be based around one thought only – how can I learn to be better?

Preliminary assessments of the work of aspiring creatives are increasingly being made online, via specialist portfolio websites, blogs and personally created websites. Whilst the days of sleek, black portfolio cases are far from over, increasing numbers of agencies and their creative directors are requesting work digitally ahead of a first meeting. *Campaign* writer Matt Williams quoted one creative director in an article written in September 2008, and now on www.campaignlive.co.uk:

> 'I'd say that about two-thirds of portfolios I look at now are websites,' one executive creative director says. 'Graduates are so used to working with digital now that when they're creating their portfolios they're thinking: "Well, why wouldn't you do it online?" It's so much more effective.'

Foliomatch is a new service designed to help creatives to find the contacts and opportunities they need to break into the industry. The website was built by a graduate and a placement-year student from the University of the West of England, and was launched in 2009. Students can use Foliomatch to upload a portfolio of their work and show everyone what they are up to. They can search for events and opportunities that could make a difference to their portfolio, such as work experience and competitions; find information on career-related issues; collaborate with other students and get approached for commission work.

Foliomatch is open to all types of creative student and can be found at www.foliomatch.co.uk. Interestingly, it is not limited to advertising and as well as presenting your own work you can sneak a peek at creative work produced by interior designers, illustrators, textile designers, graphic designers and photographers. So it is good for the head as well as your career.

Matt Williams wrote on www.campaignlive.co.uk about the experiences of Lucy-Anne Ronaynes, who recently graduated from Central Saint Martins College of Art and Design in London and got herself a job at Work Club:

> She identifies her digital portfolio as a key reason why the agency was keen to take her on, and urges other graduates to do the same. 'I think any junior who doesn't have one is at a massive disadvantage. Even if you don't have the means to build a ".com", the web is full of free blogs, so there's no excuse,' she says.

The purpose of a digital portfolio is no different from its hard-copy counterpart. It simply allows for more creativity, gives greater technological scope and makes things a darn sight more manageable for the people you're trying to impress, and it's simply

a case of sending the interviewer a link. It's a hell of a lot easier than storing a great big portfolio book on an already overcrowded desk. From a graduate's point of view, it also means the portfolio will be easier to manage and edit, and any new work created can be added at the drop of a hat. With the idea of showcasing talent online no longer a novelty, graduates are being put under even more pressure to shine in the digital space. This, in turn, means a greater need for candidates to get their creative juices flowing in order for their portfolio to impress.

My, how times have changed. Before computers, there was no other way to get your work seen by the right people than by plucking up the courage and calling someone who actually worked in advertising.

What followed was an equally nerve-wracking wait in a glamorous agency reception. People milled around looking cool. You felt like a tramp. All part of the process of getting your work seen. Now all you do is build a website.

My partner Steve and I see most creatives this way now – it's so easy to store the URLs in a folder for a rainy day. They said computers would never catch on. They were wrong. The digital portfolio – soon we'll all have one.

Darren Bailes – Creative Director, VCCP

Screenshot from a student online portfolio at Carbonmade.com.

It seems that for graduate teams in particular, the single purpose of an online portfolio must be to sell themselves and their ambitions. Do I think they are good at doing that? Well, I love them if they're fabulous digitized books, a feast of the many things the team wants to say.

They're also great if they allow me to very quickly gain an opinion as to whether I can reject or accept them instantaneously. Yet I know that if I only see the work and not the people that made it, I could miss out on someone very special. I met an art director once who's one of the craziest fuckers I've ever known. His work was shit, but his thinking was inspiring. He's now a very good planner.

If I'd only looked at his online book, I'd never have gained the benefits of his random thoughts and he'd never have got my help in turning him to planning. So, as always, it depends on how you use an online book. One worry I have is that they are used too often as simple calling cards, rather than as backdrops to a crit or interview.

This might be because a great digitized book needs huge amounts of time to make it live. Scanned scamps and small windows of film don't really help

with the impact of the work and, for the most part, teams just make their conventional flat books into conventional flat online books.

Marc Giusti – Creative Partner, GT

The learning should never stop

Naturally all portfolios, digital or otherwise, need continual nurturing, developing and refreshing by their owners. If your digital work is lucky enough to be viewed, then the daunting face-to-face meeting is still the next step. So, don't forget, agencies want junior creatives who are keen and willing to learn, not know-it-alls and prima donnas. If you have creative talent – and I know you do – you should find yourself on a creative placement anytime soon. Once you are there, learn, learn, watch and learn about:

- how to be briefed by account management teams
- target audiences and clients' businesses
- how to work better with your copywriter/art director partner
- how to present ideas to your creative director
- how to best pitch ideas to clients
- how to create visuals that communicate your ideas most effectively
- how to commission and brief designers, photographers, illustrators or film-makers
- how to evaluate and enhance their work
- how to advise new creatives, review their portfolios and manage their placements.

Once you have learned to do all these things and your reputation for creative thinking and conceptualizing is becoming known, you are an advertising creative. You know what you need to do, what's stopping you?

The last word goes to Gwyn Jones – Chief Operating Officer at Bartle Bogle Hegarty. Again, this quote comes from www.campaignlive.co.uk:

In September 1987, I started my career in advertising as one of the first three graduate trainees ever taken on by Bartle Bogle Hegarty. Twenty-one years later, I am still there. It is probably a fair assumption that something went OK in training. The problem with this assumption is that it was a long time ago and if I am certain of one thing, it is that things have changed a lot since then.

With this in mind, I decided to check the views of some of our more recent recruits, all superstars of the present, let alone the future. A couple of things immediately became clear. First, there is no way I would even be a contender among this lot. Second, despite that, some themes do appear consistent with my own memories, so maybe some tips will stand the test of time.

It goes without saying that it helps to be in a good company and to have good teachers. Listen to them well, write stuff down and accept their feedback. As a member of the inaugural graduate-training scheme at BBH, we benefited from the fact that the agency was keen to put on a very good show. We sat at the feet of legends and were afforded the chance to have a go at everything the agency had to offer.

In truth, we were horribly spoilt and I suspect, by the time we started working on accounts, it showed. Matthew Melhuish, my first boss and a subsequent founder partner of the excellent BMF in Sydney, was at pains to point this out to me: 'You think you're pretty special, don't you, Mr Fancy Pants Footlights College, BBH Graduate Trainee? Well, let me tell you something. Right now you are lower than the shadow of shark shit!'

Which you will recognize as being Australian for 'reasonably far down the pecking order'. Wherever you stand on the 'short sharp shock' approach to personal development, I can tell you that this intervention worked for me very powerfully. I reckon I was diligence and humility personified for many months. I stayed until about four o'clock in the morning one night to clear and prep a room for a pitch the following day and found John Bartle's silver pipe cleaner in the process. I got a £50 spot bonus for my trouble. I was back on track.

Notwithstanding this understanding of one's position in society, I also believe that it is important to be a bit bolshie and to find a way to challenge the status quo. Whether formal or informal, all agencies will have some form of process – a way of getting stuff done that is unique to the personalities and accounts that make up that agency. It is vital that you work out how your agency works so that you can change it. Even the best-oiled agency machines do things in certain ways because they have always done it that way. Not necessarily the best way of responding to an ever-changing world. Those who see this most clearly are those who are the least indoctrinated and closest to the future – the new guys. So, not so far down the pecking order after all. Knowing how to present your challenge then becomes critical.

To gain ground quickly, seek to deal in facts first and opinions later. One of the things you will notice in meetings is that many sentences start with the phrase: 'Well, I think . . .' Typically this phrase is delivered with a tone of voice that also implies that all previous contributions to the debate have been worthless. It is a brave recruit who decides to add their own, possibly contradictory, opinion to the fray after the chief executive has just delivered his visionary thoughts. However, the killer fact is your best friend. 'But we know that the product won't actually be on shelf until November,' can change the direction of the debate in a second. People will soon look to you for the facts and maybe even the answers. This might imply the need for an anal approach. I once learned all the lot numbers of the Levi's range and, at the same time, the inner workings of the Audi 'Torsen' differential. While this did not add to my

attractiveness as a dinner party guest, I think it was a price worth paying for getting to deal in broad-brush strokes.

How do 'suits' work?

The time has come when advertising in some hands has reached the status of a science.

Claude C. Hopkins.

Account executives—making it all happen

So you want to be an account executive? To contradict my earlier irritating remarks about the value of a degree to the advertising industry, paper qualifications will be more useful to prospective account executives. Taken at face value they can offer a pretty good insight into whether you have the required skills. Entry-level skills are the ability to write well: clearly, concisely and with engaging warmth. Being able to organize the paperwork and emails generated by a campaign – so great administrations skills, in other words. Verbal communication is the big one – can you talk clearly, confidently and with authority both face to face and over the phone? Can you present creative work persuasively and with conviction? I'm sure you can, but just try this for a moment. Go and stand in front of the nearest mirror and put yourself to the test. Clearly I am not asking you to worry about your size, shape or natural features, even advertising is not that prehistoric! But look at yourself as if you were an advertising client. What would you expect? I think you should expect to dress yourself 'one notch' above the client (or interviewer to start with). Boys, the unshaven look is uber-cool I know, but there is a break point. Two or three days looks very stylish, a fully grown beard can look equally sharp. Dirty, unattended facial hair is off-putting. Boys and girls, be clean, stylish and presentable at all times. That's why creatives call you suits! Smell of *Chanel* or *Hugo Boss* not last night's lager or an old cigarette packet. The most important thing to remember at this point is that you are the face of the agency that employs you. So, mirrors are like cameras, they don't lie. If you are satisfied that you look the business then we can move on. Otherwise take my book to the hairdresser's to read while you are waiting for a sharp new look and then go shopping!

Research thoroughly, set the scene, create context, talk them through proofs and evidence, present the idea . . . hold your breath and watch for the lightbulb flick on above their head. That's the secret to a successful presentation.

Mark Terry-Lush – founder and CEO of Renegade Media Ltd

Seriously, account management teams are the heartbeat of an advertising agency. I know creatives get all the glory and planners get asked all the questions, but without

disciplined, effective account executives and managers the place would quickly fall apart. They are the link between a client and the agency staff and run campaigns on a day-to-day basis. Good account teams possess an uncanny ability to know every detail of a campaign and intuitively know what the creatives and planners are up to at any given time. They have to because, at any moment, the client could ring and ask for an update on any aspect of the work. Budgets are often under the control of the account teams too, so a degree of numeracy is essential to ensure no other department is overspending without discussion. Clients understandably are usually less than thrilled to receive an invoice way in excess of the figure they expected. So if the budget allows, say, £5,000 for photography, then make sure the creative department hasn't commissioned a photographer who will charge £10,000. Common sense, logic and calmness are personality traits all account teams possess. You may have noticed by now I am a creative by profession; far from thinking myself superior to account management teams, like many creatives, I have always been in awe of them. Their endless range of skills and ability to defuse a crisis are jaw-dropping at times. I have met plenty on my travels; all of them can make things happen no matter how the odds are stacked against them. There was Amanda, whose smile and disarming manner of speaking could lull me into staying at work half the night to revise some visuals for the following morning, without even a half-hearted argument from me. Claire is the toughest girl I've ever met; yet she could charm any already late courier driver into waiting half an hour before collecting his package several times during the same week. If I tried the same thing, I know I would be driving the visuals or artwork to the client myself. As for Gareth, his driving was shockingly bad, yet somehow he could regularly leave for a meeting anywhere in the country 20 minutes late and still arrive early. Finally I remember H.; she was really something else. She could look over concept work, decide she didn't think it was quite what the client needed, take it back to the creative director and leave him thinking that changing the concept was his idea – phenomenal people skills, that woman. These are the kind of inherent traits great account people have. So, besides possessing incredible powers of persuasion, the patience of several saints and being able to juggle more problems than a Prime Minister, what do account executives do on a daily basis? They are all able to:

- converse on equal terms with clients about their products, services, brand and advertising requirements
- arrange meetings with clients and agency staff
- brief media, creative and research staff and assist in developing marketing strategies
- maintain contact and communication with clients and key agency personnel
- oversee the smooth running of campaigns
- negotiate details and deadlines with clients and agency staff
- present creative concepts to clients

- manage campaign costs
- write reports, keep and understand records and financial details
- have an involvement in winning new business
- administer all aspects of a campaign and monitor its profitability.

There are probably a million other things too – account executives need to quickly learn to be multitasking, multifaceted, super organized communication experts. Think you can do it. Good. Who said creatives have the most difficult job in an agency? Probably creatives themselves! Advertising agencies are dynamic, rounded, all-action teams, more often than not glued together by account management teams. You will need to be quick-witted and quick to learn once you get your first break. Not only will you need to learn the techniques associated with campaign management, you will need to have command of the intricacies of a client's business and brand and develop your presentation skills. Like most aspects of agency life, account management is no place for shrinking violets. A disarming smile is pretty useful too.

In order to get your first job you will need to demonstrate your ability just as a creative does and be prepared to be confronted by the same degree of ruthlessness. The chances are your university studies will have been either creative advertising or advertising and marketing in some guise. Many successful account managers have been through my creative course and left with a thorough understanding of the creative process which, along with their bright, intelligent personas, has got them some very good positions right up to McCann Erikson level. One girl even began life as an account executive and switched into creative – almost the perfect agency employee, I guess. Her understanding of clients, strategy and creativity must make her superhuman nearly. To achieve an interview, you will have submitted a beautifully written and neatly presented cv and statement to convince an agency to talk to you. At interview your clear communication, lively questioning mind and businesslike manner will serve you very well. Perhaps you need a portfolio too. For some of you that could include creative work. For those who have studied subjects such as marketing, advertising with business or marketing and communications, show three or four campaign outlines demonstrating strategic development work and a high standard of presentation. Because your job will require you to present creative work to clients, you will need to present yourself pretty effectively to interviewers too. The best account people are extremely attractive; I don't mean physically, I mean in the sense that people are naturally drawn to them, like them and can listen to them easily.

Charlotte Driscoll, Mason Zimbler

After graduating from the University of Gloucestershire in 2007, Charlotte Driscoll was hired by multifaceted, multidisciplined Bristol agency Mason Zimbler as an Account Executive. She saw this first position as 'a stepping stone to Account Director

then Managing Director then ruler of the world!' Having taught Charlotte for three years, I've a sneaking suspicion she is not entirely joking there!

For any aspiring account executive, her views on just what it takes to do her job are forthright and very clear:

> Communication. The essence of the job is bridging the gap between the client and the creatives/designers that sometimes takes a little interpretation on both sides. I mean this both in directing a message and how you talk to people to elicit key information, present feedback, convey a sense of urgency etc. while keeping everyone happy and on side.
>
> Also, professionalism, organization, time and people management, presentation, keeping calm in a crisis, decision-making, good customer service and problem solving. This where I'm at, though, in my job. In order to get the job in the first place graduates need a range of personal qualities. Persistence, experience, be willing to start at the very bottom and do the boring stuff, good interview experience, a basic background in market knowledge and knowledge of the agency, a face that fits (sad but very true), ability to think around a problem and not be fazed by anything.
>
> To help illustrate this, the brief here is a typical example of the way we work at Mason Zimbler.

Discover the NEW FreeAgent Family and WIN

Objective

Educate resellers on the *FreeAgent Family* with an online training quiz and chance to win a *FreeAgent Go* Outbound vehicle:

- Emails sent to SPP[1] and non-SPP[2] audiences segmented into those who had and had not shown a prior interest (SPP January and non-SPP February)
- Reminder email (March)
- Static banner in monthly newsletter email (February)
- Online media – leaderboards
- CTA[3] to visit a microsite featuring five *FreeAgent* products and a quiz.
- Take the quiz to be in with a chance of winning a *FreeAgent Go*
- Download family and individual product datasheets
- Join or visit the SPP site
- All communications in nine languages

---

1 SPP refers to the Seagate Partner Program which is a recorded database of resellers/distributers.
2 A database of users who have not yet registered as SPP members.
3 CTA = Call to action.

Results

CTR[4] Result ranged from 2 per cent to a staggering 29 per cent per audience segment all above industry average. ROI[5] was £6.31 per CTA response.

4 CTR = Click through rate.
5 ROI = Return on investment.

Some of Mason Zimbler's work for *FreeAgent*.

Images courtesy of Mason Zimbler.

I get a massive buzz out of working in advertising, but on a day to day basis it doesn't get much better than making a miserable client happy, or making an unachievable deadline achievable. I now do a lot of presentations, but that was scary when I first started at Mason Zimbler. Now the success of a presentation is in the planning and discussions we have ahead of meeting the client. I sit down with the creative and talk! Then I have a little think about it and present the concepts back to the creative so that he is confident in me and I am confident in me! He gets a chance to add anything I may have missed and then I make sure to provide him full (but maybe edited) client feedback so that it feels more like sharing a job rather than handing over each time.

Account planning – art, science or black magic?

Throughout this book I have stressed the necessity for all agency teams involved in the campaign process to sing from the same hymn sheet. Account planners are by and large responsible for creating that hymn sheet – otherwise known as the campaign strategy. I have heard many senior figures describe their outstanding planning teams as the unsung, publicity-shy heroes of many of advertising's most successful campaigns. Their vision, clarity and depth of experience provide the wisdom for creatives to create from, account management teams to focus on and consumers to engage with. The best planners are highly creative people, though not in the visual or word-spinning sense of a creative team. In the larger advertising agencies, account planners have a department all to themselves, but in smaller ones it is not uncommon for planners to be account managers as well. In the world of digital advertising they sometimes operate in disguise, under slightly different names, such as brand planner or communication planner. Here the approach differs and they focus on additional factors such as the culture of communication between users across the internet or via mobile phone technologies and social media. Fundamentally, though, account planning is centred on brand positioning, to connect effectively with target consumers.

There are three divisions within the role of an advertising agency account planner, with various subtleties shaped by the clients and advertising media environments their agency operates within. It all begins with research (yes, that word again). The planner needs to research and understand the client, the brand, the audience, the marketplace and the competition. Usually planning will provide qualification for the results of quantitive data gathered by market researchers. The creative part of the job stems from searching for the big marketing idea. The skill in this creativity is developing initial thinking and then shaping it analytically and critically to boil the idea down into one single, motivating proposition. The result of this research and big thinking is the creative brief. It is the responsibility of advertising planners to write briefs that are specific in their aims, insightful in their background, and clear in the marketing and brand objectives. If any three words can combine to best describe the work of advertising agencies, they are research, strategy and creative – but then I've told you that already, probably loads of times.

Account planners enjoy great diversity in their work; each day brings a fresh problem to solve. One day may be research based, the next may be creative, strategic thinking. All planners are good communicators; many I've met have a wicked sense of humour too. Perhaps it is a mechanism to help in working equally closely with all the other agency departments. In fact, it is probably not too much to describe planners as the hub of an agency from where all creativity stems. Specific job skills are strangely varied. A direct marketing planner I worked with some time ago described himself as a creative scientist with an unhealthy obsession for alchemy.

Fundamental planning skills:

- Creative thinker
- Strategic thinker
- Investigative researcher
- Inquisitive researcher
- Interested in people and what makes them tick
- Strong written and verbal communication
- Being interesting!

The pathway into advertising planning mirrors that of the account executive really, but many have an interest in, or a qualification (A-Level for example) in Psychology or Sociology. That is because a planner needs to be totally immersed in popular culture and the zeitgeist. In other words, what are consumers doing and thinking right now? Some planners have arrived in advertising as account executives and taken on some planning roles before moving over completely. In essence, I think a good account planner is experienced. Not so much in their job, but in life. If you want to be a planner, you truly have to make yourself more interesting. Being able to talk confidently about day-to-day consumer behaviour and communication is an absolute prerequisite. So get out and do new things. Go to music gigs and the theatre. Join an arts group. Write creatively for a local newspaper or radio station. In fact, do anything that brings you into contact with a broad range of people in different environments. Once again: learn, learn, learn.

> Go out of the office and experience everything connected with the life of the customers.
>
> **David Sloly–Creative Director, Mason Zimbler**

There exists great synergy within advertising agencies between all departments, but it is fair to say that account management and planning are especially close – sometimes because each has often done the other's job. In many agencies the ultimate responsibility for communications and the management of clients and their projects falls to a client services director. Sometimes this role includes the management of account directors, sometimes it is a title used instead of account director. Agencies place different emphasis on the role of client services directors, depending on their own specific organization of staff. So whilst the job may differ from agency to agency, for graduates aspiring to a career in advertising account management or planning this is a job to reach for over a number of years. Rather like a creative director, it is the culmination of many years' experience. Ultimately the job has overall control of campaign management for agency clients. High-level presentations, wining and dining clients and a deep involvement in client strategies are all in a day's work for the client services director. They are a vital component in retaining and developing existing clients and also in the pitching for and winning of

new business. As students or graduates, your first exposure to a client services director may be at interview or discussion stage.

Louise Goldstein, BDR London

Louise Goldstein is Client Services Director at BDR London.

I am director and co-founder of BDR London, which is a full service internet advertising agency. I have worked for some of the country's top media agencies, such as Media Contacts (MPG) and TBG London. My experience covers managing multimillion-pound advertising accounts for the National Lottery, P & O, Dating Direct and Ocean Finance, to name but a few. I started my online career in email marketing whilst working for Dennis Publishing.

I love digital marketing. New technological advancements that can be used for advertising fascinate me. My job is varied, demanding and involves being analytical, copywriting, mathematical ability, presentation and sales skills. In my agency, graduates need to show promise in each of those areas, but particularly to impress me they would need to ooze confidence, have great presentation skills and a mathematical mind. Here's why.

A client came to us because they needed to grow their business – they found that their current marketing activity was ineffective. This client provides hotel bookings and they have been advertising for years through email, lead generation and PPC. We sat down and reviewed their marketing, discussing what they had done and their thoughts on how it went. We went over the performance in great detail, in terms of their creative and ROI. We established that affiliate and lead generation was not profitable and they should concentrate on PPC (pay per click). We knew that affiliate and lead generation would not be profitable, as the margins they were working to would not fit with these marketing methods. We conducted a full competitor research and landing page optimization. We compared their landing page with competitors and looked at the performance of their PPC and recommended improvements. Marketing tools are used to identify target keywords and traffic volumes. *Analytics* data is used to discover online user behaviour and make recommendations based on actual findings.

After amends were made, we conducted A/B testing – sending some traffic to the old site and some to the new site. The new site instantly produced better results. Not only this, we totally reorganized the campaign. By using a more structured approach and advanced deep-linking techniques we were able to halve their cost per lead and double the volume.

This project shows that a mixture of feedback from the client, statistical data, campaign history, competitor research and testing all play a key role in improving results.

The biggest buzz I get is when my agency surpasses expectations on campaigns. This means that the campaign you have carefully planned has gone far better than expected and often leads to repeat advertising. Our company offers digital advertising expertise across a number of different sectors. The big brand experience of our employees allows us to apply previous campaign learning to any work we carry out. As our experience extends across all digital platforms, such as search optimization, creative and design, targeted emailing, advertising within online games and other offline digital applications, this gives us a holistic approach that we can apply to our client's marketing activity.

My account teams at BDR need to be able to research and present their ideas to others whilst backing up their findings with statistical information. As a piece of free advice: when presenting ideas to clients I get examples so that the client can visualize the concepts. I also provide figures to back up the validity of the idea being presented, along with similar case studies that have been done.

Two screens showing the way the website looked and worked before optimization and after.

Images courtesy of BDR London.

Gillian Challinor, Gyro HSR

Once again, the importance of high-level thinking in research and strategy comes shining through. Gillian Challinor is also heavily involved in the management of campaigns and clients as Digital Project Manager at Gyro HSR. Unusually she began her career as a project manager in civil engineering, before moving to an account and project-management position at a web-based agency. She has been at Gyro HSR for over a year now and describes the best parts of her job as

> mentally challenging, creative, working with nice people, at the forefront of the digital age and to make clients richer! I think my most important skills are a good eye for detail, ability to multitask, ability to keep calm under pressure, ability to find solutions to problems, good people person and communication.
>
> I meet many graduates and I expect them to be outgoing, energetic, have good research skills, plenty of background knowledge and a keen eye for spotting successful campaigns. When preparing portfolios for an interview I like graduates to be short, snappy, make a statement and dare to be different.
>
> For me launching a campaign on time and getting good results is always thrilling and I am proud to be part of a team that possesses exceptional brand knowledge and people who care about the success of the business. We talk to each other about campaigns all the time and brainstorm.

Are you getting it?

Irrespective of the positions they hold, the agency people who have shared their thoughts and opinions throughout this chapter all focus on the same fundamental expectations of graduates. Their views reinforce those I have continually referred back to throughout this book. If you learn nothing else from reading this, learn these golden rules and carry them with you throughout your careers:

1. Be more interesting – seek out and learn from every facet of culture and make it your life's work to develop a keener understanding of people: their behaviour, their desires and the way in which they communicate.
2. Be bold and confident. Make advertising people believe that you can play a part in the future of their agency by having something different to say. This should shine through in your personality and in your work.
3. Be open-minded and accept that there is a lifetime of learning still to be done. Watch, listen to and absorb everything you see, and evaluate how you can be a better, more creative and more exciting person.

In considering all of these factors, once you have achieved your first placement or even your first full-time job, don't change. The agency offered you that opportunity

because of who you are. They saw in you something interesting, something different and an edge – don't lose it. The time to be competitive is also over – you have your chance now to learn to be an effective part of the team. The more a team makes each other look good the better you will look. Professionalism is still important – don't get complacent by clinging to your student habits of lateness and unreliability. This is the best way of earning a reputation for arrogance and a lack of care – not at all good. Advertising is genuinely exciting and financial rewards come with experience – your mates in high-powered law or business positions may seem to be earning loads more than you do; but go and visit the offices they work in. I guarantee you will be glad you chose to work in advertising. You have time to 'get on' – fast-track learning is so much more beneficial to you than fast-track promotions in the long term. Creatives must be patient while they work on the agency's smaller projects, and account executives should accept that there will be more to life than contact reports and competitor research. Just not yet! Talk to others – everyone else was once in your position and they will always be pleased to help and mentor you as best they can. Above all, don't stop being interesting. Continue to do the things you love outside work, you will become more experienced and retain the personal dimension that makes you different from everyone else.

Trust me, it is there for the taking. The only thing holding you back is you.

Some websites to visit

Here are some sites to help you keep up to date with a variety of recruitment and advertising news and comment. There are many more, so feel free to use Google again!

www.campaignlive.co.uk
www.guardian.co.uk/media
www.timesonline.co.uk
www.independent.co.uk
www.prospects.ac.uk
www.ihaveanidea.org
www.graphicpush.com
www.creative-cohort.com
www.brandrepublic.com
www.dandad.org
www.yeah-magazine.com
www.ipa.co.uk
www.internship-uk.com

Here is a small selection of recruitment companies who specialize in advertising:

www.profilescreative.com
www.periscopeuk.com
www.wearemustard.com
www.galleryresources.co.uk
www.creativerecruitment.co.uk
www.macpeople.co.uk
www.the-creamery.co.uk
www.agendarecruitment.co.uk
www.purple-consultancy.com
www.workstation.co.uk
www.xchangeteam.com
www.thebook.uk.com
www.creativesync.co.uk
www.majorplayers.co.uk

Here are some online portfolio sites (see what other students are doing too):

www.carbonmade.com
www.behance.com
www.deviantart.com
www.coroflot.com
www.flickr.com
www.cpluv.com
www.figdig.com
www.electronicportfolios.org
www.indexhibit.org
www.eportfolios.org

Some books to read

It's Not How Good You Are, It's How Good You Want To Be
Paul Arden

Hey Whipple, Squeeze This
Luke Sullivan

How to Put Your Book Together and Get a Job in Advertising: Twenty-first Century
Maxine Paetro

Pick Me: Breaking into Advertising and Staying There
Nancy Vonk and Janet Kestin

How to Get into Advertising
Andrea Neidle

The Fundamentals of Creative Advertising
Ken Burtenshaw, Nik Mahon and Caroline Barfoot

Advertising Account Planning: A Practical Guide
Larry D. Kelley and Donald W. Jugenheimer

Truth, Lies, and Advertising: The Art of Account Planning
Jon Steel

Perfect Pitch: The Art of Selling Ideas and Winning New Business
Jon Steel

Life's a Pitch
Stephen Bayley and Roger Mavity

Agency Account Handling: Avoiding Blood, Sweat and Tears
Michael Sims

The Art of Client Service: 58 Things Every Advertising and Marketing Professional Should Know
Robert Solomon

Get involved

Share your interview and placement experiences and learn from everyone else on my book's Facebook and Twitter pages:

- search Facebook for 'Advertising Its Business Culture and Careers'
- www.twitter.com/adculture

7 Celebrities behaving badly – opportunities beyond the advertising agency

During our recent exploration of the kinds of career opportunities within an advertising agency, I deliberately left out two vital components of the advertising and communication process – PR and media planning/buying. Whilst these are both integral to any client's advertising activity they are services that can be offered both by advertising agencies and by specialized consultancies. To complicate things further, some clients will also employ their own staff in PR and media positions. Hence, I've given them a chapter of their own. In my experience, large 'household'-name clients operating on both the UK and global marketplace will often employ several agencies, each with their own unique specialisms, to deliver their advertising content. Take Volkswagen in the UK, for example. The marketing team based in Milton Keynes had at least six different organizations working across the media to communicate brand and product messages. The 'above-the-line' advertising (television, radio, mainstream press and outdoor) was undertaken very successfully by DDB London. They were (and still are) responsible for some incredibly subtle, witty and imaginative campaigns all with a slightly offbeat, quirky edge to them. The Polo campaign featuring the very amusing singing dog I mentioned in an earlier chapter. My recent favourites were for the Passat range – these featured several executions on the creative theme of owners not wishing to mess their cars up. One commercial saw a father obviously arriving to collect his wife and child from the shops, only to drive past when he saw his young child eating an ice-cream, leaving them dumbstruck on the pavement. Another showed a man driving his Passat away from a lonely country lane in the pouring rain, only towards the end did it become apparent that he had left his wet, muddy dog to walk home by itself. It is also interesting to note that DDB London is of course a descendant of Doyle Dane Bernbach. Go back to the 1950s press campaigns Bill Bernbach's creative team of Julian Koenig and Helmut Krone created for the VW Beetle and realize that this is an agency with history and a culture of ironic, observational wit. The temptation to go off on one and start talking about fabulous advertising campaigns has once more got too much for me and I have wandered off the point. Volkswagen also used a great deal of direct mail in its campaign strategies, especially in the commercial vehicle sector. This was undertaken with great panache by Barraclough Hall Woolston Grey, a London-based specialist DM agency. Below-the-line campaigns (secondary printed advertising) were undertaken by ABA Partners, a Gloucester-based advertising agency. These included printed brochures, nationwide dealer advertising, driver packs and technical specifications. Digital media was in the hands of a Brighton agency whose name escapes me (sorry guys), and PR was delivered by a Northampton-based consultancy called Presence. On top of this, Volkswagen's media buying ranged from national and European television spots, local and national radio airtime, and national newspaper and magazine press campaigns. In addition, a large volume of local newspaper advertising space was bought on behalf of dealerships. This media strategy and buying was looked after by Carat, a London media firm working alongside DDB London and others to provide the most effective media outlets for the campaign messages. Volkswagen is far from unique and many clients take the same diverse view of their media operations.

Passat. You can't choose your drivers.

Fleet Services

One of several successful campaigns created by DDB London for Volkswagen Passat at the time of its launch.

Image courtesy of DDB London.

Celebrity gossip and church roofs – PR

Of all the media careers that operate under the broad umbrella of advertising, Public Relations has the potential to be the sexiest and most alluring to bright-eyed, star-struck students. Everyone in the public eye needs a good PR consultant by their side. Actually, many celebrity or political clients need their PR 'guru' two steps ahead of them at all times. Maybe it's unlikely that many of you will become involved in building media relationships for the famous and infamous, but let's begin there – if only because I know it will entertain you. Oddly, there are at least two PR maestros who have become well known in their own right. Max Clifford invariably appears in the public consciousness on the side of 'difficult' celebrities. Music PR specialist Nikki Chapman rose to fame due to her appearances on the judging panel of the television talent shows *Pop Stars*, *Pop Stars: The Rivals* and *Pop Idol*, the pioneering instant-fame programmes (the last of which also gave the world Simon Cowell as a media star). Judge for yourselves how far any of these examples are good things. In the world of celebrity PR, Max Clifford is a master of damage limitation. His name is usually connected with a celebrity whose public image has suffered badly (often at their own hands) and is in urgent need of some extensive repair. The media has a love/hate relationship with famous people and can be instrumental in catapulting individuals into the faces of the public, yet at a fell swoop it can also play a distasteful role in destroying that individual. There is no doubt that Jade Goody has been a darling of the British tabloid and gossip-magazine press since her appearance on Channel 4 television's *Big Brother*. Her confused, dubious opinions and desire to enjoy herself in the extreme on national television endeared her to British viewers and, most importantly for her, to the more salacious newspaper and magazine journalists. She enjoyed a considerable period of being famous for, well, being famous really. However, her subsequent appearance some years later on Channel 4 television's *Celebrity Big Brother* was a PR disaster. Her fair-weather friends in the media dined out on the lack of judgement she displayed in her performance on television, as she was damned by gossip columns everywhere as being a bully and a racist. Her private life was put under the media microscope and her perfume brand crashed through the floor. The PR machine was immediately sent into overdrive. Off she went to India, accompanied by an army of journalists, to repair her relationship with the Indian public and the Bollywood star Shilpa Shetty, whom she had appeared to bully and insult on national television. Her PR recovery suffered a tragic twist when she was diagnosed with cancer. With the help of Max Clifford, the world's media turned their attention towards documenting her terminal illness in minute detail. Jade's marriage and death in 2009 were covered extensively by press and television, and image rights were sold to the highest bidder to support her children after her death. In the celebrity arena, PR is open to significant subjective interpretation. Did PR salvage Jade Goody's public image or did it simply manage her public death? In the words of *Big Brother*, 'who knows, you decide'? In some ways, PR can also be

associated with the word 'propaganda'. Most definitions of the word suggest that it is the supply of biased or misleading information, especially in politics. Which brings us neatly on to the term *spin*. The decade spent by Tony Blair as British Prime Minister is synonymous with spin, or was it just damned good PR? Blair's Labour Government mastered the art of managing the media to great effect. The government's *spin doctor* or PR consultant, Alastair Campbell, was responsible for writing some incredibly persuasive and evocative speeches and press releases to manage and build the goodwill of the British public. The manipulation of messages and statistics was integral to the success of Blair's government, which, under its charismatic leader, oozed an irresistible *feelgood factor* across the world's media. In PR terms, the stories of Jade Goody and Tony Blair are extreme examples, yet both display some characteristic traits of just how powerful media management can be. There are many PR consultants and agencies across the globe whose business is dedicated to managing and furthering the public's perception of celebrities. They all have a trusted PR and media manager – from the glittering Hollywood megastars right down to reality-television contestants desperate to be famous whether they have any apparent talent or not. The role that PR plays in their careers is single-minded in its focus, to try to ensure there is always enough interesting material to satisfy the hungry media. When the media turns on the celebrities it has created by publishing unpleasant tales of sexual or drug-related misdemeanours, then PR is on hand to attempt to repair the damage and restore the positive images of their clients.

I suggested at the beginning of this chapter that for many, at certain levels, PR is potentially as glamorous a career as you could have (second only to the rich and famous it represents). In which other working life is it possible to spend every day writing stories about famous people? Actors, politicians and media 'wannabes' thrive on the publicity generated by their expert PR representatives. The music industry too is a head-turner for aspiring young media communicators. Here, though, PR works a little differently. At the top end of the celebrity musician scale, the public image of rock 'n' roll mavericks like Peter Doherty and (in his younger days) Liam Gallagher has been about damage limitation. The PR representatives of music's bad boys work hard to counter the stories of sex, drugs, alcohol and fights. Or do they? Is that not the reason some of music's most legendary mavericks have such an appeal to teenagers? Does PR work hard to sustain the rebellious image? Does it really try to soften and diffuse the media stories? As with every context I have mentioned so far for advertising, it is all about knowing your marketplace isn't it? Fans of Oasis became more loyal and grew in greater numbers every time Liam Gallagher was pictured fighting with his brother, Noel. Stories and images of him bleary eyed and off his face in the early hours of the morning perpetuated the myths surrounding him. Fans everywhere smirked at the outrage, as once again he was caught sneaking from the bedroom of yet another gorgeous but also famous woman. Did someone once say all publicity is good publicity?

At a more 'grassroots' level, music PR is a thriving industry of its own. Bands and artists serious about success will hire a specialist firm to promote their latest activity. A single or album release will be promoted to all that may listen. Underground, independent music publications and websites will all be sent a promotional copy of the CD with a trumpeting, persuasive press release. Similar material will also be despatched to the mainstream music press, to national newspapers and magazines that review music, and to radio and television stations which may be prepared to play the song or screen a video. Again, it is a process of steady growth. Prime-time MTV or daytime BBC Radio 1 are unlikely to play a song by an unknown artist, but a small magazine or blog site will quite possibly write a positive review. The same is true of the film and theatre industries. The common factor that runs through music, celebrity and entertainment PR is a simple one. The consultants who represent, advise and promote such clients fully understand the marketplaces in which they operate. Just to make you feel like the glitz and glamour of these PR worlds are actually achievable, I have had a student who graduated to work in a PR agency dedicated to celebrity publicity. In truth, working in entertainment and lifestyle PR firms is no different to working in any other PR consultancy essentially. You may feel that writing press and online stories about your favourite musician is a much more exciting prospect than a technology product, but the skills and creativity required are pretty much the same – only the target audience and marketplace differ. The worn-down, overworked PR person will not always be any more excited by the news of Katie Price's separation from Peter Andre than by the promotion of summer camping holidays. The reality may often be disappointing!

Let's get back down to earth. What is PR and what do people really do? There is no question that PR and other forms of advertising connect together in the context of placing brands, people and products into the minds of potential consumers. Every piece of communication activity has a unique part to play in persuading those consumers to form opinions and allegiances to brands and to allow them to enter into and form part of their lifestyles. Consumers receive messages in an array of ways, and over time snippets of information gel together to create a balanced view of a brand. No single method of advertising achieves that on its own. Repeatedly viewing a fame-building commercial, being presented with a similar message outdoors or online and then reading and hearing about it via other behaviour-linked media are what real advertising campaigns are about. It is misleading to describe PR as advertising, yet it is impossible to separate them too. Twenty-first-century advertising recognizes that a genuine multimedia communication strategy is essential to allow brands to rise above the chaotic clutter of information consumers receive on a daily basis. Creating a fashion for young people to sport FCUK T-shirts and then have print, online and television media discussing whether they should or not is advertising. Launching a mobile telephone network commercial featuring hundreds of people dancing at a London railway station, posting a YouTube film about how it was filmed and releasing interesting stories about how the idea was

157

conceived and how ordinary people reacted to the event is advertising. Devising an online, branded game and telling magazines dedicated to gaming about it in advance is advertising. It is no longer possible to say that creating television commercials and press advertisements can best sum up advertising. Similarly, PR can no longer be defined as simply writing and issuing stories to newspapers, magazines and television. The business of promotion and communicating with consumers is diverse and integrated. By now you should appreciate that a career in media communication is about understanding consumer behaviour and making strategic and creative decisions as to how best to talk to those consumers. To be successful you must be prepared to be flexible, responsive and innovative in how you can use ideas across many media platforms. Just like traditional advertising agencies, PR has recognized this too. The distribution of news and lifestyle-led stories across the printed press and television networks, and finding new, creative ways to use the online environment, are a vital part of the modern PR process.

Life in PR is varied, multidisciplined and an exciting career prospect. The work may involve a large global brand, a major sporting event, specialist communications for fashion, music and celebrity, charity organizations and even political or environmental pressure groups. Over the course of a single day you could be running a charity event, managing a crisis, schmoozing with the media over lunch or devising brand strategies and corporate image. According to the Chartered Institute of Public Relations (CIPR), PR is about managing reputation: 'The result of what you do, what you say and what others say about you'. Effective media communication can have a huge impact on reputations. Consider the celebrity downfall of the American pop singer Britney Spears, or the public perception of British singer Amy Winehouse. What effect has PR had on the reputation and rise of Barack Obama? How has the British Government in 2009 lost its reputation – what did Tony Blair have that Gordon Brown hasn't? What has been the impact of stories about sweatshops and horror working conditions in Asia been on fashion brands like Gap, Next or Primark? With the possible exception of Max Clifford, PR tends to keep below the radar in order that their clients get the credit and the coverage. But behind every brand there is a steady output of two-way PR striking balanced dialogues with their target consumers. The relationship between journalists, industry writers and PR consultants is a close one. Engaging, effective writing skills are prerequisites, as are accuracy and attention to detail. A carefully planned media communication strategy can turn quickly into a PR crisis if facts are misrepresented. Although a specialized PR agency may have a diverse client list, the consultants it employs often work on specific accounts. Penetrating media releases about technological products require the writer to have a deep understanding of what they are, how they work, what they are for and how they can integrate with other technology. Describing a television as sleek, sexy and ergonomic is great, but be prepared to write about how it works with the internet and the resolution of its screen too. Stating cold technical facts is not good enough – you will need to understand the context and benefits of the specification too. As a

graduate looking for a start in PR there are some basics to consider. First of all, where do you want to work? Basically there are two straight choices: either a PR agency or an in-house role.

The PR agency

To persuade a dedicated PR agency to employ you as a graduate takes as much energy, conviction and creativity as breaking into an advertising agency. Your studies may have included any of the following: advertising, marketing and communications, media communications, PR, journalism or even an English degree. The two fundamental abilities you need to demonstrate are creativity and writing. Bright new ways of communicating with the media and consumers are the lifeblood of PR. Inventive ideas for media strategies, events, publicity stunts and digital communications are what will make you a star in PR. Given that most of the communications you can expect to be involved in are written, you will need to do that exceptionally well. Not just in a grammatical sense but creatively too. Just as with an advertising agency, internships and placements are commonplace. Don't expect to call a PR agency and be offered a permanent job on the spot. They will want to test you and see how you make out. The rules of engagement are similar too – go for agencies that have graduate programmes and invite contact via their websites. PR consultants are typically anal and fastidious about accuracy in writing. Any covering letter, introductory email and cv need to be perfect pieces of correctly spelled and punctuated communication. Don't just rely on spellcheckers either, read the thing aloud and ensure your applications are fluid and read well.

I know it is a creative job in a creative environment, but once again be careful with gimmicky mailouts. A seasoned PR agency director is likely to have seen what you've sent before in some form or other – worse still, they have probably seen it done better too. Send something that wasn't as clever, engaging or witty as you hoped and you've tripped over the first hurdle. Consider your personal credibility as well – covering letters written in pink gel pen, on pink flowery notepaper, will impress no one. This is a business environment where instilling belief in a piece of communication is vital. If potential employers don't believe in you, you're doomed. Do your homework. If you are approaching an agency with a particular specialism in fashion, sport, music or technology, then make sure your portfolio of campaigns reflects that. If necessary, expand your campaigns with additional independent study projects to give you greater flexibility. I can't say this often enough – so I'll say it again. Be open-minded and prepared to learn. A PR internship will probably not see you responding to press coverage of a Z-List reality-television-celebrity client photographed getting out of a car without wearing any knickers (on purpose). Chances are you will be writing reports, mounting examples of coverage, scouring the media for glimmers of coverage, updating intranet or extranet sites and administering campaigns. Developing your understanding of the industry and refining your ability to meet

deadlines and cover every detail are the bedrock on which you can build your sparkling, creative PR career over time. This experience will help you overcome the basic reaction of the general public towards PR. Nip out into the street and ask the first person you see what a PR consultant does and they will probably say 'tell lies'. Actually, that is a pretty good PR exercise for you to think about right now. How can you define what PR is to a public that doesn't care and persuade them it is a valuable career? Answers on a postcard please, or better still on this book's Twitter or Facebook page. You and I both know the answer includes communicating positive messages about a brand into the public consciousness. Or engaging with consumers as part of a brand's media strategy. To the public that is psychobabble or technospeak – don't forget, though, they all know what *spin* means!

One more thing while I think of it, get yourself a digital camera and practicse with it. Especially photographs of people interacting together. Every good PR story needs a good image to go with it. If the best you can come up with either yourself or when briefing a photographer is a forced smile and a phoney handshake then forget it. PR people don't just get jobs on creativity alone – although that makes good ones exceptional – it's the detail, planning and persuasive writing that help make the perfect employee. So, can you cope with PR in its real, more usual form? How do you communicate with farmers through the pages of a specialist magazine and interest them in a new type of cow feed? How do you convince financial advisers through professional websites to once more believe in the lending institutions? How do you maintain positive media coverage for an online or console game that most people think is crap? Once you have ideas on how to present, photograph and write the message you need to get in front of a specific target audience, how do you then get the media to publish it? Two distinct levels of operation here – persuade the media that their readers will be interested, and then persuade the readers to be interested. PR is a brilliant job, isn't it? Filled with creative and persuasive challenges. Ok, let's see the highlights.

To be the perfect PR person you will need to answer yes to all the following questions:

- Are you a 'people person'?
- Can you communicate exceptionally well verbally and in writing?
- Are you organized and disciplined?
- Are you full of creative ideas and imaginative ideas?
- Do you have the ability to research and learn? Are you abreast of events as they are happening? Do you know which features magazines, newspapers and websites are running relative to your client and target audience?
- Do you have patience and loads of commonsense?
- Do you have complete belief in the brands you are publicizing?
- Can you work under pressure and hit deadlines?
- Are you confident and interesting?

You should have plenty of ticks – if so, you have a good place to start. Did you get the 'interesting' word again too? Experience everything and find out all there is to know about a brand and its consumers. While you are about it, read about what everyone else is doing too. Being conversant in contemporary issues, trends and affairs should be second nature to you. There, that should keep you busy for the rest of your career. Don't stop learning just because you've finished university – now is the time to start all over again. Think I might have said that before somewhere . . .

It never ceases to amaze me how many students do not bother to read a daily paper or watch TV News or the occasional current affairs radio or TV programme. For example, the BBC Radio 4's *Today* programme, which still sets the news agenda for many evening papers, or BBC television's *Any Questions* programme.

PR revolves around what is going on around you and the politics and current affairs of the day, both domestic and international. You cannot begin to even understand what PR is about if you are not on top of current business trends and developments. I have chaired interview panels where one of the questions to potential graduate trainees is, 'So tell me what is happening in the news today.' If they could not begin to answer the question, they had little chance of making it to the second round of interviews. So be news aware!'

Robert Minton Taylor, Senior Associate Lecturer,
Leeds Metropolitan University

It is not just me, on some kind of personal crusade, that believes students need to up their intellectual game when it comes to being more socially aware. The advertising and communications industry demands it. Maybe the above quote is a little narrow: everything it says is true, but I think you should be equally inquisitive and involved in the everyday lives of consumers too. As with other advertising, media and marketing disciplines, you have to find ways to stand out in PR too. Specialist skills can be in high demand. Lindsay is a recruitment consultant at Paradigm Staffing, and she has this to say about modern expectations in PR:

We have been getting a lot of requests for PR professionals who have experience with digital and social media. Companies are looking for communications professional who have done more than pitched a few bloggers or developed a client Twitter profile. They are looking for candidate who can strategize and implement digital media programs and integrate then with their traditional communications strategies.

She also suggests that many graduate candidates simply ignore or fail to recognize the basics at interviews:

Preparedness is the number one reason that some candidates do better than others. Recently, many of the very qualified candidates who were dismissed from the interview process had made very basic interviewing errors: talking too much, not dressing appropriately, not researching the company enough prior to the interview or not asking good questions.

PAST PERFECT VINTAGE iPOD

A very clever Oxfordshire company, Past Perfect, has for some while specialised in re-engineering popular music from the 1920s, 1930s and 1940s and releasing it on compilation CDs and MP3 downloads. And although some might argue that the hiss and crackle of 78rpm recordings is, surely, integral to mid-20th-century music, Past Perfect has proved that it is not - its recordings are still loaded with that nostalgic, antique patina, but the engineers have transformed them from black and white, you might say, to colour.

And now, Past Perfect has had the brilliant ruse of installing its entire collection at top digital quality (typically 224 Kbps) onto a customised 8Gb iPod Nano. It has thereby solved at a stroke the next present problem you face with an older relative or friend who just doesn't need another bloomin' foot spa. You also save a few bob; if you bought all the CDs on its Senior Nano individually, the music alone would cost over £600, against the £280 you pay this way, iPod included. The collection you get comprises 1,075 tracks from 290 artists ranging from Sinatra to The Andrews Sisters to Billie Holliday to Fats Waller, Stephane Grappelli and Django Rheinhardt. There are dance compilations, big bands, bebop, sax solos, second world war music and even George Formby, if you must. And you get the latest Nano's brilliant USP, the Shake to Shuffle feature by which you simply give the iPod a shake and get a new random selection of tunes.

Seriously, you do need to consider if the person you're buying this for will be able to manage its controls. The special instructions supplied are good, but I could imagine some older people finding the control wheel too fiddly. A solution would be also to buy one of the squillions of docks on the market that have bigger buttons - and a remote. *£280, from Past Perfect, www.pastperfect.com; 01869-325 052.*

A PR story released by Punch Communications and shown reproduced in *The Financial Times*.

Image courtesy of Punch Communications.

What do the PR agencies have to say, though, and what can you learn from those who are out there doing the job? Pete Goold is the Founder/Managing Director of Punch Communications. His career to date has been diverse.

I've worked at five UK-based PR agencies on a variety of projects with clients such as Microsoft, Sony PlayStation, Kellogg's and Boeing, for example. I have also been involved in crisis management for brands during the British beef crisis and the furore surrounding children drinking alcopops, before setting up Punch Communications in 2003.

Punch is different to any of the agencies that I worked at previously – which were based in Birmingham and London respectively – drawing on the good, of

which there was a great deal, and leaving aside the not-so-good. Specifically we're passionate about delivery and effectiveness, rather than simply going through the motions, which some people in this industry do, sadly. I've been fortunate to have worked throughout the first dotcom boom with brands such as lastminute.com, ft.com, excite and numerous others and Punch currently works with many leading Web 2.0 businesses, both in the UK and further afield. We currently have clients in Germany, Sweden, Dubai and the USA.

In addition to traditional PR services, we offer 'PR 2.0' services, such as SEO for example, which traditionally has been the province of web developers rather than PR agencies. Consequently, at the time of writing, we are the number one Google search result for keywords such as 'PR Company' and 'PR Agency' within the UK and number one in the USA for 'UK PR Agency', amongst other terms.

Given the above online success and other factors, in the past 18 months we've grown from two to ten people – despite the global economic downturn. So, my job has changed throughout that period. Fundamentally I'm a PR person who has managerial and financial responsibilities for the business. Nevertheless, given my character and passion for the job, there's still a large part of me that's an Account Executive at heart, which I think speaks volumes about why I do what I do.

With the greatest of respect to the creative process within the advertising industry, there is a fundamental difference between advertising and PR in that one is paid for and the other negotiated. I have been fascinated by and drawn to the intellectual and creative challenge of the PR industry since my first day in the job.

To do this job I would describe the fundamental skills as needing to have energy, enthusiasm, determination, honesty, humility, a sense of humour and finally creativity. Although members of the team have different levels of experience, Punch is very much a meritocracy. Therefore, accepting the fact that there are some aspects of my job which are about the running of the business, the Account Executive's role overlaps greatly with that of the Account Manager and the Account Director. My advice to graduates is very much to work hard, learn from every available source inside and outside of work and seize every opportunity.

Whilst qualifications are of course fine, be prepared to relearn from the ground up from day one. We see such arrogance amongst some graduates who truly believe they can teach the world how PR should be done. I get far greater satisfaction from working with – and indeed learning from – the hardworking, humble, creative graduates that want to excel and know it's going to take hard work to do so.

One project that we have worked on since the beginning of 2009 is for a Web 2.0 business called Qype (www.qype.co.uk), a business based in Germany and backed by venture capital. We have undertaken a number of activities but in

particular we have been promoting an Apple *iPhone* application called Qype Radar, which is free-to-download and offers Qype's reviews and recommendations for functionality on the go. Our strategy has been to take journalists to the streets, give them an Apple *iPhone* loaded with Radar and set them challenges.

We have done this recently with members of the editorial team from *FHM* (results of which can be seen here: http://london.blog.qype.com/?p=703 and here: http://www.fhm.com/video/all-in-a-days-work/qype-orienteering-fhm-tests-a-new-iphone-app-20090408), *The Financial Times, BA Business Life, The Daily Mail* and *WebUser* magazine.

Ever since the very beginnings of my 15 years in PR, being able to show a client a piece of press coverage or some other result which will make a difference to their business in some tangible way still excites me. At the moment the real differentiator is the ability to call upon leading-edge PR 2.0 services which help raise client visibility online and dovetail with traditional PR. To any graduates who want to do my job, you simply need determination.

Qype updates its mobile reviews app for Android and iPhone

Comments (0)

Reviews site Qype has updated its mobile app 'Radar' with a new version for **Google Android** and a new **iPhone** version due out next week. The major new feature is the ability to post reviews directly fro the app rather than just searching them, which makes absolute sense when most users will want to review while they are at a venue.

Qype's latest mobile app, Radar v2

Reviews can include multiple photos from their phone, and the freeapp saves reviews while they are being written in case someone phones before it has been posted or, as has been known more than a few times, your phone battery dies.

The next step for Qype's app is to include real-time reviews being posted nearby, thus entering the holy grail of location-based and real-time tools in one step. But perhaps external developers will start exploring what's possible there through Qype's API

Posted by Jemima Kiss Thursday 9 April 2009 18.07 BST guardian.co.uk

A larger | smaller

Technology
Mobile phones · iPhone · Research and development · Internet startups

Media
Digital media

More from PDA on

Technology
Mobile phones · iPhone · Research and development · Internet startups

Media
Digital media

More blogposts

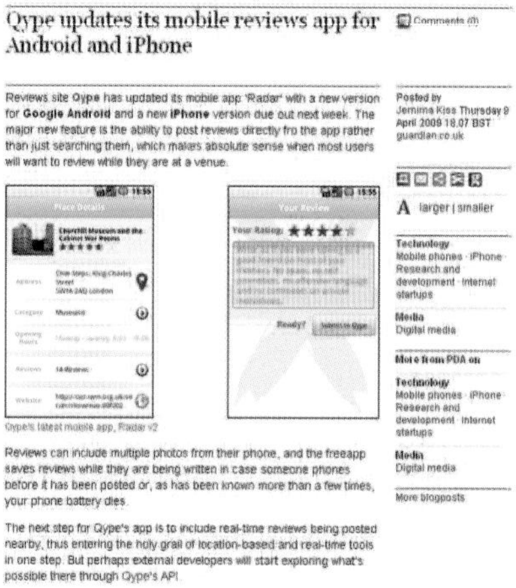

A PR story released by Punch Communications and shown reproduced in *The Guardian* newspaper.

Image courtesy of Punch Communications.

Mark Terry-Lush has been working for 20 years in communications, particularly business-to-business marketing and PR. He has worked both 'in-house' and for several global PR organizations, and was instrumental in launching the UK's first digital TV channels and the sports network Rivals.net. His experience extends into sport too, where he helped Carlsberg build its reputation as a major sporting sponsor, most notably in football with Liverpool Football Club and England. Whilst working with Foster's, the beer brand, he maximized their involvement with Formula 1 motor racing, placing images and stories into several male-orientated magazines. Mark founded Renegade Media in 2001 with a client roster of digital brands and trade organizations. This quickly expanded to include other creative agencies and media companies. Renegade Media now works across many business sectors, including automotive, entertainment, technology and retail, and its current client list features high-profile brands such as Mitsubishi, Sony Ericsson, Sara Lee and Douwe Egberts.

Why does he love his job?

> I ask myself that every day . . . because I'm unemployable elsewhere! I love media, I love the evolving media landscape – I feel plugged in. I also get to travel – China, USA, Europe, Wales . . . I'm my own boss too. But to do this job I need a sharp enquiring mind, skin like a rhino, a mouth like a machinegun and creative flair somewhere between a circus ringmaster and theatre impresario.
>
> Graduates need the same but also to know everything there is to know about the 'next big thing' in media. For me, seeing an idea/angle/concept that one of my team or I came up with end up in print makes it all worth while. As a company we offer clients dedication, passion and understanding of the market and sector. From graduates I need a combination of outstanding writing and creative skills with insight and an open mind.
>
> This is an indication of the kind of work we do for clients at present. Under Armour – launch of first football boots in UK, Ireland, Germany and Austria. We're focused primarily on maximizing the exposure of the launch of two Under Armour football boots and the Under Armour 11 Test Team.

Activities include (but are not limited to)

- **Seeding.** Essentially online PR – getting content published via placing or linking to UA's assets (video, websites, text etc.) published on websites, blogs, forums, social networks of influential interest groups.
- **Search Engine Optimization (SEO).** Ensuring that the Under Armour UA11 site gets as high as possible in search engines, i.e. first pages, and is found when people search for UA football boots.
- **Blogging.** Under Armour's endorsers. We will spark and manage appropriate conversations.
- **Online reputation management.** Monitor the internet for articles, comments and posts that influence the perception of the UA brand/product. We will advise on strategies for dealing with negativity.
- **Blog nesting.** Negotiating for editorial content to be displayed inside or on a blog (so that it appears 'approved' by them) in return for Under Armour assets or product.
- **Social media marketing.** Create and deliver a strategy enabling us to interact with the Under Armour's target audience, make them aware and spread the word about the UA football boots and UA11.

We also represent China's largest advertising and entertainment agency, DMG, and our brief is to *make them famous* in the USA and Western Europe. They've gone from being invisible to being sought after in less than two years.

Mark Terry-Lush, founder and CEO of Renegade Media Ltd

Working 'in-house'

Whilst the principles of communication, reputation building and media management are the same as for PR agencies, working 'in-house' is a totally different, more insular environment. It could be argued that life in a PR agency is more flexible, more diverse and with greater long-term opportunities for promotion. However, working in an in-house PR team is potentially more complex, more stable and sometimes pays better. It is likely that your range of skills will need to be more rounded too – an 'in-house' PR specialist does not have the luxury of a large team to fall back on so you may need to be involved in every activity. In evaluating whether an agency or 'in-house' environment might better serve your career goals ask yourself this: How important is variety to you? Agency clients may be from different market sectors or several different clients in a specialist sector. Working 'in-house' will limit you to promoting the interests of one brand and its range of products, services or messages. Admittedly, that could be almost anything from a mobile phone network to a cinema chain or a breakfast cereal manufacturer to an engineering widget company. The key functions will differ slightly from those of an agency too. Naturally, communicating with the brand's existing and potential consumers will be a major requirement; but so too will communicating with staff, possibly on a global basis, and other suppliers and associates. In addition to external consumer communications, an in-house PR team will maintain the company's intranet and create printed or online newsletters to communicate information to staff about training, vacancies, brand developments and also to organize social events to build staff morale and loyalty. The trick here is to create a sense of security and belonging to assist the brand with staff retention. It may also be necessary to organize business conferences to bring the brand's departments and geographical offices together. Just as an aside, many advertising agencies have an in-house PR team. This serves to communicate news about the agency's account wins and campaigns to the industry and potential clients and to manage external enquiries from the media about issues relating to advertising campaigns. Sometimes it is also necessary to provide spokespeople to appear on television or in the press to speak on broader advertising subjects. I have done this myself in a small way. On two occasions recently I have been interviewed live on local radio to provide 'expert' advertising opinion on behalf of my university. I have spoken about digital advertising in the recession and about an advertising campaign promoting a newly opened designer retail outlet in Gloucester. Occasionally advertising agencies also generate PR coverage on behalf of its clients. Trevor Beattie is particularly good at maximizing creative advertising campaigns by

speaking to the media about them too. Especially the ones that use swear words and cause traffic jams!

As I have stated many times, this book is not a 'how to do', it is a what do you need to know to do it. I think I can best illustrate the possibilities of an in-house PR role by focusing on the activities of an organization that relies heavily on PR to promote and raise awareness of its work. Oxfam is a familiar name in the charity sector and now involves itself in a wide range of global issues. Sam Barratt is Head of Media and has run Oxfam's in-house media unit since 2005. Based in Oxford, the team comprises 15 members of staff who lead on Oxfam's international media campaigns raising public awareness of trade, humanitarian disasters, aid and debt as well as a UK PR team for 750 shops and individual appeals.

Sam has worked for Oxfam since 2000, and been involved in many of Oxfam's highest-profile campaigns as well as events such as Oxfam's response to the tsunami disaster in Indonesia, the WTO meetings in Cancun and the war in Afghanistan. He has travelled and worked widely across the world, spending a year developing Oxfam's media and campaign work in East Africa. Prior to working for Oxfam, Sam worked for more than three years in corporate public relations. Like virtually every advertising and media professional I have ever met, Sam loves his work:

> I enjoy the breadth, international politics that swirl around it and the difference that campaigning and our programmes can make to poor people. I do this with tenacity, by influencing and by being creative. In my experience, graduates need to demonstrate an ability to do lots of different jobs that demonstrate energy and impact in their work and have genuine drive. When preparing for an interview they must really know what job they are applying for and drag up all their relevant experience which shows why they can do the job.
>
> I never fail to be excited by my work and press coverage that really stirs things up or emergencies that mean that you have to think and respond fast give me a huge thrill.

Even though Sam is employed 'in-house', the diversity of work presented by Oxfam's far-reaching involvement in world affairs is every bit as challenging as the variety of client accounts held by PR agencies. Don't get sniffy, an 'in-house' PR post is a job to be cherished and should form an integral part of your post-graduation get-a-job strategy. Here are just a few snapshot examples of campaigns Sam has been responsible for over the past year or so. They are extracts from 'live' media releases created by Oxfam's PR and media team and are reproduced as they were written and subsequently posted by their recipients.

Image courtesy of Oxfam GB.

YouTube if you want to

Oxfam's YouTube advertising contest on climate change is inspiring young filmmakers to create great work, Ian Sullivan reports.

840 videos. 48 hours. One massive issue and one huge meeting to mobilize people around. I've spent two days watching them and they've got two weeks to get them viewed as many times as possible.

It's the YouTube *Cannes Young Lions* advertising contest and people have been making videos about the *UN Climate Change Summit* in Copenhagen this December. You know the one – it'll decide our fate.

My friends don't have any sympathy for me when I tell them that I've been watching YouTube at work – constantly – but it has been a challenge. Video, after video, after video we've watched. There's the totally random, plenty of superheroes, great animations and the completely daft. There was also a lot of toilet humour. The link between bodily functions and climate change is disturbingly strong in some people's heads.

But mostly we've been totally amazed at the thought, skill and effort that's gone into them. Go to YouTube *Cannes Lions* and have a look. It's well worth it.

There's another week to go until we find a winner. So have a look and forward the ones you like onto your friends. You could make the difference as the aspiring filmmakers try and get their video viewed.

I really want to put in links to my favourites but I'll have to wait at least a week so that we don't get accused of favouritism.

Get involved: *climate change*

Control Arms campaign

The unregulated international arms trade fuels conflict, poverty and serious human rights abuses around the world. It's enough to make people want to campaign – hard. So they do.

Killer facts

1. In an average year, small arms kill around a third of a million men, women and children – and leave hundreds of thousands more injured, disabled, traumatized and grieving
2. 1,000 people die each day from armed violence, and hundreds of thousands more are displaced, maimed or lose their livelihood.
3. Seven of the G8 countries are among the biggest global arms exporters.

Press photograph for the launch of Oxfam's Control Arms campaign.

Image courtesy of Oxfam GB.

Why campaign on the arms trade?

Armed violence – whether in the form of war, community conflict, or domestic abuse – seriously limits people's ability to earn a living, grow crops and benefit from education.

The result is that years of development are rapidly undone, and spending on arms diverts billions of dollars that could be spent on vital services like health and education.

Without tougher controls, arms will continue to fuel violence, perpetuate war, human rights abuses and poverty worldwide.

How we're doing it

In 2003, Oxfam launched its Control Arms campaign in alliance with IANSA & Amnesty International – part of a global push for tighter regulation of the arms trade.

Since then, countless publicity events, demonstrations and high-level lobbying initiatives, including our Million Faces visual petition, have kept leaders and decision-makers under pressure to act, and control the flow of weapons around the world.

Success

In June 2006, our Million Faces petition was presented to UN Secretary General Kofi Annan.

And in December of that year, three years of tireless campaigning finally paid off – 153 governments voted at the UN General Assembly to begin work towards an historic, legally binding international Arms Trade Treaty.

What now

Getting agreement to work towards an Arms Trade Treaty is truly fantastic progress.

During the negotiation stages to come at the UN, however, some governments will try to weaken any treaty – as they're against stricter controls on the arms trade.

We need to keep pressing them, to make sure they don't succeed.

Double-edged prices: lessons from the food price crisis – 10 actions developing countries should take

October 16, 2008 at 12:01 am.

Bangladesh floods – Ibrahim Khalil taking up rice seedlings for replanting elsewhere.

Image courtesy of Jane Beesley/Oxfam GB.

The recent sharp increase in food prices should have benefited millions of poor people who make their living from agriculture. However, decades of misguided policies by developing country governments on agriculture, trade and domestic markets – often promoted by international financial institutions and supported by donor countries – have prevented poor farmers and rural workers from reaping the benefits of higher commodity prices. As a result, the crisis is hurting poor producers and consumers alike, threatening to reverse recent progress on poverty reduction in many countries. To help farmers get out of poverty while protecting poor consumers, developing country governments, with the support of donors, should invest now into smallholder agriculture and social protection.

Push the Prime Minister to Copenhagen

7 December 2009. Copenhagen. A momentous time and place on the journey to fight climate change. The date when the world will choose how to replace the Kyoto Treaty – the existing international treaty for tackling climate change.

The stakes couldn't be higher. 15,000 officials from 200 countries will gather. But as it stands, there will be one or two sad-looking empty chairs.

Nudge him in the right direction

Key world leaders haven't yet made a commitment to attend the UN Climate Change Conference. Gordon Brown is one of them.

We need you to send the Prime Minister an urgent message telling him he must be there to make sure any deal on climate change puts poor people first.

Your email will go directly to Number 10. Every email gives the PM another nudge. Every nudge pushes him one step closer to Copenhagen.

May 2008 TBC: Oxfam launches 'She Changes Lives' campaign

This celebrity-backed campaign will highlight the importance of women health and education workers in the developing world and call for greater investment. Photographs and quotes from high-profile female celebrities, including Rachel Stevens, Mariella Frostrup and Edith Bowman, will be available.

Image courtesy of Oxfam GB.

So there you have it, real-world PR and media releases from a global, campaigning charity – all generated from a creative, dynamic team who are absolutely dedicated to their work. Of course, a career as part of an 'in-house' PR team doesn't always begin for graduates (or even end) with a job at such a high-profile organization. That is not meant to be disparaging in any way; equally dedicated, creative media campaigns are implemented from the PR office of an almost limitless variety of businesses. Chris Pitt was a graduate from my first-ever Advertising teaching group. Whilst his story may not from the outside appear quite as glamorous, he is just as

inventive and just as dedicated to promoting his organization as anyone else and finds his work just as valuable and fulfilling.

When I first left university I joined Cheltenham & Gloucester, the mortgage provider, as a communications executive. I was responsible for many aspects of internal communications, including writing and overseeing production of a staff magazine. I made a move to the company's PR department, where I wrote press releases and feature articles, met journalists and helped to manage C&G's external profile. I then moved to join Ecclesiastical Insurance, the leading insurer of Church property. I started as a press officer tasked with maintaining profile as a Church insurer but also building the profile of the company as a leading insurer of care homes, charities, schools and heritage properties. I was also responsible for promoting the company's personal insurance products, such as wedding cover and financial advice service, including a range of ethical investment funds. I am now PR Manager at Ecclesiastical responsible for managing external reputation, dealing with issues and giving the company a bigger and clearer voice in the outside world.

I enjoy writing so I looked for a career that involved this skill. PR was a natural choice. It's also a people business, so it's all about building and maintaining relationships. I'm passionate about making a difference through your work. I saw an opportunity to play an important part in a company through a PR role.

To be successful in PR above all else you need good written and verbal communications skills. Your written and spoken words need to inform and influence. You need to have the confidence to state your case to senior managers and you need to set out clear communication strategies that work.

You need a journalistic nose for a story and you must be tenacious in pursuit of interesting issues regardless of how elusive or complex they are.

In the past, PR people have rarely come from a PR training background. This is mainly because there wasn't any formal PR training, but also because a wide experience, open mind and strong communications ability are more important than on-paper qualifications. However, more recently university degrees and CIPR courses are teaching the right technical skills, which complement natural ability. So, increasingly, formal qualifications are important. However, a good creative ability, strong writing skills and impressive interpersonal skills are all-important.

Understand a company inside out – examine the issues it is facing, those it might face in the future and prepare some thinking about how you might tackle them. You don't need answers, just clear thoughts about how you might generate and maintain the right kind of debate which will support that company's future. Show your ability to understand complex issues quickly and interpret them. Impress with your passion for communicating.

A typical project for me would run something like this.

Press images showing spokesperson Ian Wainwright for Ecclesiastical's Metal Theft campaign for churches.

Images courtesy of Ecclestiastical Insurance.

Metal Theft campaign for churches.

Following a massive surge in thefts of metal from churches (mainly lead from roofs) we launched a campaign to help churches protect themselves. We linked up with a high-tech security company, SmartWater, to supply churches with security-marking kits. These kits permanently and uniquely marked lead so it could be traced back to the exact church it was stolen from. We launched the campaign at several churches in the most hard-hit areas of the country. Media interest was massive: Sky News, BBC, ITV, national newspapers, specialist trade magazines, local and regional papers all featured the story and interviews with Ecclesiastical spokespeople. The campaign reassured and supported the Church and helped to reduce thefts.

For me, changing minds and behaviour is the biggest thrill of working in PR. Bringing an important issue to the public's attention, encouraging people to act differently or unearthing an issue which should not be ignored. Without good publicity (and I emphasize good) the really important issues in this world wouldn't reach the surface. Equally, PR creates a great deal of 'noise' that draws attention away from what is actually worth hearing about. The challenge is to cut through this and make yourself heard.

As an 'in-house' PR my 'client' is Ecclesiastical. PR helps Ecclesiastical to build a better understanding with its customers. PR complements the full creative mix of advertising and marketing. I'm a little biased, but I believe PR goes much further. It doesn't just inform, it discusses. Which means you're not just telling customers, you're inviting them to share their views with you. It creates a much more inclusive relationship that strengthens the bond you have, increases advocacy and encourages customers to stay with you longer.

To my mind the most important skills I need are perseverance. Life isn't simple. The media debate is complicated. To be in PR you have to want to be part of it. So you need to raise issues and deal with criticism. There are rarely any clear-cut or simple answers, so you need to maintain your enthusiasm in the midst of a complicated and evolving debate.

Chris Pitt – PR Manager, Ecclesiastical Insurance

The media messiahs – media planning

The final piece in the career puzzle, which works both within the advertising agency and at specialist external agencies, is the art of media planning. The most direct definition of media planning I can come up with is: the achievement of marketing and advertising objectives by the creative selection of media platforms. Clearly, whether the media planner is working for an advertising agency or has been commissioned, the relationships and decision-making are the same. The process has a

synergy with the creative development of campaign ideas and also with the proposition devised by the account planners. The media suggested by and subsequently bought by the media planning and buying agency or team has to reflect the strategic, creative and budget objectives exactly. The job of a media planner may include analysing target audiences, keeping abreast of media developments, reading market trends and understanding motivations of consumers (often including psychology and neuroscience). This is starting to get boring now. Actually no it isn't. Notice how media planning shares precisely the same criteria as an account planner, a creative team or a PR consultant – understand everything that is going on in media and with consumers, and make yourself more interesting with a range of cultural and social experiences up your sleeves. If I have to say that again, I will scream. I am painfully aware that in a face-to-face teaching environment students do not wholly take this message on board – because I have now said it so often, you will, won't you? Please. It's for your own benefit.

You may find on your hunt for opportunities in media that media planners are actually not even called that any more. Brand planners, communication planners, strategic planners – if media is your passion look out for those job titles and descriptions. Most media experts would also agree that the job has got a whole lot more challenging in recent times. The days when media planning was about booking television spots when there were only two channels to choose from and suggesting a few poster sites and magazine titles have gone forever. This reflects a shift away from 'traditional' media planning to a more holistic approach. The planner now has to consider above-the-line media such as TV, print, radio and outdoor, PR, below-the-line media, in-store, digital media, product placement and other emerging communications channels. The objective is always to ensure the client's advertising budget is well spent, as well as adhering to the overall marketing and advertising strategy devised by agencies, consultants or the clients themselves. The demands on time and the pressure have gone through the roof for media planners – negotiating a great rate for television spots, though still part of the process, is not enough any more. As I said, many media planners operate from within advertising agencies. Global organizations of the calibre of Initiative Worldwide, Carat, ZenithOptimedia, Starcom, Mindshare and OMD are examples of stand-alone media-planning agencies for consumer brands. The burgeoning increase in media and ever-emerging technologies has created an increasingly fragmented range of media platforms for advertising to take advantage of. Many media companies now specialize in what are known as 'vertical markets' – for example, Communications Media Inc. is known and respected in advertising for its creative use of media in the pharmaceutical industry and the complex legal issues that burden advertising within that sector. Others may emphasize their great planning and buying strengths as being in the digital lead-generation market; others may have extensive knowledge of multilingual campaigns. Strategic Media in Washington DC specifically handles political campaign media buying, which requires special expertise due to legal restrictions on advertising expenditure and other campaign finance regulations.

Simon Williams is head of digital strategy at Carat Ltd, one of London's highest-profile media agencies. His journey into media is an interesting one:

> I went straight out of college into media at Capital Radio in London. After two years learning about the industry (sales, audience analysis, research, creativity, planning) I joined Carat, one of the biggest media agencies, as a planning executive. I've been there ever since, though I'm now the head of digital strategy.
>
> I'm lucky. While my job can be frustrating, I'm actually interested in the industry I work in and get a lot of leeway as to how I decide to move things forward. To do my job I need to be able to understand and make sense of a lot of contrary data very quickly. To frame complex issues in simple terms. To present arguments compellingly. To be interesting.
>
> Graduates wishing to get into media need to have quick thinking, be ambitious, very curious and constantly looking to absorb new knowledge. I guess they would probably already be cultivating a role and a reputation in communities and planning conversations online. However, I am the worst person to give advice on interview techniques. I suck at interviews. People tell me that the best thing to do is write out a bunch of questions you could get asked and that you want to ask them about, and then have a go at writing answers.
>
> Recently I've been leading a project to create a game for 10–12-year-olds with the DfT (Department for Transport). It's basically designed to get kids applying their knowledge of the green cross code (which they find boring and baby-ish) in a new, fantastical context. The idea is that by reframing this simple behaviour as something they *want* to do (to succeed in the game) they will apply it more generally in real life. The process of solving a problem/getting buy-in to a really big idea is what I enjoy most.
>
> In media and at Carat, I think it is important to offer challenges to clients' view of the world, a complete focus on their consumers' real behaviour and attitudes, and the ability to make stuff happen. I do that by being curious, thinking quickly and being adaptable to changing circumstances.

As with PR and to some extent advertising creatives and planners, experts in digital media are in particular demand. As advertising continues to explore bigger, better and even more effective digital strategies, media will continue to change rapidly. Future areas of digital specialization, especially in the advertising-savvy USA, are beginning to become reality with a new breed of media planners understanding and implementing behavioural planning techniques, advertising network marketing specialists, social media specialists and SEO/SEM/PPC experts. The frenzied growth

of the digital market has created a new generation of media *bright-young-things* who offer clients only online media solutions – most notably Avenue A, Razorfish and Centro, who managed the digital media buying for Barack Obama's successful Presidential campaign. There's that man Obama again, plum in the middle of all that is new and exciting in media communications. A new type of politician for a more sophisticated media landscape.

The combination of innovative media thinking and consumer-focused analysis and research is at the core of effective media strategies. Complex programmes of online communication that challenge and test the creativity of media planners can easily be followed the next day by sourcing a nationwide campaign of taxi advertising. As with all creative media professions, variety is very much the spice of life. Broadly speaking, the skills required to rise high in media fall into two activity areas: preparation and implementation. Put simply, researching and working out how to do it, then doing it imaginatively and with style. Here's a quick list of what you might expect to do if media planning is your thing:

Preparation

- working with the client and the account team to understand clients' business objectives and advertising strategy
- liaising with the advertising agency team, clients and consumers to develop media strategies and campaigns
- making decisions on the best form of media for specific clients and campaigns
- applying detailed knowledge of media owners in a range of geographical locations
- thinking creatively about ways to represent particular clients
- undertaking research using specialist industry resources
- researching and analysing data to translate ideas into a quantifiable task
- identifying target audiences and analysing their characteristics, behaviour and media habits
- presenting proposals, with media and cost schedules to clients.

Implementation

- recommending the most appropriate types of media to use, as well as the most effective time spans and locations
- working with colleagues, other departments and media buyers either in-house or in a specialist agency
- making and maintaining good contacts with media owners, such as newspapers, magazines and websites (and taxis!)
- managing client relationships to ensure respect and trust in your judgement
- proof-reading advert text and content prior to release

- maintaining detailed records
- developing evaluation techniques for your campaigns.

The kind of university courses aspiring media people consider are the same as agency account teams and PR people. Advertising, media communications, marketing and communications are all good places to start. The funny thing is, in my experience students are often only dimly aware that media planning even exists prior to choosing a course, and get turned onto media during their learning process. Some don't even know they want to do it until they get offered a job. This happened with a student I knew, who, after graduating from my advertising course, got her first job in the media department at MTV. Have and develop the right skills. You will need to know plenty about advertising – including a deep understanding of brands, products and media platforms. Media planners know about branding and can be heavily involved in strategies to brand or rebrand specific products. You should have great people skills, as you will be working closely with clients and advertisers to make a campaign happen, quite literally.

Get some experience and start building it from different directions if necessary. Media planners often start at advertising agencies working in account management or planning. If you can, take an internship or placement with an advertising agency. It does not have to be directly related to media planning right away. What is more important is that you get experience working in the industry, understanding how every aspect of it works, and then climbing the ladder to hit your own personal highs.

To get a job all the basic rules we've discussed elsewhere in this book apply, and yes you too will need a portfolio. One that explores a range of media strategies for a wide spread of brands.

In easy-to-assimiliate terms, a media strategy may include these elements:

- take the campaign briefing from the client and build the business strategy by liaising with the creative team, the client and consumers
- identify the target audience
- identify the best media for advertising a particular product or service
- set advertising budgets and oversee costs
- liaise with media sales staff and arrange for the advertisements to be seen and heard by the highest possible number of the target audience at the lowest possible price
- assess the effectiveness of the campaign.

In some advertising and media agencies, planning and buying are separate departments and are carried out by different individuals. So if you think you can wave your creative wand across a rapidly changing and emerging media world and make brilliant creative concepts come alive in front of as many consumers as possible, maybe media is for you.

According to the COI (Central Office of Information, a UK government department) Chief Executive Carol Fisher, an integral part of their advertising policy is to create an equal partnership between creative and media-planning agencies.

> There is a need for media planning to move up the agenda. Creative agencies and media planners need to recognize the increasing importance of specialist audiences and make this central to their strategic planning.

Mindshare is a global media agency which was formed from the media departments of Ogilvy & Mather and JWT in 1999. It is renowned across the world for its inventive and highly effective media strategies. To conclude this chapter and to put into context the impact creative media planning can have on advertising around the world, I have reproduced below some campaign case studies from Mindshare's portfolio. Notice how they stray into PR territory too.

Nike Human Race

The challenge was to promote the Nike *Human Race* in Istanbul to a population that did not see running as part of their sporting culture. The solution involved creating a paid-for media partnership including traditional advertising spots on TV, in newspapers, in magazines, online and on mobile phones with 'out-of-home' activity on 150 bridges in Istanbul. Results were astounding, with over 30,000 people applying to take part!

Human Race was the first big running event in Turkey, a country with a non-existent running culture. Nike wanted to use this global event to get a non-running nation think and talk about running, create a base for upcoming running campaigns and activities, and build a direct association between the sport and their brand. The primary challenge was getting 10,000 people to run.

We needed to encourage the local population, whilst maintaining alignment with the global strategy for the *Human Race*. It was decided that to inspire the city, the impactful use of media wasn't enough. A campaign involving celebrities with whom the target audience associate themselves was designed.

Platform/idea

Nike *Human Race* 2008 was a global phenomenon and this was a truly localized version of that event strictly catering to the Turkish market. We knew that the target audience of non-athletes would need reminders of their lack of motivation and so we tailored the strategy around this idea.

A cross-media partnership facilitated this process. A deal of this type was unique within the local market. The Dogan Group agreed to a central deal for all the media

we needed in the campaign. They gave us their celebrities, agreed to produce, promote and air the celebrity spots, engaged their columnists to write about the event and integrate the event story into their programmes, serials, news and talk shows. Our online strategy included both display and social networking advertising. The outdoor campaign raised awareness with strategically placed messages at busy traffic spots.

Government support came from the ability to harness the event to promote the nation's health. Government endorsement further raised the profile of the event as we were given permission to run over the famous Bosphorus Bridge for the first time ever. Streets were closed down on the day of the race. This endorsement promoted the merits of the campaign to an even wider audience.

Consumer journey

Our partnership with Dogan included access to nine television stations, five newspapers, 13 monthly magazines and six online sites.

Each of the television stations produced customized spots promoting the event with their in-house talent. The same message ran through all the TV material, that this was an opportunity to get involved in a local event that was part of a global spectacle. The script editors were instructed to include reference to Nike *Human Race* in programming wherever possible. On one of the Dogan music channels (the largest TV broadcaster in Turkey), the planning and preparation of every Video DJ for the event was filmed and shown on-air to increase the exposure.

Five newspapers and 11 columnists were involved in the promotion of the experience, each columnist putting a different spin on the event. The PR surrounding the event appeared in all local media, including editorial pieces on television, in print and online. The celebrity association was key in creating the level of interest and coverage.

Online we used interactive banner ads to promote the event and encourage people to do more than just observe. The event was also integrated as a mini-game into one of the biggest social networks. Mobile was used for location-based MMS messaging, which was sent to the Nike database. Wap banners also led to an event Wap page where people could find Nike *Human Race* videos and event information.

A major wow factor was that the municipality-owned bridges and overcrosses were used for the first time by any brand: 150 bridges and overcrosses throughout the city were dominated by the *Human Race*.

Results

On the day, the full 10,000 places were taken for the *Nike Human Race* in Istanbul, countering the cultural norm. The event was three times oversubscribed in this

supposedly lethargic city and, due to the promotion, 860,000 individuals visited the bespoke Nike *Human Race* website.

The uplift in sales of Nike Plus (Nike's iPod compatible running product) was beyond expectations, with 5,000 Nike Plus kits sold in Istanbul over three months during the campaign – the equivalent to the total amount of units sold during the previous two years. Overall this was a spectacular achievement, with the whole city embracing the brand, the event and the sport, paving the way for similar activity in the future on both a personal and city-wide level.

Everest: Beyond the Limit

Two climbers spent two weeks living, eating and sleeping on a 7.2 metre platform extending from a billboard advertising the Discovery Channel's new series called *Everest: Beyond the Limit.*, 16 metres above a busy Budapest road junction.

Press image from Mindshare's
Beyond Everest PR campaign.

Images courtesy of Mindshare.

The Discovery Channel was looking to promote its groundbreaking six-part docu-soap, focusing on a group of mountaineers ascending to the roof of the world in *Everest: Beyond the Limit*, in the cluttered Hungarian marketplace.

The channel and the programme aimed to increase recognition among young urban males and to ensure awareness of Discovery's core values of taking the viewer to the extreme. They also aimed to prove 'Discovery is now closer, more connected and relevant to Hungarian viewers.'

To cut through, the campaign needed to stand out from the competition; this was achieved in a very literal sense. Discovery brought endurance to life.

Creative execution

Whilst on the platform, the two climbers kept a daily blog written on laptops with wireless connections and also replied to SMS messages from the public. The experience was featured in the Budapest *Metro* newspaper and in a regular radio slot on a Budapest-based radio station.

Target audience

The Discovery Channel was looking to engage young urban males not only to *Everest: Beyond the Limit*, but also to its wider programming and channels.

This was achieved through the combination of the extreme-sport representation of the campaign, online and SMS applications, PR exposure in urban print titles targeting young professionals and the Roxy Radio segment, which targeted young urbanites. These elements combined to make a highly focused campaign.

Effectiveness

The outdoor campaign showed that perception of the Discovery Channel was up 87.8 per cent, with total preference up by 155.1 per cent and total activation increased by 178 per cent compared to the category average.

The programme attracted a 400 per cent increase in the target young urban male audience, according to AGB/Advantedge.

Virgin Mobile – 'Think Hatke' – 'Think Differently'!

A 'live' Bollywood film as a brand launch vehicle! In a market with significant mobile network players, a 'Hatke' or 'Different' approach was needed to launch Virgin Mobile and to cut through to the Indian youth target. Research revealed that Indian youth has a fascination for Bollywood and celebrities. The team in India planned the launch around the world's first 'live shoot and broadcast' of a Bollywood flick!

The draws for the film were the beautiful star Neha Duphia and a mysterious International Celebrity (eventually unveiled as Sir Richard Branson). A young, star cast was selected from across the country via auditions with a huge media build-up. The movie was titled *Andaz Apna Very Hatke* or *We are Very Different*. Channel V was the chosen media partner in keeping with its popularity amongst the Indian youth.

Creative execution

Like any mega blockbuster release, a marketing blitz preceded the premiere. On D-Day, the TV viewers got a sneak peek into the rehearsals, make-up and last-minute panic before the 'live' film was aired on Channel V.

The film shot as a single sequence featured seven magnificent sets with continual action captured by 50 cameras and a crew of 500.

The typical Bollywood potboiler featured a poor boy–rich girl romance, with the father forcing her to marry the rich villain. The villain kidnapped the unwilling girl, and the boyfriend rushed to her rescue. When overpowered by the villain, Sir Richard, the saviour, came crashing through a glass door to their rescue. He got shot, but was saved as the bullet struck his Virgin Mobile handset. The lovers are reunited, thanks to Virgin Mobile and Sir Richard Branson!

Target audience

Virgin Mobile is aimed at Indian youth aged 15–24 – a tough target to reach given the barrage of messages they face across various media platforms. The idea was to speak to them in a very 'Hatke' (different) manner, yet build an immediate connection that they found relevant.

The media blitz across appropriate platforms offered them a unique opportunity to act alongside a Bollywood heroine and an international male celebrity or to view the telecast 'live' on TV.

The build-up lent a high talkability quotient even as the promotion of the film started. PR, online, radio and TV combined to build word of mouth, raise anticipation levels and ensure tune-ins.

Effectiveness

The 'live' Bollywood flick featuring Richard Branson and the brand at the climax ensured lasting impact. It is estimated that the piece was viewed by 10 million people, and the PR value was priceless, maximizing brand recall, connection and relevance among consumers.

There is a career choice to be made within PR and media planning, but the good news is that you can change at anytime. Whether you work inside an advertising agency or for a specialist PR or media agency is entirely up to you. If you prefer to ply your PR and media trade directly for an organization and work 'in-house', feel free. The land of opportunity is yours to visit. Remember, the skills and experience you develop will allow you to move from agency to 'in-house' and back again if you wish.

Some websites to visit

Here are some sites to help you keep up to date with a variety of PR and media news and comment. There are many more, so feel free to use Google and YouTube if you want to!

Information and news sites

Oxfam UK www.oxfam.org.uk
Chartered Institute of Public Relations www.cipr.co.uk
International Public Relations Association www.ipra.org
The Press Association www.pressassociation.co.uk
The Foreign Press Association www.foreign-press.org.uk
News Associates www.newsassociates.co.uk
American News Project www.americannewsproject.com
Cable News Network www.cnn.com
USA Today www.usatoday.com

Interesting PR agencies to start your ball rolling

Punch www.punchcomms.com
Renegade Media www.renegademedia.net
Golly Slater www.gollyslater.com
Pink Mango www.pinkmangopr.com
PHA Media www.pha-media.com
10 Yetis www.10yetis.co.uk
Alison Brod PR www.alisonbrodpr.com
Supersonic www.supersonicpr.com
Weber Shandwick www.webershandwick.co.uk
Edelman www.edelman.com
BBC www.bbc.co.uk/radio1/onemusic/pr
Lander PR www.landerpr.com
Fashion PR www.fashionpr.co.uk
Boudoir PR www.boudoir-pr.com

A selection of media agencies

The Specialist Works www.TheSpecialistWorks.com
TCS Media Planning www.tcsmedia.co.uk
Space & Time Media www.spaceandtime.eu.com
MindShare www.mindshareworld.com
Carat UK www.carat.co.uk

Industry magazine websites

www.prweek.com
www.mediaweek.co.uk
www.medialifemagazine.com

Some books to read

PR Power: Inside Secrets from the World of Spin (Virgin Business Guides)
Sir Richard Branson (Foreword), Amanda Barry (Author)

The New Rules of Marketing and PR: How to Use News Releases, Blogs, Podcasting, Viral Marketing and Online Media to Reach Buyers Directly
David Meerman Scott

PR 2.0: New Media, New Tools, New Audiences
Deirdre Breakenridge

The Fall of Advertising and the Rise of PR
Laura Ries and Al Ries

PR in Practice: Public Relations: A Practical Guide to the Basics
Philip Henslowe

Press Releases Are Not a PR Strategy
Linda B. VandeVrede

The Media Handbook: A Complete Guide to Advertising Media Selection, Planning, Research and Buying
Helen Katz

Advertising Media A-to-Z: The Definitive Resource for Media Planning, Buying and Research
Jim Surmanek

Get involved

Share your interview and placement experiences and learn from everyone else on my book's Facebook and Twitter pages:

- search Facebook for 'Advertising Its Business Culture and Careers'
- www.twitter.com/adculture

8 Big sticks and chocolate – life as a client

On the whole, students who choose to study advertising and media communications in all the guises I have looked at so far, tend to dream of life in an agency environment. The 'work hard, play hard' culture inherent in all those I have encountered in my career is attractive to young people. The jeans and T-shirt dress code of creative studios, where music plays all day long, is a world away from the offices perhaps your parents work in. There is a streak of rebellion that flows through agency culture and the inhabitants are fiercely proud of the creative environment they spend their days in. Clients visiting agencies often feel slightly jealous of the liberating atmosphere and somewhat anarchic working practices. Working in an agency is fun – it has to be to sustain and nurture the creativity the work demands. However, particularly when exploring the roles of PR and media people, we have seen that a career in advertising does not necessarily have to be agency based. If your career road leads towards brand management or marketing management, then you will not work in an agency environment. Not as an employee anyway.

A good grounding in advertising, marketing and communications can move your chair around to the other side of the desk – the client side. This is an attractive prospect to some students who crave the cut and thrust of the advertising industry but who do not see themselves working in an advertising agency. A position in brand or marketing management in some ways offers the best of both worlds – strategic thinking about a brand and the opportunity to work with advertising people. There is one big difference – you would be the client and hold all the aces. The incessant, chaotic and generally noisy advertising agency can change in an instant when clients are in. It's a bit like the Queen visiting your school; suddenly all the hedges get trimmed, the kerbstones are painted and the broken window is mended. Perhaps less of a facade is necessary if an agency has worked with a client for a long time – then the culture, dress code and ambience of the agency are familiar and accepted. If prospective new clients visit, then expect big changes. The account management team will be dressed to kill, the fresh coffee machine is dusted off and the technology for the presentation will be tested to within an inch of its life. Every agency has its own way of looking after clients; some are even very involving, inviting clients to 'away' days and 'fun' days. A direct marketing agency I once worked at was famous among its clients for cakes. They were 'custom' made for client meetings by a bakery around the corner and designed for the occasion. This usually involved colour coding them to the client's brand colours. Also, lunches, drinks and dinner at fancy restaurants are the norm when it comes to schmoozing clients. Back at the agency, working lunches are good news for all staff because this usually involves left-over plates of sandwiches and cakes finding their way into the studios of ravenous creatives and designers.

Often, an advertising agency's first exposure to a new client is an invitation to present creative work at a 'pitch'. There are a couple of variations on the pitch process – a large client may issue a media release to the advertising and marketing press inviting agencies to register their interest in pitching for the business. Typically the media release will go something like: 'Brand X to put £20 million soap powder account out to pitch'. Income of that size is very attractive to agencies, and the time and money invested in a competitive pitch can be well worth the risk. Once the client has reviewed the agency responses, it will create a shortlist. Alternatively, some clients prefer to define their shortlist first, quietly, and then invite a small number of agencies to pitch. I have a copy of a television documentary that I show to students about the pitch process. It tells the story of a marketing team from Psion, the 'palm' or hand-held computer company. The team's approach was to firstly create a shortlist of three agencies against specific criteria. They decided that this should include their existing advertising provider, a very large, well-known agency and a new, energetic advertising agency. They conducted what are known as 'chemistry' meetings first of all. This involved visiting their selected agencies (often last thing on a Friday afternoon to ensure wine and not coffee was on the boardroom table) to assess how they felt about the agency staff they would be working with and the kind of professional relationship they might expect. Personal chemistry is a totally subjective issue, but in my experience a stimulating and close business relationship with a client usually produces the best creative results – getting on with someone on a personal level and having mutual respect is the soundest basis I know for long-term business interaction. Following the 'chemistry' meetings, the Psion team issued a pitch brief to the agencies and arranged a day for the presentations to take place. These were to be held at Psion's headquarters. The cost of pitching can be high for agencies – £15,000–£20,000 and beyond is not uncommon. Larger agencies often involve themselves in pitch 'theatre', going just that bit further to impress possible clients.

Psion's brand image relies on strong visuals and putting the product at the forefront.

Image courtesy of Psion Teklogix.

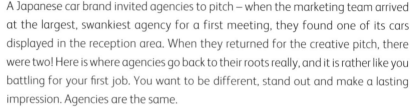

A Japanese car brand invited agencies to pitch – when the marketing team arrived at the largest, swankiest agency for a first meeting, they found one of its cars displayed in the reception area. When they returned for the creative pitch, there were two! Here is where agencies go back to their roots really, and it is rather like you battling for your first job. You want to be different, stand out and make a lasting impression. Agencies are the same.

Agency.com creative director takes her turn to speak in the infamous Subway pitch video.

Image courtesy of Agency.com.

Another client decided to run all its chemistry meetings in one day just before Christmas. By the end of the third meeting they were flagging after three large plates of mince pies had been presented to them. The fourth and final agency was smart and anticipated this. They gave their prospective clients reviving mulled wine instead. The moral of the story? A little thought can go a very long way. The agency pitch will be based around the ideas that have been developed both strategically and creatively to further the client's perceived business objectives. After all, there is no other reason for any organization to prepare a marketing plan that involves a large sum of money being committed to advertising, than to increase awareness of their brand and sell more products. Needless to say, even the pitch process can inspire agencies into new dimensions of creative thinking and draw huge amounts of attention and controversy along the way. In the USA, Agency.com were invited to pitch ideas for the digital advertising account of Subway, the take-away sandwich and food brand. Their pitch 'concept' was based around a nine-minute film, uploaded to YouTube, of the agency trying to pitch for the account. The film showed Agency.com staff interviewing consumers on the street; they got involved with students at the renowned Miami Ad School; ordered and ate plenty of Subway products; and a couple of the Agency.com team even got jobs at Subway. Hard to fault their approach to research! Then it fell apart. An industry debate raged at Agency.com's decision to film a re-creation of a client pitch. It seemed, to YouTube viewers, that the agency was parodying the pitch process. Agency.com no doubt employs lovely people that are witty, strategically smart and highly creative. What the film portrayed was people overdoing the cool, hip agency thing. Some of the phraseology was straight out of the George W. Bush repertoire – using terms such as 'tasked them on the fly' and 'you know, if we roll, we roll big', sounded rather like a television sitcom set in an advertising agency. The sight of creatives trying to 'do' marketing speak was pure comedy. Subway is the world's largest sandwich brand and the fourth largest take-away food provider. Is footage of a creative describing the brand as 'having a lot of potential' doing Agency.com any favours? Is the creative director, Kate, really helping her agency's case by explaining how a copywriter once described her as a 'combination between Grace Kelly and Rodney Dangerfield'? Even the footage of the two agency staff working at Subway didn't rise to the expected levels of interest, fun and humour. Surely this is viral advertising gone wrong, isn't it? Another creative director, Tom, stating that 'if we have our way, the whole world's gonna know about it', is probably not the agency's greatest ever pitch line. The film is entitled *Going To Work For Subway: Part 1* and it got over 17,500 hits

on YouTube. American cynics suggest that 16,000 of these were other advertising people rejoicing in the damage another agency was inflicting on itself. Whilst Subway asked for a 5-minute film to be submitted as part of the pitch, it has been hotly debated as to whether this was entirely the conceptual approach such a strong global brand required. Hit the YouTube search engine and decide for yourselves. Pure genius or pure self-indulgence? The blog sites are less than complimentary; what do you think?

If you are fortunate enough to land a brand or marketing management position at a major client, then during your career you will be involved in many creative pitch meetings. You will also enjoy the added thrill and heartache of being part of the final decision-making. Do not believe for one moment that working on the 'clientside' is any less ruthless and pressured than working in an agency. Hiring an agency and commissioning and approving creative work that fails in its strategic and marketing objectives is a crime. The punishment will be an inglorious blot on your career cv. I can hear it now at subsequent interviews you attend, 'So, you were involved in *that* campaign were you?' Working as part of a client marketing team has two essential parts: devising a strategic and marketing plan to grow the brand, and commissioning outside agencies to help implement it. Am I scaring you yet?

Defending the brand and planning an attack

> Starting a marketing career means gaining a breadth of experience early on and then focusing on your area of interest. To be a good brand manager means being able to keep lots of plates spinning at the same time and effectively deliver projects involving teams of very different personalities.
>
> **Katharine Mansell – Brand Manager, Utterly Butterly, Dairy Crest**

Assuming that I haven't totally put you off, what does a brand manager do? Essentially, the role carries direct responsibility for either the brand as a whole or a product within the brand's 'portfolio'. It is the brand manager's job to ensure that the brand has the correct presence in the marketplace; in other words, that it stands out from the crowd. This will include an involvement in the packaging design, advertising, building the brand message, developing the brand personality and telling the brand story at every opportunity. It is reasonable to expect that, in achieving these goals, brand managers will work closely with design consultancies on packaging design and corporate identity development and management. They will be directly involved in advertising campaigns and strategies with perhaps more than one agency across television, outdoor and digital media (and more besides). PR too will be under their remit, communicating closely with either an agency or an in-house team. In fact, a career in brand management will take you through virtually all of the environments I have discussed so far in this book. It is necessary to be conversant in all types of media strategy and to have a direct input into the briefing, commissioning

The Utterly Butterly brand extends its marketing and strategic plans beyond traditional advertising and media communications. This image features a heavily branded stunt plane!

Image courtesy of Dairy Crest.

and even hiring of communication agencies for all media platforms. The brand manager leading the advertising and media communication for their brand will be accountable for maintaining, developing and enhancing its values. This is not just about selling more products (though that is important), it is having responsibility for everything the brand stands for in the eyes of the consumer. The brand will be your baby – to protect, to grow and to understand the value of both the brand as a physical asset and its intellectual properties. A job in brand management is one to be proud of and is not easy to get. If a diverse range of skills and a strong desire to be part of market-research activity and product development, and to work with advertising agencies, designers, marketing teams and PR consultants, sound like your thing, then here's what you need to do. Actually, the personal attributes should be quite familiar-sounding by now, because, guess what? You need to be analytical, a good listener, a great communicator, culturally aware, entrepreneurial, creative and visionary. Just about the same list that applies to every job in advertising and media communications. Armed with these skills, the entry-level jobs your communication degree (whether it is advertising, marketing, PR or whatever) will equip you for, are likely to be joining an in-house marketing team or a more specific position as brand executive. These are generic job descriptions, as brand managers ultimately come from diverse backgrounds – from client marketing teams through to advertising agency account management. All are equally valid places to start. As with all professional media and marketing positions, variety is the spice of life. Expand your cv with as diverse a range of brand management and marketing experiences as possible. Gain work experience in research, marketing and even an advertising agency account management team or, better still, account planning, to broaden your scope. Learn about strategy and media, and absorb as much as you can about digital advertising and online marketing techniques. The more you know, the better your cv and the more attractive a graduate you become. Understand what brand managers really do. A senior brand manager may have overall responsibility for the brand as a whole. For example, a food manufacturer such as Dairy Crest will have senior staff at director level overseeing all of its brand communications. Yet several other brand managers may have the job of developing a single brand within the product range, such as Utterly Butterly in the case of Katherine Mansell (whom I quoted above).

It is difficult to offer a definitive outline of exactly what you can expect from a career in brand management. Each organization has its own structure and strategy, and the job description varies accordingly. At the highest level, global brands of the stature of Unilever, Nike or Nestlé have many hierarchies of sub-brands and products. Smaller, more tightly focused brands may have one overarching brand proposition to develop and sustain. The common factor, though, is that all brands are businesses in their own right and a brand manager needs to run them accordingly. Irrespective of an individual company's marketing and strategic structure, a brand manager will always be involved in the following activities and processes:

- Monitoring and understanding the marketplace in which a brand resides
- Developing strategies to exploit existing and new market opportunities
- Executing those strategies with in-house teams and external agencies
- Familiarization with and delivery of sales volumes, market share and profit targets for the brand.

The business process is continually evolving for brand managers, and business plans and communication strategies can change regularly. For instance, if the global oil price has an influence on the cost of a brand's products, then the business and marketing plan will be volatile and need to be amended periodically to suit the current manufacturing or transportation cost. In equal measure, brand managers focus on the detail of sales reports and invent new, big ideas to excite and involve consumers in the brand vision and lifestyle. Managing a brand and ensuring consistency and innovation in communicating its story to consumers are an integral

part of business and marketing. The ever-increasing channels of media available to tell the brand story means that good brand managers are in demand. A word of caution, though – every business recognizes the importance of marketing and brand management, but as communication strategies become ever more complex and emerging technologies present new challenges and opportunities, some businesses are outsourcing their marketing and brand management to, yep you guessed it, advertising agencies. As I write against a background of worldwide recession, the creativity and resourcefulness of brand managers is being tested to the limit as they strive to retain the competitiveness and profile of their brands with a much reduced marketing budget. The distance between a dream job and a nightmare one can be narrow. On the one hand, a brand manager will enjoy ownership and ultimate responsibility for a brand. On the other, if the strategy and communication plans go awry the buck stops firmly at their door. But then all work carries its own trapdoors for people to fall down. Creatives with no good ideas, PR consultants who can't get stories in the media, planners who fail to understand the target audience – any position in advertising and media communications is performance related; it goes with the territory.

With the correct levels of personal and work experiences to draw on and natural creative and communications skills, all of you who are keen on brand management stand a chance of a varied and interesting career. If you can prove yourself capable of leading and inspiring cross-functioning, multitalented teams of people then your career will also be a successful and rewarding one. As you grow into the role and learn, you will quickly move from implementing the marketing plans of others to devising your own. But enough of me telling you how and what you need to be a brand manager, the people out there doing the job are best placed to give you hope and inspiration. Peter Harbour is a Brand Marketing Manager in the Middle East at the giant Unilever Corporation, one of the world's largest FMCG (fast moving consumer goods) brands:

> There is nothing quite like working in a developing market with high growth and different cultures everywhere you turn. As a role, this one is more diverse than anything I have done before and more business related. Across the Middle East, markets are growing at double digit, and Unilever, like its other FMCG counterparts, are launching into new sectors and the pace is high. I look after the Dove Skin business in the Middle East, which involves complete P and L [profit and loss] analysis. You get to know all the elements that make up your business. What impact does importing your product from India have on the margin you make? Do you make an advert in Arabic or English? If it's Arabic, what dialect do you use? Is it traditional Arabic? Is it Lebanese dialect? Do you focus your launch on the wholesale sector or the modern trade sector of the market? You interact with Middle Eastern, Asian and European cultures through all aspects of the business and it is a sure-fire way of learning to use your

relationship skills to their optimum as well as understanding the different cultural values that people adopt.

Living in another country can be a lot of fun as well as making a difference to your job. I am based in Dubai, and who would have thought that before you launch a product you need to do a special transit test for Arabia to ensure that your product can withstand the 50-degree-plus temperatures that we experience in the summer.

The beauty of a brand management career is the sheer breadth and diversity of the brands that graduates, like you, can get to work with. This next short insight into the job comes from a Senior Brand Manager at PG Tips, the tea brand:

> As the Senior Brand Manager I led all marketing activation. At the beginning of 2005, PG celebrated its 75th anniversary. I delivered a new TV advert to the market as well as overseeing a PR campaign that featured the world's most expensive teabag ever made (£7,500 worth of diamond-encrusted tea leaves). We featured in loads of newspapers and I had to spend a day on the phone giving radio interviews and even an interview to ITN News.
>
> Recently I have overseen the *Wallace and Gromit* link-up. The only bespoke TV advert featuring the tea-drinking heroes globally, as well as over a million *Gromit* mugs with a thermo-changing nose in-store. Chuck in a PR campaign that featured a *Wallace and Gromit* inspired *readywhenUR* kettle (a kettle that turns itself on when you text it) and you have an activation campaign that is varied and great fun to work on.

See what I mean about diversity, being involved in the creation of advertising activities featuring *Wallace and Gromit?* How cool is that? On a totally different note, here are some thoughts from a brand manager for Vaseline Intensive Care (see, I told you it was varied!):

> Just me and the brand, a chance to travel to and work with my European innovation team in Hamburg, Germany and the global brand centre in New York. A brand that everybody in the company loved and a brand that everybody wanted to see do well. I had autonomy, I was involved in a global advertising brief, worked on the packaging design for a new product and had a brilliant (mainly female) Skin Cleansing and Care team in Kingston that I worked with. I loved it. As a brand manager you end up being very protective over your brand. Once you understand your target consumers and you begin to truly understand what your brand is capable of, you start telling everybody about it. As a marketing team, the skin-care team were always eager to tell everybody who would listen about our plans for the year, and working in a team with such passion motivates you to achieve even more.

In modern business, brands really are king. Advertising and brand awareness run deep through popular consumer culture. Shopping is a key part of many consumer lifestyles, and the continuing expansion of digital communication possibilities mean a career in marketing, brand management and advertising in one of its many guises is a seriously smart career choice for any young, hungry student. Even in difficult economic times, the growth of internet marketing shows no sign of slowing down. The competition for ways into advertising and media communications, whether agency, in-house or 'clientside', is stiff though. Standing out from the crowd and having something different to offer are vital; I cannot stress that enough. Brand management is just as tough to break into as any other advertising and media discipline.

> Be creative and always keep up to date with new technology. Try to experience a variety of different media, product sectors and audiences to become as well rounded as you can be.
>
> **Lindsay Strachan – Brand Consultant, Scottish Widows**

I talked about diversity of brands and the career opportunities earlier. Calm down girls, this next interview is with a guy doing a job many of you would simply die for – working with chocolate. Neil Anderson is Marketing Manager for Cadbury World, part of Cadbury plc. Here is his story:

> I have been at Cadbury for nine years now, joining in 2000 after leaving university having gained a BA (Hons) in Media and Communications Studies and Spanish Studies.
>
> I originally started in Commercial Services – a department required to support the sales and marketing functions. After 14 months the business half-funded an MA in Mass Communications, which I studied at the same time as working. I then moved into the Customer Marketing Team, leading the project management, procurement and development of display solutions to support key temporary, promotional, tactical and seasonal activity. This 'below the line' advertising has always been important to our business. Confectionery is often bought on impulse and it is important that, in order to support the messages and awareness generated by 'above the line' activity, our display solutions are aligned and consistent – reminding the consumer of our products in store with innovative and eye-catching point-of-sale equipment.
>
> Alongside point-of-sale manufacturers, designers, agencies and our own consumer marketing and sales teams, I worked on diverse projects throughout the next three years. These included the launch of *Cadbury Dream, Maynard's Wine Gum Sours, Trebor 24–7, Bassett's Fruit Allsorts*; the

A bright, vibrant execution from Big Communications helped position Cadbury World more effectively.

Image courtesy of Cadbury World.

relaunch of the Trebor and the Cadbury *Dairy Milk* ranges; as well as our key seasonal activity at Christmas and Easter. In order to support this role I gained a Certificate in Point of Purchase from POPAI (Point of Purchase Advertising International) accredited by the Chartered Institute of Marketing.

In 2004 I moved to our sales team and held a number of positions including business development and account management, working alongside a variety of customers from local retailers, food-service regional wholesalers, vending and leisure customers as well as leading players in the quick-service restaurant area. Bringing a confectionery focus to these varied businesses always included the need to understand the customer and often the customer's customer requirements, and work alongside their own marketing teams or agencies to deliver our joint business plans.

At the end of 2008, I moved on from focusing on the consumers of a leading FMCG product and joined Cadbury World as Marketing Manager. Whilst still working for Cadbury plc, my focus has now shifted from FMCG to the leisure sector. With responsibility for the marketing strategy, promotions and our all-important education team and product, I now find myself promoting and talking about all aspects of everything 'Cadbury'. Not just our products – but our heritage and corporate social responsibility agenda – in order to bring visitors through the door of Birmingham's leading leisure attraction.

I love working for Cadbury. It is a great company to be a part of. In this day and age it is difficult to find such a large organization as committed to the environment, the community and the wellbeing of its employees as it was nearly 200 years ago. When I tell people that I work for Cadbury, a big smile appears on their face and they're really interested in learning more.

I love talking to customers and consumers, taking new ideas and repackaging or reworking existing products or concepts and bringing them to the attention of new people. Being able to get a message out there in various channels and through various media and seeing people respond is really satisfying.

Confectionery and Cadbury, the brand, are not as easy to market as people might think – it's a competitive world out there – but creating the message around 'more moments of pleasure', 'pleasure is good for you', and supporting that with our organization's rich heritage, make it incredibly enjoyable.

I think having an open mind helps me in my job. You need to be open to new suggestions and new ways of operating. An idea can strike you in the unlikeliest of places, and what may seem completely unrelated to your industry, product or sector could have a transferable application.

You also need to be able to communicate effectively with people from all levels and walks of life. In addition to this, you need to be quite a creative thinker, not just to help with the formulation of briefs and working with agencies, but also in terms of what value you can get out of a certain campaign and the most cost-effective ways of maximizing your budget.

I think, fundamentally, a graduate needs a sound understanding of the theory behind why the creative industries work in the way they do: what has gone on before, and the reasons why campaigns run in the way that they do. If they are looking to go into a specific area or discipline – such as being at the communications forefront of modern technologies – then a thorough understanding of that subject is essential.

More importantly, particularly in today's environment, they need genuine experience of using the skills required (commercial, finance, creative acumen etc.). This can be particularly difficult whilst studying full time. Vacation work, gap years and internships are the best option, but helping to run a college/university newspaper or radio station,or promoting guild events, look good on the cv also. Some experience of using these skills in a practical environment and the demonstration of transferable skills are absolutely essentially and will put a graduate at the top of a recruiter's shortlist. Every employer will be scoring a candidate against a list of desirable and essential criteria – the more boxes the graduate ticks the better – and actual experience will help. If the graduate is unlucky enough not to be able to secure a position straightaway, they should think about what would make for 'good cv reading'. During vacations or a gap year, there are plenty of charities out there who require these types of skills and services, or new businesses starting up who may jump at the chance of somebody volunteering.

Don't overlook the interview process either. Research is absolutely essential! Just as the graduate would study for an exam or an essay, they will need to develop their own research style. It is important that they know the company they're going for, why they are successful, who their customers or clients are, what their USPs are, how they have performed etc.

Conducting a SWOT or PEST analysis may help the graduate determine what the top line points are. Think about the potential interview questions and how you would answer them. Use the S(T)AR (outline the *Situation* or *Task*, the *Action* taken and then the *Result*) format and make your responses as concise and as powerful as appropriate. There are plenty of websites out there to help with interview technique, nerves and situations. A majority of them also have example questions.

Remember also to ask the interviewer questions at the end of the interview – the best ones, I find, are the ones which help you to understand the interviewer's motivations for doing the job they do and the company they work for. Don't forget that this is a two-way process: it is essential that you like the feel of the place and that you are comfortable with the people you may be working with. If you don't get the job – ask for feedback and see if there is anything you need to do differently next time.

Even though Cadbury World has been around for nearly 20 years, we are very much intrinsically linked to the workings, operations and reputation of the main

business. We also have to benchmark ourselves against other leisure attractions and consider what it is that a potential visitor might require from a great day out.

There has always been a great deal of confusion around what Cadbury World was: was it a museum, a theme park and who was it targeted at?

Recently we have done some work to build the actual 'brand' of Cadbury World in order help potential consumers avoid any confusion. Working with an agency who developed the creative (Big Communications in Leicester), we finally feel that we now have a brand for Cadbury World. We can build on this as time goes on, whilst still ensuring that the potential visitor is not confused as to what Cadbury World is about (Cadbury World: Where Chocolate Comes to Life. Fourteen Amazing Zones, One Fantastic Day Out).

It's still a huge thrill for me seeing a campaign come to life. From initial idea through to execution, and having the target audience respond in the right manner – whether that's buying a product or visiting the attraction.

In achieving this I expect our agency to completely and utterly understand our products and services and deliver high levels of service. I insist upon regular scheduled fortnightly or monthly 1–2–1s as well as constant open communication.

I feel to do my job it is necessary to be able to visualize (if not fully and completely) what it is you're trying to achieve and who you're targeting.

Start with that end goal in mind and work backwards – mentally go through stages that need to happen and anticipate any challenges or obstacles and actively think how they could be overcome.

Brand or marketing management? What's the difference?

For those of you considering a 'clientside' career, your future job title is almost certain to include the words 'brand' and/or 'marketing'. Is there a difference and, if so, what is it? In concise terms, the role of a marketing manager is to formulate an organization's marketing strategy. Operating in conjunction with sales and marketing teams, the marketing manager identifies and estimates the marketplaces for, and the consumer's demand for, its range of products and services. Part of the role may also involve setting the selling price of these products and services to maximize the organization's profit and to get consumers interested. Many marketing managers have had a background in sales, although brand managers and advertising agency account managers have also successfully made the switch. I think it is probable that the word 'sales' provides the key definition, if there is such a thing, that separates brand and marketing management. Whilst brand managers and marketing managers work very closely together, the marketing role extends into the sales team on a more regular basis. In fact, many organizations combine two roles to create the position of Sales and Marketing Manager. There is no specific definition, nor is there any specific separation – brand and marketing go hand in hand. Some people would suggest that sales staff taking on marketing is a mistake as the role demands creativity, subtlety and cross-functioning communication. Others would argue that sales staff are the best placed to take on marketing strategies. It is also fair to say that many senior figures in business have a background in sales, which may also influence the thinking behind and definition of the position of marketing manager. There is enormous crossover here, but the following list might typify a marketing manager's working day. Read through it and spot the differences and similarities:

- Formulating, directing and co-ordinating marketing activities and policies to promote products and services, working with advertising, brand and promotion managers
- Identifying, developing and evaluating an organization's marketing strategy, based on a knowledge of its objectives, market characteristics, costs and profit factors
- Directing the hiring, training, and performance evaluations of marketing and sales staff and overseeing their daily activities
- Evaluating the financial aspects of product development, such as budgets, expenditures, research and development appropriations, and return-on-investment and profit-loss projections.
- Developing pricing strategies, balancing firm objectives and customer satis-faction.

Kind of strays into brand-management territory doesn't it? The two roles can be combined sometimes and very distinctly separated in others. There are no golden rules. Read the job descriptions very carefully to ensure you move in the appropriate direction for you. In the minds of many businesses, the same confusion exists between advertising and marketing. I hope you have learned enough from reading my book so far to understand that advertising is a component part of the marketing process (albeit an important one). Yet marketing is centred round market research, media planning, PR, pricing, distribution, customer care and support, sales strategy and even community activities. Some of those functions are undertaken by or supported by an advertising agency or other media-communication agency, clearly some are not. That list perhaps also spins off into a distinct career path of its own: that of market research. In modern marketing and advertising (the two are almost inextricably linked for most large organizations), research provides the basis and the safety net for brand development and subsequent media communications. Since being championed by David Ogilvy and other Madison Avenue advertising pioneers, most agencies and their clients dare not speak without researching what they are to say first. The process of understanding cultural, lifestyle and buying habits is the launchpad of creative communication. It defines the direction of marketing and is the core of developing a brand personality. It is very important and so will you be if you can do the job well. The good news is market research is graduate-led in many ways. Understanding markets, behaviours and social opinions thrives on new techniques and innovative, fresh input. New product development, rebranding, politics and business strategies all rely heavily on market research.

I know what some of you are thinking right now. Surely all a market researcher does is stand in the street with a clipboard or telephone people when they are eating their dinner. Wrong, very wrong. Whilst these are tasks performed by market-research companies, they are the job of interviewers not researchers. These activities gather the information; they do not form opinions about it. It may well be a useful source of weekend spending money to do such a job when you are studying, but it is not how I would define a career in research. Graduate researchers are more likely to find themselves in managing a complete project – from the planning process, through data collection, to analysing results and communicating to the clients what these mean for their business or organization. Once again, market research offers graduates a diverse exposure to different market sectors and industries – financial services, retail or healthcare, to government policy-making and understanding existing and emerging markets in the UK and abroad.

It is an exciting career that will allow you to spot trends almost before they happen, or even to predict them – a skill that makes you highly employable. Every organization wants to know what could be the next 'big thing'. Researchers play a vital part in marketing, advertising and brand strategies and market research offers a specialist career path that can equally lead back to marketing and brand management later in your career.

> Throw your body and soul into the role, seize every opportunity to gain experience and build a reputation for honouring your promises.
>
> **Tim Dixon – Head of brand, More Th>n**

It is reasonable, but not wholly true, to suggest that to creatives, designers and even planners or strategists, a portfolio of campaigns is their main weapon. To 'clientside' marketing and brand managers, I guess a cv is the thing you should lovingly craft and nurture. I am not going to outline a perfect cv for you: you will have had that lesson many times at school, college and university. Needless to say, it should be focused, targeted and motivating to all that read it. I am going to make one common-sense observation though – your email address. You are selling yourself to a professional, businesslike organization. If your email address goes something like sexyfunbird@hotmail.com, think about changing it, huh? It may seem stupid, but I've heard all about weird and wonderful email addresses killing some great cvs stone dead. Assuming your cv and interview techniques have been honed to perfection, you will get your job, but be patient. In March 2007, American marketing guru Rob Engelman of Engelman Management Group Inc. wrote the following internet article for *The Wiglaf Journal,* discussing what a marketing department does, it is well worth a read. Here are some highlights:

> For starters, the responsibilities of a Marketing Department vary based on several factors including business size, industry, corporate structure and more. To complicate the matter, a Marketing Department's role will undoubtedly be different for organizations where the department is considered to be a 'cost centre' versus a 'revenue centre'.
>
> The following are my thoughts on 9 core activities/responsibilities a Marketing Department must handle. They are not listed in any particular order, as they all should be accomplished if an organization wants to grow the value of its business.

> 1) Focus on the Customer. Marketers should spend time listening to their customers (and prospective customers) in order to understand their needs and wants regarding a particular product or service. Soliciting thoughts and input from internal stakeholders such as Sales and Customer Service is also appropriate, as these departments are typically closest to the customer.
>
> 2) Monitor the Competition. Learning about, and understanding the competitive landscape is also an important function of the Marketing Department. Marketers should be the 'go to people' within an organization to answer the following types of questions: Who is the competition (both direct and indirect)? What do they communicate? Which customers do they serve? Why do customers choose the competitor versus you?
>
> 3) Own the Brand. The perceptions and feelings formed about an organization, its products/services and its performance, are what is known as its brand. The Marketing Department is responsible for creating meaningful messages through words, ideas, images and names that deliver upon the promises/benefits an organization wishes to make with its customers. Furthermore, the Marketing Department is responsible for ensuring that messages and images are delivered consistently, by every member of the organization.
>
> 4) Find & Direct Outside Vendors. Internal Marketing Departments do not create magic alone. Therefore, Marketing needs to source and oversee a group of outside resources (a.k.a. 'partners') such as copywriters, graphic designers, web designers, database specialists and printers so that a company can get the most bang from its marketing efforts.
>
> 5) Create New Ideas. Whether it's customer acquisition campaigns, keep-in-touch programs, new product promotions, retention efforts, or something in between, the Marketing Department should ultimately be responsible for developing new ideas that generate revenue for the company. This

does not mean that the Marketers have to come up with every idea on their own; however, they need to identify, cultivate, and work with others (see point #4) to execute programs that will create revenue.

6) Communicate Internally. It is important that the Marketing Department communicates with all departments inside an organization. Since any employee (regardless of position) can support (or damage) a brand, value proposition or even specific program initiatives, the Marketing Department needs to take responsibility for disseminating information throughout the organization (this includes internal education and training when appropriate).

7) Manage a Budget. Establishing and communicating messages to the marketplace costs money. Therefore, Marketing Departments should be responsible for estimating the anticipated expenditures associated with marketing activities. Once set, Marketers should be held responsible for meeting all budget projections.

8) Understand the ROI (Return on Investment). Since marketing activities are an investment – an investment in time, money, and effort – they should be monitored and measured against specific concrete goals and objectives. Marketing Departments should constantly ask themselves . . . 'What's my expected return?' Answering this simple, yet often overlooked question, will result in better, more accountable decisions.

9) Set the Strategy, Plan the Attack, and Execute. One of the key activities for a Marketing Department is to integrate an organization's goals, strengths, channels of distribution, competitive environment, target markets, pricing, core messages and products into one cohesive document known as the Marketing Strategy. As part of the strategy, the Marketing Department should also develop the list of tactical ideas such as direct mail, print advertising, and search engine optimization that will enable the organization to communicate its message to customers and prospects. With a strategy and tactical ideas in hand, the Marketing Department is now ready to take on the responsibility of executing the programs and initiatives to drive sales and revenue for the organization.

Courtesy of www.wiglafjournal.com

The respective roles of brand managers and marketing managers cross over in many areas. The essential aim of both jobs is to build a brand, strike up an on-going dialogue with consumers and sell more products as a result. Brand management is focused on the brand itself, its presence in the marketplace and the personality it adopts to persuade consumers to 'buy in' to its lifestyle. In many organizations, this can be the job of a marketing manager. We are dealing with business terminology here and unravelling job descriptions from the job titles organizations choose to give their staff. Positions you may apply for either on work experience, as an intern or on a permanent basis need careful research on your part. As students of advertising or media communications in its various forms, you are well equipped to aim for a career in brand management for the most part. Marketing management can be different. When the job description indicates responsibilities closely aligned to brand managers – strategy, brand building and liaison with external communications agencies – you are on reasonably safe ground. If the detail of the job requires an understanding of, and a background in, sales, then you could find you are not fully equipped. Go for the role that asks for creative, strategic thinking.

Martin Moll is Head of Marketing at Honda (UK) and he has outlined his career to date and explained his personal views on just what it took for him to rise to that position. Here's what he has to say:

> Most recently my commercial experience covers three core industries: Automotive, Advertising Agency and Power products – for example, Marine, ATV (Quad bikes), Generators and Lawn and Garden. Within those industries my roles have included:
>
> - Regional Sales management – looking after car-dealer network
> - Press & PR Manager for Honda (UK) – responsible for all UK media contact, including product launches
> - Marketing – all elements of marketing mix, in the role of Head of Marketing.
>
> My university education includes: a BA (Hons) Business & Marketing and a Masters degree in Business & Leadership.
>
> I love my present job and do it because I am passionate about being involved at the forefront of commercial activity, and seeing ideas blossom into action, and then being able to see the commercial impact and benefit of those decisions come to life.
>
> Personally I think tenacity, determination, focus, resilience, flexibility, adaptability and empathy (towards other areas of the business and to the customer – be it to the retailers or importantly the customers) are the skills I have developed to do my job effectively and to the best of my ability.
>
> Graduates should demonstrate an inner belief and a real desire to add value. Formal qualifications are actually not critical (but more a filter process for employers to see who has applied themselves). They need to understand the wider business (commercial awareness) and how marketing links to sales function and the bottom line (otherwise it is just an *expense* or cost centre). Be passionate. Let others see how you think, feel, respond to external stimuli and what makes you tick. ALWAYS look at things in 3D contextually – especially in terms of customer viewpoint – on anything and everything (i.e. you might be passionate about something, but don't just rely on your view).

Graduates who genuinely believe they can demonstrate those skills should then prepare for interviews like this:

- Know the brand you are approaching. Have a view, and don't be afraid to speak openly on delicate issues. Just do it empathetically.
- Know YOUR brand – who are you, what are you and what do you stand for? I always use the rule of 3 – create 3 'brand' statements about yourself, and how you want the world to see and perceive you. They should be stretching, evocative and 'attractive' to employers. THEN, make sure all your behaviours are in line with this, so it is conveyed clearly.
- Be clear that Marketing is 2nd to sales function. It's a support function, and not the 'core' function. Anyone 'doing' marketing, without a real appreciation of cost versus benefit, is going to fail – quickly.

Here is an outline example of the kind of communications work I am involved in:

- Delivering a core message on lawn and garden product within a cluttered market place.
- Mechanism – direct mail.
- USP: created a completely biodegradable mailer piece. The customer letter was 100 per cent biodegradable paper, made of flower seed. Even the ink was soya based . . .
- Impact: within the letter construction, customers were reminded *how Honda was as green as the gardens we provided product for* . . . once the letter was read, customers were asked to scrunch up the paper (including the envelope), douse it in water and then plant the letter anywhere in the garden. Within weeks the letter would reappear as a flower.
- Result/measure: customer feedback incredible. Not just in terms of sales impact, but positive and 'warm' reaction to our brand.

Projects like this give me a real buzz. It's all about impact . . . making a tangible, measurable difference by taking an idea and seeing it through to fruition – adding value and improving the bottom line. I regularly work with advertising agencies and I expect them to have an understanding of our business, commercially, as well as the people, culture, relationships and direction/strategy. I respond best to simplicity . . . complicated creative that needs explaining and putting into context will definitely fail. Customers do not hang around to try and learn. Some creatives get too close or caught up in their imagery. It is a business and a personal relationship, so agencies must show transparency, integrity, honesty and empathy. Many talk about providing this, but, surprisingly, many are actually more geared towards 'self' rather than 'partnership' or indeed who is the real customer.

Brand managers and marketing managers form close relationships with external communications agencies. These work best when there is a mutual respect and trust. This is also a mandatory job requirement. In choosing to study advertising or another strand of media communications you will be well equipped to manage these relationships if you choose to work on the 'clientside'. You will have developed an understanding of strategic and creative processes; therefore you will be familiar with the ways in which advertising and other communications agencies work. That is a strong place to start when you embark on your career as a client. There is a position of power in that, though stay grounded and do not get carried away with it. If you are working in an agency you will become used to account managers emailing you and saying, 'the client wants to know when they can see something'. You could be that client. Experience will allow you to know when to wield the big stick if agencies are dragging their feet. When to search for new agencies to freshen and move your brand further forward. When an agency has not given you as much as you expected and when they have done brilliant work that breaks new ground. We are also dealing with human nature here. If you work closely with your agencies and they really produce the goods and there is a dramatic increase in your brand awareness and product sales, you will share in the glory. Your boss will love you. Equally, if you are involved in an underperforming campaign that cost a fortune, prepare to get your butt kicked and learn how to take it out on the agencies too.

I shall close this chapter with a few thoughts on the relationships between clients and their agencies. These are the views of people who pay the fees at the end of a strategic and creative campaign development process. Both examples come from the website of Business Link, an organization that provides advice to small and medium businesses across the UK.

Sheactive specializes exclusively in sportswear and activewear for women. The company has an online shop plus stores in Brighton and Covent Garden. Marketing director Johanna Fawcett describes how Sheactive worked with its advertising agency to produce a campaign that has raised brand awareness and increased sales.

Some of the campaign advertising for Sheactive.

Images courtesy of The Think Tank/Sheactive.

Our aim has always been to create a brand, so our first advertising campaign had to do more than just show our products. To ensure we could brief agencies properly we assessed competitors' advertising and went through magazines pulling out images that captured what Sheactive is about.

We took these to three agencies we shortlisted through contacts and research. We presented to them and asked them to propose ideas for a print campaign to attract customers to our website. We also asked for proof of their experience in producing campaigns on a tight budget. The time spent preparing

for and briefing the agencies proved invaluable. It ensured we were dealt with professionally and gave us a basis upon which to judge responses.

The agency we chose, The Think Tank, had some great case studies and the rapport was good from the start. We began brainstorming immediately to decide key visuals that would translate into future ads and support materials.

As agreed, they then came back with visuals for us to respond to. It pays to be really specific with your feedback. For example, if you feel a colour isn't right, don't be vague – state that you want it changed, why and to what.

We didn't have a huge budget, but we still wanted quality, so we were open with The Think Tank and asked them to look beyond the short-term fees, which they did. Another important point was that we negotiated doing the media buying ourselves. Agencies usually do the buying and take a cut, but you can get it cheaper by going direct. Our agency was also prepared to help us cut costs in other ways – we used friends as models and didn't pay for locations.

Ultimately, their creativity and execution made it look like we had spent a lot more than we actually had. Customer research in the month after the first ads appeared showed that sales rose by nearly 20 per cent and a third of visitors to the website had seen Sheactive in a magazine.

Although we got excellent value for money, we should have been clearer about exactly what we could afford from the start. An agreed monthly retainer would have helped us control costs. Our deadlines were tight, so we didn't have the luxury of getting to know the agency first. In an ideal world, we would have held more brainstorming sessions to get us working as a team.

Michael Welch started his business, Black Circles, in November 2001. The company, based in Scotland, links more than 700 independent tyre fitters across the UK. When contacted through its call centre or website, it locates the customer's nearest and cheapest tyre fitter.

We needed to start advertising from day one to attract customers. I started by looking for places to advertise which I thought would reach our target market, such as car magazines like *Revs* and *Max Power*. The readers of these magazines are a captive marketplace. As fast-car enthusiasts and owners they need to buy tyres regularly. I got the circulation figures and the demographics of the people that were reading these magazines. This included information such as their salary, age and the type of car they drive. I then broke our potential customers down into similar categories and decided which magazines would target them best.

We spend around £25,000 to £30,000 a month on advertising and our turnover is £3 million. We manage to convert about 70 per cent of our advertising spend into sales. After a few months of a particular campaign we analyse how it is working and then either pull it or continue to do more. Our sales team always ask new customers how they heard about us, so we can tell which advertisements work.

When they start out, many businesses don't think they can compete with larger firms when it comes to advertising, but they can. As long as you are clear about the message you want to get across and know which media is right to reach your target market, a small business's advertising can be as successful as anyone else's. We use an advertising agency but I oversee all of the work they do. In the early days I thought that they were the professionals and they knew best, but ultimately you need to have control of the advertising messages and your brand image. In the beginning our unique selling point was that we were cheap. but we wouldn't sell at those prices now. Our USP now is excellent customer service and value and all our marketing is designed to reflect this. Our strapline is *Think tyres, think Black Circles,* and all of our advertisements are black and white. We try to keep it simple and we had some campaigns that weren't as successful in the beginning because we didn't have much experience. Now we have the luxury of having the time, money and knowledge to be able to experiment and find out what works. The key is not to bet too much on one campaign but to build up slowly. I would definitely like to do some radio and TV advertising in the future because it will expose us to a much bigger market.

In retrospect though, perhaps I would have extended the magazine advertising sooner and thought about brand development earlier. However, the cost of advertising means that what you would do in an ideal world isn't always possible in the beginning.

Some websites to visit

Here are some sites to help you keep up to date with a variety of PR and media news and comment. There are many more, so feel free to use Google and YouTube if you want to!

Information and industry sites

Chartered Institute of Marketing www.cim.co.uk
ACIM – American Chartered Institute of Marketing www.a-cim.org
Advanced Marketing Institute www.aminstitute.com
Business Link www.businesslink.gov.uk
Chartered Management Institute www.managers.org.uk
Employer Brand Institute www.employerbrandinstitute.com
Direct Marketing AssociationUK – www.dma.org.uk USA – www.the-dma.org
www.getin2marketing.com
www.ico.gov.uk

www.marketingdonut.co.uk
www.social-marketing.org
www.marketingweek.com
www.engelmanmanagement.com
www.wiglafjournal.com
www.thinktank.org.uk
www.bigcommunications.co.uk
www.cadburyworld.co.uk
www.honda.co.uk

Some books to read

The New Strategic Brand Management: Creating and Sustaining Brand Equity Long Term
Jean Noel Kapferer

Harvard Business Review on Brand Management
Harvard Business Review

Strategic Brand Management
Larry Percy and Richard Elliott

Strategic Brand Management: Building, Measuring, and Managing Brand Equity
Kevin Keller

Strategic Brand Management: A European Perspective
Dr Kevin Lane Keller, Dr Tony Aperia and Mats Georgson

Brand Management
Dr Rik Riezebos

Brand Management: Theory and Practice
Tilde Heding, Charlotte F. Knudtzen and Mogens Bjerre

Brand Management: 101 Lessons from Real World Marketing
Mainak Dhar

Building Strong Brands
David A. Aaker

Marketing Management
Philip Kotler and Kevin Lane Keller

Marketing Management and Strategy
Peter Doyle and Phil Stern

CIM Coursebook Marketing Management in Practice
Chartered Institute of Marketing

Strategic Marketing Management: Planning, Implementation and Control
Richard M.S. Wilson and Colin Gilligan

Marketing Strategy and Management
Michael J. Baker

Marketing Communications: An Integrated Approach
Paul R. Smith and Jonathan Taylor

Marketing: Essential Principles, New Realities
Jonathan Groucutt, Peter Leadley and Patrick Forsyth

Qualitative Research: Good Decision Making through Understanding People, Cultures and Markets
Sheila Keegan

Get involved

Share and learn with everyone else on my book's Facebook and Twitter pages:

- search Facebook for 'Advertising Its Business Culture and Careers'
- www.twitter.com/adculture

9 The way ahead

Some people take no mental exercise apart from jumping to conclusions.

Harold Acton

Actually, the way ahead is a particularly stupid choice of closing chapter title on my part. If you have been patient enough to read this far (and I thank you for that) you should be pretty clear in your own mind what represents the way ahead. If you are not yet confident enough or experienced enough in your studies, you should at least have a good grasp of the opportunities and challenges that are before you. I also tried very hard to find the perfect nugget to lead into my summary and crystallize the thinking I have attempted to impart. I expected it to come from one of advertising's big hitters. It didn't. The quotation from Harold Acton, the Italian-born writer, sometime gay activist and leading patron of Evelyn Waugh, however, seems to put my essential message of learning and cultural and social experience into context. Likewise, if you ask me to give you one single overriding piece of advice, I couldn't. Apart from to say enjoy the world around you, observe it, evaluate it and then feed it back into your creative work processes. You simply must never close your mind, accept that you know enough and rest on your laurels. There is always something new to learn.

Consider this, then choose to laugh at it, ignore it or think, yeah, maybe he has got something there.

It is hard to genuinely surprise me professionally. In my quarter of a century as a practising designer and art director I have been there, done it and use most of the T-shirts as dusters. In my decade as an advertising lecturer I've met most 'types' of students and seen brilliant, mediocre and totally awful work from them. During the summer of 2008 I met Aileen, my long-suffering editor. She was visiting universities on the look-out for ideas for student books – clearly advertising was on her agenda when she came to my department. In our meeting I threw some ideas around as to what I thought I could say in a book loosely about the advertising industry and how to get into it. Surprisingly for me, she seemed to like what I said and invited me to submit a proposal for writing a book on my ideas. To my continuing amazement, she liked that too and offered me a contract to write the thing. At that point my blood turned to ice. Me and my big mouth, I thought. I have talked this up so much; I have talked myself into it. Where the hell do I start? I've never written anything approaching a book before and, if I'm honest, my graphic design courses nearly 30 years ago didn't even require me to write a dissertation. I can't and don't 'do' academic, so what can I possibly say that any student wants to hear? Bouts of grunting, mumbling and snoring aside, Tina, my wife, tells me that nothing wakes me once I'm asleep so I can't pretend that I stayed awake all night worrying about it, but I thought long and hard. In particular, I went over and over in my mind the techniques I use to teach. I think my students quite like me really and respond well to and enjoy what I have to say. At the same time, especially during the first few weeks of the course, they think (quite rightly) that I am from the Planet Idiot. The thinking exercises I throw at them and my constant 'going on' at them about how they don't know enough about life and people leaves them thinking 'he's mad'.

Finally, my mind cleared and I remembered what I say to students on their first day and also to teachers on the courses I run on the theme of introducing advertising into design and media courses. I say this: 'I am not a trained teacher, neither am I an academic. The only way I can teach you anything is based on my own experiences of working in advertising, design and other media communications.' That was my 'eureka' moment. I jumped out of my chair, ran around the room for a bit and got excited. Exactly the same feeling I have when I have a great idea for an advertising campaign or piece of marketing communication. So that is what I have tried to do. Tell you how the industry is and what you should strive for in order to establish yourself within it.

The real point of this story though is this. Even in my mid-forties, I haven't lost the desire to learn something new and rise to interesting challenges. That is how it must be for you too. As a direct result of writing this, I will be a far better teacher. Why? Simply because I have learned a lot that is new. So I won't be relying on tried and trusted techniques and briefs I have been using for years. I'll be sharing all that I have discovered over the past few months with students, both in my teaching and in this book.

Please do not become a student of the Google generation. By that I mean one who is narrow-minded and one-dimensional. Students who can recite to me everything that, say, Ogilvy, Bernbach, Hegarty or Beattie have achieved, mechanically and in parrot fashion will not have a particularly successful advertising, marketing or media career. That is all too easy. Searching online and finding only one answer is not good enough. I don't want to be told that Trevor Beattie was born in the Midlands and was creative director at TBWA. I want to hear something new. I want students to tell me about the influence he exerted upon consumer thinking and, above all else, I want to know about the effect his work had on students personally. Then I want to know how that can inspire you to have ideas in a different way. After all that, probably what I would be most impressed with is a student that began with Beattie and finished somewhere completely different. The whole ethos of communicating with consumers should be the search for something new to say. Read books, watch movies, watch TV, surf the web and go out and experience people in many different environments. Whatever you do, don't do this to order. Don't just do it because I've said so, or as part of a student project, do it because you are genuinely excited by the prospect of a job in advertising, marketing and media communication.

Make yourself more interesting. I did.

Further reading

Here are some of the books and websites that inspire me.

Books

Confessions of an Advertising Man
David Ogilvy

Ogilvy on Advertising
David Ogilvy

Open Minds: Twenty-first Century Business Lessons and Innovations from St. Luke's
Andy Law

Adland: A Global History of Advertising
Mark Tungate

Twenty Ads that Shook the World
James B. Twitchell

Advertising and New Media
Christina Spurgeon

Lateral Thinking Techniques
Edward De Bono

Standing on the Shoulders of Giants
Hermann Vaske

FURTHER READING

It's Not How Good You Are, It's How Good You Want To Be
Paul Arden

Hey Whipple, Squeeze This
Luke Sullivan

The Fundamentals of Creative Advertising
Ken Burtenshaw, Nik Mahon and Caroline Barfoot

The Advertising Handbook
Sean Brierley

Copywriting
Robert Bowdery

Websites

www.ipa.co.uk
www.adage.com
www.yr.com
www.ddb.com
www.ogilvy.com
www.campaignlive.co.uk
www.brandrepublic.com
www.adweek.com
www.business.timesonline.co.uk
www.prospects.ac.uk
www.ihaveanidea.org
www.cipr.co.uk
www.prweek.com
www.mediaweek.co.uk
www.cim.co.uk
www.businesslink.gov.uk
www.dandad.org
www.cst.com

And a million other agency websites, anecdotes and people . . .

Index